IN SHORT

by Judith Kitchen

NONFICTION

Only the Dance: Essays on Time and Memory

Understanding William Stafford

POEMS

Perennials

IN SHORT

A COLLECTION OF
BRIEF CREATIVE
NONFICTION

edited by
Judith Kitchen
and
Mary Paumier Jones

W · W · Norton & Company
New York   London

Since this page cannot legibly accommodate all the copyright notices,
pages 321–27 constitute an extension of the copyright page.

The text of this book is composed in 11.5/14 Adobe Garamond
with the display set in Bodega Serif Medium
Composition and manufacturing by the Haddon Craftsmen, Inc.
Book design by Margaret M. Wagner

Library of Congress Cataloging-in-Publication Data
In short : a collection of brief creative nonfiction /
edited by Judith Kitchen and Mary Paumier Jones.
         p.   cm.
    Includes index.
    ISBN 0-393-03960-9—ISBN 0-393-31492-8 (pbk.)
      1. American essays—20th century. 2. College readers.
  I. Kitchen, Judith. II. Jones, Mary Paumier.
  PS688.I5 1996
  814'.508—dc20   95-39350

W. W. Norton & Company, Inc.
500 Fifth Avenue, New York, N.Y. 10110
http://web.wwnorton.com

W. W. Norton & Company Ltd.
10 Coptic Street, London WC1A 1PU

1 2 3 4 5 6 7 8 9 0

For help and support, we wish to thank the talented writers collected herein, the Rochester Public Library, our editor Carol Houck Smith, and our families—most of all, all ways and always, Stan and Jim Edd.

Contents

Contents

Contents

Contents

Contents

Contents

Contents

Preface:
The Disproportionate Power
of the Small

I had seen Salvador Dali's *The Persistence of Memory* in dozens of reproductions, but it wasn't until my freshman year of college that I was able to visit the Museum of Modern Art in New York to view the painting firsthand. Throughout high school I possessed an endless appetite for the disquieting juxtapositions and biomorphic forms of surrealism, and I raced through the museum eager to find Dali's landscape, a flaccid watch draped over the limb of its single tree. Distant cliffs, sulphurous light, and elongated shadows—this unpeopled world had so impressed me with its engulfing, dreamlike perspective that I passed the tiny painting several times before a guard finally pointed it out. I'd expected a huge canvas, believing that only a work of art as monumental as a mural could contain the sense of the infinite I'd come to associate with Dali's masterpiece.

The Persistence of Memory turned out to be only 9½ by 13 inches. But once I stood before it, the painting did not disappoint. In fact, compressed and intensified like the view through the wrong end of a telescope, the eerie vista exerted an even stronger psychic pull.

Another artist who understood the value of smallness was Joseph Cornell. Each of his boxes, with their spare groupings of found objects—fossils or marbles or glass vials—suggests an entire lifetime of melancholy. Confined by wooden walls, isolated behind glass, Cornell's assemblages are willfully insular and fragmentary. Yet the containment of his art is the very source of its drama, in much the same way haiku is made all the more acute by its brevity.

Miniatures have a peculiar impact, in low art as well as high. A hobby store in my city sells boxes of the little figures that inhabit model-train landscapes. The smallest scale is "N," and the people come six to a box, each figure floating in his or her own vacu-formed compartment. The people within the boxes are related by some prosaic theme: commuters reading newspapers, guests at a party, men and women walking to work. At arm's length the people look like plastic slivers. Only when you bring the boxes close can you begin to make out the cut of a jacket, the length of a skirt, and closer still—though you have to squint in speculation—the expression on a face. I find this Lilliputian populace to be every bit as wistful and evocative as the wide sky on a starry night; holding the boxes up to the light reminds me anew how small we are, how alone in our separate compartments, how elusive our traits to the naked eye.

•

While studying fine art in college, it dawned on me that any image I wanted to work with could be conjured solely through words. An ardent reader, I'd grown more and more interested in the medium of language. And so, after many sleepless nights, I decided to abandon the visual arts in order to pursue the craft of writing.

During those years of apprenticeship, I had no preconceived notions of the kind of work I wanted to write, but I did retain some respect for possibilities inherent in the small, the concise. My early efforts took the form of poems, but the rigors of line breaks and scansion made my poems stodgy, constricted, not the lively things I wanted them to be. I tried short stories, too, and though I found prose liberating, I wanted to write from my own point of view rather than from a character's. As a visual artist there had been no mask, no fictional filter through which to sift content. More important, I felt a sense of fidelity to people I had known and things that had actually happened. My debt, in short, was to memory. And its persistence.

I was living in a small apartment in Los Angeles at the time, teaching freshman composition at a local college, resigned to the possibility that I might never stumble upon an appropriate genre, might never be capable of work that made me truly proud. I was thirty-three, a fact I kept repeating to myself like the refrain of a sad song. To compound matters, the firestorm of AIDS had begun to claim friends and acquaintances; grief and fear and illness pervaded daily life, and the world seemed more irrational, more untenable than ever before. I dislike immensely the notion that despair breeds art, but I think it was precisely my heightened sense of mortality, my outrage at the fact of transience—blink, and someone, something is gone—that spurred me, finally, to do my best work.

One summer afternoon, feeling irritable and empty, I sat down to write. I wrote about my mother telling me, when I was a child, how she swam from Russia to America. She was two, she said, the ocean salty and cold. How could I have believed her? What had caused her to indulge in such a preposterous lie? I had to have these questions answered and I had to have them answered in a hurry because my life was running out as my mother's had. It didn't matter if what I was writing turned out to be brief or if it resisted definition. My concentration was sharp; I felt wholly present, yet somehow selfless. Within hours the four pages were complete, and all the paragraphs seemed to mesh like the gears in a pocketwatch.

After that day I was determined to find a place in my work for every memory that obsessed or baffled or stirred me: paint-by-number landscapes, my father's bathrobe, the voice of my Filipino barber. The windows of my writing room were choked with ivy, and in that dark room, in the dead of summer, I was introduced to the bright theater of an inner life. I had arrived, it seems to me in retrospect, at a genre as self-contained as a Cornell box: the short personal essay. A fitting form for the understanding that drove me to write: Life is over quickly, and art is elegiac.

What a pleasure, years later, to read and be a part of *In Short*. This collection includes several writers whom I consider mentors, whose voices have sustained me from the very beginning: Tobias Wolff, Gretel Ehrlich, Scott Russell Sanders. It also includes writers whose efforts in the short nonfiction form served as models, precedents that gave me courage along the way: Albert Goldbarth's hybrids of science and autobiography and current events in *A Sympathy of Souls;* Cynthia Ozick's passionate distillations of personal and literary history in *Metaphor & Memory;* Michael Ondaatje's inventive, patchwork memoir *Running in the Family.* What allies both the new and seasoned writers in this collection is that they have tried their hands at a difficult and anomalous form. The results are as rich as they are precise.

Judith Kitchen and Mary Paumier Jones have arranged their anthology into thematic patterns, patterns that are all the more salient because the pieces are brief. At its core, *In Short* is a book of exigencies: the pull of love, the power of nature, the dissonance of urban life, the labors of language, and the inevitability of loss— these emerge as shared concerns despite the fact that they are addressed by vastly different sensibilities. Although the writers gathered here represent diverse classes, ethnicities, geographies, and sexual orientations, this is not an identity-based or didactic anthology; the essays have been chosen first and foremost for their economy, their capacity to evoke pleasure and to inform by unexpected means—an editorial aesthetic that makes this a particularly affecting and humane collection.

An instructive collection, too, in that it suggests countless ways that shortness can be employed by the writer of nonfiction. For some of the authors represented here, brevity is the result of a restless spirit. "Get in, get out. Don't linger," Raymond Carver once advised writers. In an act of swift engagement with his or her subject matter, the skilled essayist can imbue even the briefest text with the immediacy, momentum, and intellectual agility one expects from a longer work. Take David James Duncan's "Rose Vegetables," in which the author recalls watching a parade along with hundreds of spectators when a dairy wagon, drawn by a team of black Clydesdales, crushed the skull of a man who had fallen beside the horses. What ensued was a mass faint. In fewer than three pages, Duncan is able to touch upon the unruly nature of fate, the chasm between civic pride and private grief, and the haste and inauspiciousness with which so many are dispatched to the hereafter—subjects culled from a single moment and conveyed in a rush that approximates the shock one would feel in witnessing such a scene. Other writers have simply heeded the dimensions of a precise subject, and allowed an essay to be only as long as it needs to be. In some instances, the writer may even wish to forego resolution altogether. For example, Vivian Gornick's "On the Street," a meditation on the transient encounters that punctuate the author's daily walks through her New York neighborhood, is an appropriately fleeting literary experience. Gornick shows how city dwellers are constantly grazing the lives of other, ultimately unknowable people, and she does so more pointedly than she might have in a longer and more exhaustive essay. The lonely resonance of "On the Street" stems, in part, from its modest scale, its intentional lack of closure. Still other writers are able to create vitality and tension by compressing varied subject matter into a tight frame, as in Bill Capossere's "A Wind from the North." With the death of an uncle as his point of departure, –Capossere veers seamlessly from family anecdotes to meditations on anonymity to a riff on the Eskimo words for snow; he fashions an essay that, in its brisk and meandering path, mimics the wind of the essay's title.

To write short nonfiction requires an alertness to detail, a quickening of the senses, a focusing of the literary lens, so to speak, until one has magnified some small aspect of what it means to be human. To read *In Short* is to experience, in essay after essay, the disproportionate power of the small to move, persuade, and change us.

—*Bernard Cooper*

Editors' Introduction

Something is going on out there. Almost simultaneously, many fine contemporary writers are writing in a new form: a non-fiction form, literary rather than informational, and short—very short. This new short form has no name, and partly because of this, frequently has trouble finding a home. We suggest calling these pieces simply "Shorts" and giving them a home in this anthology.

Like many another new thing, the Short is in some ways not really new. A short essay form has been around since the days of Bacon and Addison, with fine examples bequeathed to us by writers like W. E. B. DuBois and Virginia Woolf. Today, however, many different kinds of writers are independently reinventing the short form and putting it to new single, mosaic, and punctuational uses—writers of different ethnic backgrounds, established and emerging writers, traditional and experimental, rural and urban, young and old, men and women, journalists, fiction writers, and poets, as well as essayists.

We don't pretend to know why all of a sudden so many diverse writers are writing Shorts. We can only offer some tentative speculation. Twenty years ago a nonfiction piece one or two pages long would have been extremely rare, a book with a two-page chapter unheard of. Writers felt obligated to set the scene, develop the plot, and provide the transitions. Today, writers skip or condense much of that, and readers, schooled by the quick takes of television and movies, translate what they have learned there to the written page. Writers take advantage of that, further schooling readers, and on it goes. We see the development of the Short as part of that wider cultural trend, and as one part—one fascinating part—of the experimentation in the burgeoning field of what is coming to be called "creative nonfiction."

We had been writing Shorts, using them in teaching, and reading them for a long time before we began to think of the Short as a form in itself. The idea for an anthology then followed quickly. Each of us already had favorite pieces and knew of writers we wanted to contact. We were struck again and again by the responses. "I love the idea of the very short essay. I realize I have longed for it, for ages." . . . "I've written such pieces for more than a decade but have never known what to call them or where to place them." . . . "I was never comfortable thinking of this as either a short story or a prose poem."

The writers we contacted initially were also generous in suggesting others who were writing Shorts, giving us the opportunity to discover new voices—or in some cases, to discover the prose nonfiction voices of writers whose previous work has been in other genres. We continue to come upon new pieces and we know—to our sorrow—that there are wonderful writers we have missed.

As we have gone along, we have naturally refined what we think a Short is—a process by no means complete. Our approach has been to trust our instincts and then try to figure out why we made one or another instinctive choice. We unequivocally and enthusiastically wanted "Nature's See-Saw" by Edward Hoagland and

"Proofs" by Richard Rodriguez, for example, though the word count for each is almost two thousand. Being of a pragmatic bent, we established our outer word limit at two thousand, and eventually realized that those two pieces exemplify the kind of density and depth we see as essential to a Short. It is a matter of proportion—how much the piece *does* for how long it is.

A Short, as we see it now, can be an essay, or an anecdote, or a description. It can be a journal entry, or a commentary, or an inventive foray into language. Whatever it is, the writer has taken the time to *make* it short, though shortness alone is not enough. These pieces are also deep—a whole world created with just a few strokes. In this they are like poetry or "flash fiction"—with the difference that here the people, the places, the events, are real. Shorts are also complete in themselves. To borrow a definition from the librarian Helen Haines, they are "unicellular prose organisms." No matter how brief, everything needed is there; an initial something moves somewhere, taking as long as it takes and no longer. Length, depth, and wholeness, then, are the characteristics of Shorts.

In form, the Shorts here reflect almost every way in which nonfiction can be written. Those by Pico Iyer and Maxine Kumin exhibit the meditative qualities we associate with the traditional essay form. Diane Ackerman's piece on hummingbirds has a sharp focus of attention, while Tim O'Brien captures a fragmented moment. Charles Simic emphasizes his intent by naming his pieces "memory fragments," and Denise Levertov, whose latest book is called *Tesserae* (the individual tiles that make up a mosaic), moves from memory to "supposition." Vivian Gornick and Kim R. Stafford speak in a storytelling voice while Franklin Burroughs is formally elegant. David James Duncan delights in language even as he deplores its distortions. Many (among them Michael Dorris, Jane Brox, Paul West, Naomi Shihab Nye) move from the specific to the abstract, although some travel in the opposite direction (Tobias Wolff and Gretel Ehrlich). Some, brief as they are, are built in mosaic fashion of even smaller parts—note the number which have individual sections. Others, like those by Marvin Bell and Albert Goldbarth, are single but far-ranging romps.

Some of these Shorts were written expressly for this anthology. More have been published singly in literary magazines or have appeared in full-length collections by the individual authors. A few have surprising origins: "Proofs" by Richard Rodriguez originally introduced a book of photographs; August Wilson's three paragraphs set the scene for a play; Andrei Codrescu's piece was spoken on National Public Radio; and David Huddle eventually used his as a brief scene in a much longer fictional story. Jerry Ellis's piece opened his book while Tobias Wolff's closed his.

Several of the writers included here have made entire books from sequences of Shorts, among them Bernard Cooper, Denise Levertov, Michael Ondaatje, Bia Lowe, and Susanna Kaysen. In these works, the pieces can accumulate meaning much as a collection of poems adds up to more than the sum of its parts. But just as a collection of poems is different from one long poem, a book made up of short pieces is different from a continuous narrative. The self-sufficiency of the individual parts is emphasized by the fact that they do stand alone, they can be read separately, and they have individual titles and pages. Emily Hiestand uses a similar method of construction, indicating each new "tile" with a marginal notation. Other writers employ periodic Shorts as a transitional glue or punctuation between longer pieces. Kathleen Norris used this technique as a kind of counterpoint, and Stuart Dybek inserted short nonfiction pieces on contrasting color pages within a collection of short stories.

Occasionally, a Short can be found buried within a longer work, self-contained even as it serves the larger piece. We found such buried Shorts in the work of Deborah Tall, Fred Setterberg,

Li-Young Lee, Franklin Burroughs, Rita Dove, Teresa Jordan, Art Homer, Ian Frazier, and Henry Louis Gates, Jr. The writers all have made such slight adjustments (adding a title, deleting a phrase, etc.) as were necessary to underscore the self-sufficient nature of the piece. The singularity of these particular Shorts was made even more evident when we discovered that not all books using the mosaic method would offer up a selection; try as we might, we could not separate the individual parts of William Least Heat Moon's *PrairyErth* from the whole.

As you might expect, the themes in this collection are as varied and unique as the individual writers themselves. Sometimes pieces fell together in what seemed like self-ordained sequences. There are, for example, Vietnam experiences in the essays of Norma Elia Cantú, Tobias Wolff, and Tim O'Brien, or "quiet heroes" in the essays of William Kittredge, Gwendolyn Nelson, Ted Kooser, and Judson Mitcham. Some essays cluster around a single image or idea: tea, snow, the night sky, weather, jazz. Other themes recur like rhythms: margins, courage, flight, nostalgia. Certain threads—family, ethnic diversity, feminism, travel, and especially nature—weave their way through the collection in surprising permutations. Finally, the Short as "snapshot" is emphasized by the sheer number and variety of essays based on photographs.

The physical geography of these pieces ranges from the Alaska of John Haines to the New England of Donald Hall and Edward Hoagland, with a taste of the South, the Southwest, and the Great Plains as well. One sequence moves steadily west, continually refocusing our understanding of geography, geology, and American identity. The emotional terrain is equally varied— these ninety writers offer a mixture of humor, irony, nostalgia, thoughtful contemplation, speculation, deep sadness, joy.

We feel certain that *In Short* will attract as many different kinds of readers as it has writers. Busy readers, certainly. Nonfiction readers, of course. And, we hope, readers of poetry and fiction, who will find here the imaginative play and aesthetic satisfaction they look for in literature. You can pick up this book, open it, and read it in any order. Or you can follow the connective tissue we have played with in our arrangement. We believe that these pieces speak to each other in interesting ways, but we would recommend that you also discover them in their original contexts. For that purpose, we have included in the Biographical Notes titles by each author—hoping you will reacquaint yourself with old favorites and discover someone new.

—*Judith Kitchen and Mary Paumier Jones*

IN SHORT

STUART DYBEK
Lights

In summer, waiting for night, we'd pose against the afterglow on corners, watching traffic cruise through the neighborhood. Sometimes, a car would go by without its headlights on and we'd all yell, "Lights!"

"Lights!" we'd keep yelling until the beams flashed on. It was usually immediate—the driver honking back thanks, or flinching embarrassed behind the steering wheel, or gunning past, and we'd see his red taillights blink on.

But there were times—who knows why?—when drunk or high, stubborn, or simply lost in that glide to somewhere else, the driver just kept driving in the dark, and all down the block we'd hear yelling from doorways and storefronts, front steps, and other corners, voices winking on like fireflies: "Lights! Your *lights!* Hey, lights!"

REGINALD GIBBONS
All-Out Effort

I have cleaned off the old radio and put new batteries in it. I have brought up the old boots from the basement and cleaned and polished them. I have brought the old rocker down from the attic and repaired the arm that was broken. I have washed and ironed the old khaki pants and the old soft green shirt that were hanging at the back of the closet for so long.

Out the kitchen door, on the back landing, three floors above the trash cans filled with this week's garbage, I've put the rocker, I've set the radio down beside it and turned it on softly to the right music. I've put on the pants and shirt and boots, I have sat down in the neighborhood afternoon in the quiet time just before the working day is going to end.

To prepare myself, I brought back to mind the unseeable green of a meadow where we stood at night one time, where we could see the reassuring lights and sounds of a crowded lit room, and no one could see us: that moment, and others like it.

I've brought back to my mind the words I said to you, and I've spoken them again, wearing these same clothes that I wore then. Many times I have had lots of ideas and I started off with many thoughts, but none of them was able to reach a resting place, or find what I was after. Even though I chose a summer day for this, or it chose me, I know enough to know this green shirt may not be warm enough, because there are frozen fields and cold streets to cross, just as many of them as of those furnace nights buzzing outside with cicadas and tree frogs, sirens and shouts and engines.

But I'm wading and flying, now, I'm off, I'm headed into a place of ago, the radio's getting fainter, a little wind of time is starting to whip my pants legs and sleeves and make my eyes smart. Let the tears come! This rocker is gathering some speed. I'm going back, I'm going to rescue all of it!

JUDITH ORTIZ COFER
Volar

At twelve I was an avid consumer of comic books—
Supergirl being my favorite. I spent my allowance of a quarter a
day on two twelve-cent comic books or a double issue for twenty-
five. I had a stack of *Legion of Super Heroes* and *Supergirl* comic
books in my bedroom closet that was as tall as I. I had a recur-
ring dream in those days: that I had long blond hair and could
fly. In my dream I climbed the stairs to the top of our apartment
building as myself, but as I went up each flight, changes would
be taking place. Step by step I would fill out: my legs would grow
long, my arms harden into steel, and my hair would magically
go straight and turn a golden color. Of course I would add the
bonus of breasts, but not too large; Supergirl had to be aerody-
namic. Sleek and hard as a supersonic missile. Once on the roof,
my parents safely asleep in their beds, I would get on tip-toe, arms
outstretched in the position for flight and jump out my fifty-
story-high window into the black lake of the sky. From up there,
over the rooftops, I could see everything, even beyond the few
blocks of our barrio; with my X-ray vision I could look inside
the homes of people who interested me. Once I saw our land-

lord, whom I knew my parents feared, sitting in a treasure-room dressed in an ermine coat and a large gold crown. He sat on the floor counting his dollar bills. I played a trick on him. Going up to his building's chimney, I blew a little puff of my super-breath into his fireplace, scattering his stacks of money so that he had to start counting all over again. I could more or less program my Supergirl dreams in those days by focusing on the object of my current obsession. This way I "saw" into the private lives of my neighbors, my teachers, and in the last days of my child-ish fantasy and the beginning of adolescence, into the secret room of the boys I liked. In the mornings I'd wake up in my tiny bedroom with the incongruous—at least in our tiny apartment— white "princess" furniture my mother had chosen for me, and find myself back in my body: my tight curls still clinging to my head, skinny arms and legs and flat chest unchanged.

In the kitchen my mother and father would be talking softly over a café con leche. She would come "wake me" exactly forty-five minutes after they had gotten up. It was their time together at the beginning of each day and even at an early age I could feel their disappointment if I interrupted them by getting up too early. So I would stay in my bed recalling my dreams of flight, perhaps planning my next flight. In the kitchen they would be discussing events in the barrio. Actually, he would be carrying that part of the conversation; when it was her turn to speak she would, more often than not, try shifting the topic toward her desire to see her *familia* on the Island: *How about a vacation in Puerto Rico together this year, Querido? We could rent a car, go to the beach. We could* . . . And he would answer patiently, gently, *Mi amor, do you know how much it would cost for the all of us to fly there? It is not possible for me to take the time off.* . . . *Mi vida, please understand.* . . . And I knew that soon she would rise from the table. Not abruptly. She would light a cigarette and look out the kitchen window. The view was of a dismal alley that was littered with refuse thrown from windows. The space was too narrow for anyone larger than a skinny child to enter safely, so it was never cleaned. My mother would check the time on the clock over her sink, the one with a prayer for patience and grace written in Spanish. A birthday gift. She would see that it was time to wake me. She'd sigh deeply and say the same thing the view from her kitchen window always inspired her to say: *Ay, si yo pudiera volar.*

Around the Corner

When I was small, maybe seven or eight, I noticed some crinkled leather boots in my mother's closet, some I knew I had never seen her wear. She told me they were for horseback riding, and showed me some funny-shaped pants. "They're called jodhpurs," she said, and spelled it for me. She said she'd ridden when she was in college. She had taken archery, too. She had planned to major in journalism so she could meet with world leaders, and she had interviewed the university president for the student newspaper. She had taken Spanish, and sometimes spoke phrases of it around the house: "You're *loco in la cabeza,*" she would say to my father, and she had taught me to count from *uno* to *diez.* She also knew another language: shorthand. Her mother had made her take it because it was practical, and my mother had used it when she worked as a secretary at the truckline. She wrote her Christmas lists in shorthand—and anything else she didn't want me or my father to read, like her diary. It was a little red leather book with gilt-edged pages, and I was most intrigued by its little gold lock. As I remember it, my mother showed it to me, and maybe even read some passages to me. Looking over her shoulder I could see that some parts were in shorthand. When I asked what they said she just laughed and turned the page.

My mother seemed to treat the diary—and the boots and jodhpurs, the glamorous pictures of herself that she had sent to my father overseas, her dreams of becoming a famous journalist— as relics of a distant past that no longer had much to do with her. She had left them all behind for life with my father, and me, and eventually my two brothers. I loved my mother, and thought she was beautiful. I was grateful for the sort of mother she was—she had milk and cookies waiting when I came home from school, packed my lunchbox each morning. Every holiday was full of treats and surprises: a present by my plate on Valentine's Day, eggs hidden all over the house on Easter morning, Kool-Aid in my thermos on my birthday. Yet at the same time that I basked in the attention my mother lavished on me, I was haunted by the image of the person who seemed to have disappeared around the corner just before I arrived.

MAXINE KUMIN
Enough Jam for a Lifetime

January 25. Three days of this hard freeze; 10 below at dawn and a sullen 2 above by midday. After the morning barn chores, I start hauling quart containers of wild blackberries up from the basement freezer. I am a little reluctant to begin.

Last August, when the berries were at their most succulent, I did manage to cook up a sizable batch into jam. But everything peaks at once in a New England garden, and I turned to the importunate broccolis and cauliflowers and the second crop of bush beans, all of which wanted blanching and freezing straight-away. Also, late summer rains had roused the cucumber vines to new efforts. There was a sudden spurt of yellow squash as well.

Victor went on picking blackberries. Most mornings he scouted the slash pile along upturned boulders, residue from when we cleared the last four acres of forage pasture. We've never had to fence this final field, for the brush forms an impenetrable thicket on two sides and deep woods encircle the rest.

We've always had blackberries growing wild here and there on the property, good-sized ones, too. But never such largess, such abundance. I wondered what this bumper crop signified, after a drought-filled summer. Were the Tribulation and the Rapture at hand?

Long ago I wrote in a poem, "God does not want / His perfect fruit to rot," but that was before I had an addicted picker on my hands—whose enthusiasm became my labor. It is the habit of the deeply married to exchange vantage points.

Even the horses took up blackberries as a snack. Like toddlers loose in a popcorn shop, they sidled down the brambly row, cautiously curling their lips back so as to pluck a drooping cluster free without being stabbed in the muzzle by truly savage thorns. It was a wonderful sight.

Making jam—even though I complain how long it takes, how messy it is with its inevitable spatters and spills, how the lids and the jars somehow never match up at the end of the procedure—is rich with gratifications. I get a lot of thinking done. I puff up with feelings of providence. Pretty soon I am flooded with memories.

My mother used to visit every summer during our pickling, canning, freezing, and jamming frenzy. She had a deep reservoir of patience, developed in another era, for repetitive tasks; she would mash the blender-buzzed, cooked berries through a strainer until her arms were as weary as a weight-lifter's at the end of a grueling workout. She prided herself on extracting every bit of pulp from the purple mass.

I find myself talking to her as I work. I am not nearly as diligent, I tell her, thumping the upended strainer into the kitchen scraps pile, destined for compost. I miss her serious attention to detail.

Scullery work used to make my mother loquacious. I liked hearing about her childhood in the southwestern hilly corner of Virginia at the turn of the century, how the cooking from May to October was done in the summer kitchen, a structure loosely attached to the back of the house, much as many New England sheds and barns connect to the farmhouses they supplement. I liked hearing about my grandfather's matched pair of driving horses—Saddlebreds, I gather, from the one surviving snapshot that shows my mother's three youngest brothers lined up on one compliant horse's back. My mother talked about the family pony that had a white harness for Sundays. I wonder aloud what a white harness was made of in the 1890s. Perhaps she had imagined this item, but fabricated it lovingly so long ago that it had become real.

One spectacular late summer day we took my mother down North Road along Stevens Brook in search of elderberries. We hiked up and down the sandy edge of the water in several locations before coming upon an enormous stand of the berries, ripe to bursting, branches bent double with the weight of them. After filling the five-gallon pail we had brought with us, greedily we started stuffing whole racemes of berries into a spare grain bag.

I had not thought much about dealing with the booty until we had lugged it triumphantly home. Mother sat at the kitchen table well past midnight, stripping the berries from their slender finger filaments into my biggest cooking pot. Even so, the great elderberry caper took two more days to complete. We prevailed, eventually boiling the berries with some green apples from our own trees so that the released pectin would permit the mass to jell. I don't believe in additives and scorn commercial pectin, but I will lean on homegrown apples or rhubarb in order to thicken the berry soup.

It was amazing what those elderberries had reawakened in my mother; she was transported. There was the cold cellar, there stood the jars of pickled beets, the Damson plum conserve larded with hazelnuts; there, too, the waist-high barrel of dill pickles weighted down with three flatirons atop a washtub lid. Potatoes and sweet potatoes, carrots, onions and apples were stored in areas appropriate to their needs—apples in the dark far corner which was the driest (and spookiest) and so on. There was the springhouse, where milk from the family cow cooled unpasteurized in a metal can set down in a cavity of rocks, and a butter churn which took hours of push-pulling the paddle to turn the cream into a finished product.

It was never an idyll Mother described. She remembered sharply and wryly the labor, the peonage of childhood, when the most menial and least absorbing tasks were invariably assigned to the smallest children, especially the girls. She could not escape the chores of housekeeping for the imagined dramas of field and barn. But interestingly, chickens seemed always to have been relegated to the care of females.

Mother loathed the chickens that pecked her feet when she went into the coop to scatter their scratch. She detested egg gathering, having to shoo brood hens off their nests and then be quick about plucking the eggs into the basket; eggs from which fluff, feathers, and bits of crusty manure had to be removed. I never saw my mother eat an egg, boiled soft or hard, poached, or sunny-side up. They were a bit too close to nature for her taste.

Another kitchen thing I hear my mother say as I work, this cold January noon: "Warm the plates!" she croons to me from the Great Beyond. She abhorred the common practice of serving hot food on cold china. *Common* is the epithet she would have applied to it, a word that carried powerful connotations of contempt.

This wintry day, then, I reduce five gallons of blackberries to serviceable pulp, measure out three cups of sugar to every four of berry mash, and set it boiling. We will have successive batches on the stove the rest of this day. I have already rummaged for suitable jars from the cellar shelves and these I will boil for fifteen minutes on a back burner. Toward the end I will grow more inventive about jars, for there are never enough of the good, straight-sided variety.

But for now, the jam puts up lacy bubbles, rolling around the top third of my giant cooking pot at a full boil. Despite candy thermometers, the only way I trust to gauge when the jam is ready is dip and drip. From a decent height, off a slotted spoon, I perform this test until the royal stuff begins to form a tiny waterfall. This is known as sheeting; all the cookbooks describe it, but it's a delicate decision to arrive at. Stop too soon and you have a lovely blackberry sauce to serve over ice cream, sponge cake, or applesauce. Continue too long and you have a fatally overcooked mess of berry leather.

There is no quality control in my method. Every batch is a kind of revisionism. It makes its own laws. But the result is pure, deeply colored, uncomplicated, and unadulterated blackberry jam, veritably seedless, suitable for every occasion. After it has cooled, I pour melted paraffin on top of it, tilting the glass to get an airproof seal. Modern science frowns on so casual an approach to shutting out microbes, but I don't apologize. If the wax shows a spot of mold growing on top after a few months on the shelf, I can always remove it, wipe the sides clean, and pour a new layer of wax over all.

My mother would go home from her summer visits with a package of pickles and jams for her later delectation. When she died, there were several unopened jars in her cupboard. I took them back with me after the funeral. We ate them in her stead, as she would have wanted us to. Enough jam for a lifetime, she would say with evident satisfaction after a day of scullery duty. It was; it is.

An Unspoken Hunger

It is an unspoken hunger we deflect with knives—one avocado between us, cut neatly in half, twisted then separated from the large wooden pit. With the green fleshy boats in hand, we slice vertical strips from one end to the other. Vegetable planks. We smother the avocado with salsa, hot chiles at noon in the desert. We look at each other and smile, eating avocados with sharp silver blades, risking the blood of our tongues repeatedly.

BHANU KAPIL
Three Voices

I

The bath heated by pans of water from the stove, the
man's glistening mouth when he pours the water over my belly,
the oil in my hair, the ice snapping in the tree outside my room,
and then, after the green and brown night, I drink hoji-cha, eat
toast with black cherry jam, eat a banana, and answer the man's
questions. There are phones ringing beyond Beethoven. It is
eleven in the morning, and already the day has backed up farther
and farther inside me. Today, I cannot shake the lump of coal
out of my body. The man wants to go to the supermarket to buy
fresh fruit, and some milk. Okay, okay.

A bowl of avocado meat, softened and pressed by the back of
a spoon, is my pleasure. Beneath the pleasure, the hunger that's
made of eggshells, and pieces of cloth. Perhaps it is simply a matter of studying and exercising. Okay, okay. But I am not in the
mood to read novels, or spend time with friends, or sing. No. I
think I want to sing. But what's this? My voice is a stone in my

chest. It doesn't stream. I am filled with music! But I can't swallow.

I am not writing about myself as a rational human being. I'm writing about the substances of an animal and female life: magic, pain, the cracked nails of four feet, and the days like this one, when it is difficult to speak to a good-looking man. He returns with sesame seeds, unleavened bread, ginger and coriander powders, coffee, chives, chocolate, yoghurt, onions, cucumbers, potatoes, and a quart of milk. He thinks I am a woman, because he bathes me, and puts his hands on the sides of my face, and tells me I am beautiful. Yes. Okay. But there is something hard between my lungs. It is the size of a blood orange from northern California.

II

And then, one woman, she cannot breathe from her stomach, tells the man: "I am not in love with you. Next year, I will be twenty-five years old, and perhaps I will panic, and perhaps I will not tell you the truth about my heart. And listen, don't ask me about it unless you want to hear about the piece of stale bread I ate one day, when you were sleeping in my bed. I don't know how this happened. Enough!"

The man is not stupid. He's noticed how, in her own sleep, she rubs her palm between her breasts. He replies: "What the hell do you want from me?"

And the woman starts to speak. There is an orange-colored wave rising up her spine.

III

I am blessed. Even in this loneliness, I am blessed. I open the Spanish dictionary at random to "algun" (someday), and "marriage" (matrimonio). I open a book of symbols to "crane," which is connected to pine trees and the sun. And Neruda, in his memoirs, writes: "She gave up her husband, and she also gave up the soft lighting and the excellent armchairs, for an acrobat in a Russian circus that passed through Santiago."

There are not many Russian acrobats in upstate New York. But here is an orange on the kitchen table. I will learn to juggle it on the tips of my fingers. No. I think I'll place it on the front step. A stranger passing by will, perhaps, noticing it, come into my rooms. He is the coming power of the future.

Anhelo: longing. My life: joven. Joven: young woman. Stranger: Angel. Naranjo: orange. Wonder: milagro. My life: sagrado. Sagrado: sacred.

RICHARD RODRIGUEZ
Proofs

You stand around. You smoke. You spit. You are wearing your two shirts, two pants, two underpants. Jesús says, if they chase you throw that bag down. Your plastic bag is your mama, all you have left; the yellow cheese she wrapped has formed a translucent rind; the laminated scapular of the Sacred Heart nestles flame in its cleft. Put it in your pocket. The last hour of Mexico is twilight, the shuffling of feet. A fog is beginning to cover the ground. Jesús says they are able to see in the dark. They have X-rays and helicopters and searchlights. Jesús says wait, just wait, till he says. You can feel the hand of Jesús clamp your shoulder, fingers cold as ice. *Venga, corre.* You run. All the rest happens without words. Your feet are tearing dry grass, your heart is lashed like a mare. You trip, you fall. You are now in the United States of America. You are a boy from a Mexican village. You have come into the country on your knees with your head down. You are a man.

•

Papa, what was it like?

I am his second son, his favorite child, his confidant. After we have polished the DeSoto, we sit in the car and talk. I am sixteen years old. I fiddle with the knobs of the radio. He is fifty.

He will never say. He was an orphan there. He had no mother, he remembered none. He lived in a village by the ocean. He wanted books and he had none.

You are lucky, boy.

In the nineteenth century, American contractors reached down into Mexico for cheap labor. Men were needed to build America: to lay track, to mine, to dredge, to harvest. It was a man's journey. And, as a year's contract was extended, as economic dependence was established, sons followed their fathers north. When American jobs turned scarce—during the Depression, as today—Mexicans were rounded up and thrown back over the border. But for generations it has been the rite of passage for the poor Mexican male.

I will send for you or I will come home rich.

In the fifties, Mexican men were contracted to work in America as *braceros,* farm workers. I saw them downtown in Sacramento. I saw men my age drunk in Plaza Park on Sundays, on their backs on the grass. I was a boy at sixteen, but I was an American. At sixteen, I wrote a gossip column, "The Watchful Eye," for my school paper.

Or they would come into town on Monday nights for the wrestling matches or on Tuesdays for boxing. They worked over in Yolo county. They were men without women. They were Mexicans without Mexico.

On Saturdays, they came into town to the Western Union office where they sent money—money turned into humming wire and then turned back into money—all the way down into

Mexico. They were husbands, fathers, sons. They kept themselves poor for Mexico.

Much that I would come to think, the best I would think about male Mexico, came as much from those chaste, lonely men as from my own father who made false teeth and who—after thirty years in America—owned a yellow stucco house on the east side of town.

The male is responsible. The male is serious. A man remembers.

The migration of Mexico is not only international, South to North. The epic migration of Mexico and throughout Latin America, is from the village to the city. And throughout Latin America, the city has ripened, swollen with the century. Lima. Caracas. Mexico City. So the journey to Los Angeles is much more than a journey from Spanish to English. It is the journey from *tu*—the familiar, the erotic, the intimate pronoun—to the repellent *usted* of strangers' eyes.

Most immigrants to America came from villages. The America that Mexicans find today, at the decline of the century, is a closed-circuit city of ramps and dark towers, a city without God. *The city is evil. Turn. Turn.*

Mexico is poor. But my mama says there are no love songs like the love songs of Mexico. She hums a song she can't remember. The ice cream there is creamier than here. Someday we will see. The people are kinder—poor, but kinder to each other.

Men sing in Mexico. Men are strong and silent. But in song the Mexican male is granted license he is otherwise denied. The male can admit longing, pain, desire.

HAIII—EEEE—a cry like a comet rises over the song. A cry like mock-weeping tickles the refrain of Mexican love songs. The cry is meant to encourage the balladeer—it is the raw edge of his sentiment. HAIII—EEEE. It is the man's sound. A ticklish arching of semen, a node wrung up a guitar string, until it bursts in a descending cascade of mockery. HAI. HAI. HAI. The cry of a jackal under the moon, the whistle of the phallus, the maniacal song of the skull.

●

Tell me, Papa.
What?
About Mexico.
I lived with the family of my uncle. I was the orphan in the village. I used to ring the church bells in the morning, many steps up in the dark. When I'd get up to the tower I could see the ocean.
The village, Papa, the houses too . . .
The ocean. He studies the polished hood of our beautiful blue DeSoto.

●

Mexico was not the past. People went back and forth. People came up for work. People went back home, to mama or wife or village. The poor had mobility. Men who were too poor to take a bus walked from Sonora to Sacramento.
Relatives invited relatives. Entire Mexican villages got re-created in three stories of a single house. In the fall, after the harvest in the Valley, families of Mexican adults and their American children would load up their cars and head back to Mexico in caravans, for weeks, for months. The school teacher said to my mother what a shame it was the Mexicans did that—took their children out of school.
Like wandering Jews. They carried their home with them, back and forth: they had no true home but the tabernacle of memory.

•

Each year the American kitchen takes on a new appliance. The children are fed and grow tall. They go off to school with children from Vietnam, from Korea, from Hong Kong. They get into fights. They come home and they say dirty words.

The city will win. The city will give the children all the village could not—VCRs, hairstyles, drum beat. The city sings mean songs, dirty songs. But the city will sing the children a great Protestant hymn.

You can be anything you want to be.

•

We are parked. The patrolman turns off the lights of the truck— "back in a minute"—a branch scrapes the door as he rolls out of the van to take a piss. The brush crackles beneath his receding steps. It is dark. Who? Who is out there? The faces I have seen in San Diego—dishwashers, janitors, gardeners. They come all the time, no big deal. There are other Mexicans who tell me the crossing is dangerous.

The patrolman returns. We drive again. I am thinking of epic migrations in history books—pan shots of orderly columns of paleolithic peoples, determined as ants, heeding some trumpet of history, traversing miles and miles . . . of paragraph.

The patrolman has turned off the headlights. He can't have to piss again? Suddenly the truck accelerates, pitches off the rutted road, banging, slamming a rock, faster, ignition is off, the truck is soft-pedalled to a stop in the dust; the patrolman is out like a shot. The cab light is on. I sit exposed for a minute. I can't hear anything. Cautiously, I decide to follow—I leave my door open as the patrolman has done. There is a boulder in the field. Is that it? The patrolman is barking in Spanish. His flashlight is trained on the boulder like a laser, he weaves it along the grain as though he is untying a knot. He is: Three men and a woman stand up. The men are young—sixteen, seventeen. The youngest is shivering. He makes a fist. He looks down. The woman is young too. Or she could be the mother? Her legs are very thin. She wears a man's digital wristwatch. They come from somewhere. And somewhere—San Diego, Sacramento—somebody is waiting for them.

The patrolman tells them to take off their coats and their shoes, throw them in a pile. Another truck rolls up.

As a journalist, I am allowed to come close. I can even ask questions.

There are no questions.

You can take pictures, the patrolman tells me.

I stare at the faces. They stare at me. To them I am not bearing witness; I am part of the process of being arrested. I hold up my camera. Their eyes swallow the flash, a long tunnel, leading back.

Your coming of age. It is early. From your bed you watch your Mama moving back and forth under the light. The bells of the church ring in the dark. Mama crosses herself. From your bed you watch her back as she wraps the things you will take.

You are sixteen. Your father has sent for you. That's what it means: He has sent an address in Nevada. He is there with your uncle. You remember your uncle remembering snow with his beer.

You dress in the shadows. Then you move toward the table, the circle of light. You sit down. You force yourself to eat. Mama stands over you to make the sign of the cross on your forehead with her thumb. You are a man. You smile. She puts a bag of food in your hands. She says she has told *La Virgin*.

Then you are gone. It is gray. You hear a little breeze. It is the rustle of your old black *Dueña,* the dog, taking her shortcuts through the weeds, crazy *Dueña,* her pads on the dust. She is following you.

You pass the houses of the village; each window is a proper name. You pass the store. The bar. The lighted window of the clinic where the pale medical student from Monterrey lives alone and reads his book full of sores late into the night.

You want to be a man. You have the directions in your pocket: an address in Tijuana, and a map with a yellow line that leads from the highway to an "X" on a street in Reno. You are afraid, but you have never seen snow.

You are just beyond the cemetery. The breeze has died. You turn and throw a rock back at *La Dueña,* where you know she is—where you will always know where she is. She will not go past the cemetery, not even for him. She will turn in circles like a *loca* and bite herself.

The dust takes on gravel, the path becomes a rutted road which leads to the highway. You walk north. The sky has turned white overhead. Insects click in the fields. In time, there will be a bus.

I will send for you or I will come home rich.

Tino & Papi

I. TINO

In the photo, he stands to the side with his hand out as if pointing a gun or a rifle. Everyone else, sisters, cousins, friends, neighbors crowd around me; the piñata in the shape of a birthday cake sways in the wind above our heads. Everyone's there: aunts, uncles, cousins, the neighbors, my madrina, everyone, even Mamagrande Lupita from Monterrey. I'm holding the stick decorated with red, blue, yellow tissue paper that we will use to break the piñata. And at age nine he holds out the imaginary gun, like a soldier. Only ten years later, 1968, he is a soldier, and it's not a game. And we are gathered again: tías, tíos, cousins, comadres, neighbors, everyone, even Mamagrande Lupita from Monterrey, and Papi's cousin Ricardo who's escorted the body home. We have all gathered around a flag-draped coffin. Tino's come home from Vietnam. My brother. The sound of the trumpet caresses our hearts and Mami's gentle sobbing sways in the cool wind of March.

II. PAPI

On the wall, the image of the Virgen de San Juan, a pale rose background, grayish black outline, shines like silver in the dark. Bueli lights candles when Tino is so sick el Doctor del Valle, the doctor across the river in Nuevo Laredo, fears he will die. He's only three. The illness has taken over. But Papi cries in front of another image of our Lady. It's a calendar from Cristo Rey Church with the image of Nuestra Señora del Perpetuo Socorro. He prays, he weeps, hits the wall with his fists, like he would hit the mesquite tree in the backyard with his head sixteen years later like a wounded animal, mourning, in pain, that morning when Tino's death came to our door. But the child Tino survives the illness; the injections, the medication, the prayers, the remedios— something works, and Papi frames the calendar image in gold leaf, builds the image a repisita—a shelf for candles. In 1968, in his pain, tears running down his face, he'll talk to the image, "For this, you spared my son," he'll take the image down from its place on the wall, cannot bear to see it, to be reminded. On the wall, a rectangle of nothing, the color of the wallpaper Mami had hung for Tio Moy's last visit three years ago, like new—lines of green fern leaves on dusty beige. The votive candle on the tiny shelf is left burning to an empty space.

TOBIAS WOLFF
Last Shot

George Orwell wrote an essay called "How the Poor Die" about his experience in the public ward of a Paris hospital during his lean years. I happened to read it not long ago because one of my sons was writing a paper on Orwell, and I wanted to be able to talk with him about it. The essay was new to me. I liked it for its gallows humor and cool watchfulness. Orwell had me in the palm of his hand until I came to this line: "It is a great thing to die in your own bed, though it is better still to die in your boots."

It stopped me cold. Figure of speech or not, he meant it, and anyway the words could not be separated from their martial beat and the rhetoric that promotes dying young as some kind of good deal. They affected me like an insult. I was so angry I had to get up and walk it off. Later I looked up the date of the essay and found that Orwell had written it before Spain and World War II, before he'd had the chance to see what dying in your boots actually means. (The truth is, many of those who "die in their boots" are literally blown right out of them.)

Several men I knew were killed in Vietnam. Most of them I didn't know well, and haven't thought much about since. But my friend Hugh Pierce was a different case. We were very close, and would have gone on being close, as I am with my other good friends from those years. He would have been one of them, another godfather for my children, another big-hearted man for them to admire and stay up late listening to. An old friend, someone I couldn't fool, who would hold me to the best dreams of my youth as I would hold him to his.

Instead of remembering Hugh as I knew him, I too often think of him in terms of what he never had a chance to be. The things the rest of us know, he will not know. He will not know what it is to make a life with someone else. To have a child slip in beside him as he lies reading on a Sunday morning. To work at, and then look back on, a labor of years. Watch the decline of his parents, and attend their dissolution. Lose faith. Pray anyway. Persist. We are made to persist, to complete the whole tour. That's how we find out who we are.

I know it's wrong to think of Hugh as an absence, a thwarted shadow. It's my awareness of his absence that I'm describing, and maybe something else, some embarrassment, kept hidden even from myself, that I went on without him. To think of Hugh like this is to make selfish use of him. So, of course, is making him a character in a book. Let me at least remember him as he was.

He loved to jump. He was the one who started the "My Girl" business, singing and doing the Stroll to the door of the plane. I always take the position behind him, hand on his back, according to the drill we've been taught. I do not love to jump, to tell the truth, but I feel better about it when I'm connected to Hugh. Men are disappearing out the door ahead of us, the sound of the engine is getting louder. Hugh is singing in falsetto, doing a goofy routine with his hands. Just before he reaches the door he

looks back and says something to me. I can't hear him for the
wind. What? I say. He yells, *Are we having fun?* He laughs at the
look on my face, then turns and takes his place in the door, and
jumps, and is gone.

TIM O'BRIEN
LZ Gator, Vietnam, February 1994

I'm home, but the house is gone. Not a sandbag, not a nail or a scrap of wire.

On Gator, we used to say, the wind doesn't blow, it sucks. Maybe that's what happened—the wind sucked it all away. My life, my virtue.

In February 1969, 25 years ago, I arrived as a young, terrified pfc. on this lonely little hill in Quang Ngai Province. Back then, the place seemed huge and imposing and permanent. A forward firebase for the Fifth Battalion of the 46th Infantry, 198th Infantry Brigade, LZ Gator was home to 700 or 800 American soldiers, mostly grunts. I remember a tar helipad, a mess hall, a medical station, mortar and artillery emplacements, two volleyball courts, numerous barracks and offices and supply depots and machine shops and entertainment clubs. Gator was our castle. Not safe, exactly, but far preferable to the bush. No land mines here. No paddies bubbling with machine-gun fire.

Maybe once a month, for three or four days at a time, Alpha Company would return to Gator for stand-down, where we took our comforts behind a perimeter of bunkers and concertina wire.

There were hot showers and hot meals, ice chests packed with beer, glossy pinup girls, big, black Sony tape decks booming "We gotta get out of this place" at decibels for the deaf. Thirty or 40 acres of almost-America. With a little weed and a lot of beer, we would spend the days of stand-down in flat-out celebration, purely alive, taking pleasure in our own biology, kidneys and livers and lungs and legs, all in their proper alignments. We could breathe here. We could feel our fists uncurl, the pressures approaching normal. The real war, it seemed, was in another solar system. By day, we'd fill sandbags or pull bunker guard. In the evenings, there were outdoor movies and sometimes live floor shows—pretty Korean girls breaking our hearts in their spangled miniskirts and high leather boots—then afterward we'd troop back to the Alpha barracks for some letter writing or boozing or just a good night's sleep.

So much to remember. The time we filled a nasty lieutenant's canteen with mosquito repellent; the sounds of choppers and artillery fire; the slow dread that began building as word spread that in a day or two we'd be heading back to the bush. Pinkville, maybe. The Batangan Peninsula. Spooky, evil places where the land itself could kill you.

Now I stand in this patch of weeds, looking down on what used to be the old Alpha barracks. Amazing, really, what time can do. You'd think there would be something left, some faint imprint, but LZ (landing zone) Gator has been utterly and forever erased from the earth. Nothing here but ghosts and wind.

JUDITH KITCHEN
Culloden

AUGUST 6

This is where Scotland's dream was dashed. Windswept moor, purple with blooming heather. Bog land. Our shoes keep sinking into watery peat. We wander this high stretch, shading our eyes to see the mountains in the distance. From here, you could sight your enemy. You could prepare.

At first they are imperceptible, a part of the natural terrain. Then the eye discerns a series of long, low, grass-covered mounds. Near each is a plaque: Clan Chattan, Clan Cameron, MacDonells of Glengarry. And behind these, more—then more. The mass graves of men without names. Buried together, identified only by tartan.

It's not hard to imagine: 1746, the field strewn with corpses and Bonnie Prince Charlie already headed for the sea and Skye. You hear the whistle of wind over grasses. A silence like this one. Under foot, the treacherous water. Bog land. Hardly fit for farming. Hardly worth fighting for.

Time is the trickster. Today I woke up half a century old. I am not ready. Too much yet to do. Too much everyday living. Too much left unsaid, unimagined.

Late afternoon. The sky hunkers down, presses, like a lover, against the land. Small sounds. A far sheep, faint barking. Time to drive on, toward Strathpeffer, friends, a phone call from my father.

Late afternoon. In upstate New York, the sun will be high in the sky. The morning newspapers will be screaming my traditional birthday headlines: HIROSHIMA. A kind of national guilt— or, at least, a national doubt.

This land is at the root of my family tree. Duguids and Murrays—"cleared" from these mountainsides—settled in Cherry Valley, New York, in 1774. They left behind their peat fires, their few cows. Left behind the stories—yet to become legend—of their exiled prince.

The road twists upward. In the Scottish summer, the sky never quite goes black, just deeper and deeper blue. We enter its sea. The crofts are all gone now, but there are lights in the few white-washed cottages we pass. Few. And far between.

They moved on to Ohio and the flat lands of southern Michigan. Their farms flourished. Not a mountain in sight. The names grew steadily American. My grandmother was Mary Ellen Duguid, but she was called Mayme. Her sisters were Maud and Myrta Belle. The boys, John and Dennis and Otto. Stories begin to attach themselves to the names. Soon they come to me firsthand. Mayme marries blue-eyed Benjamin Pendell—the grandfather I will never know. One summer day he will fall from the hay wagon, dead before he hits the ground. Mayme's grand-daughter will live for two years in Scotland. She will marry a man she meets there. They will have sons. Thirty years later, she will return with someone else. There will be lights in the cottages, human constellations.

Early evening. At home it is full afternoon. Hard to keep track. Three hours earlier, in Seattle, where William and Matthew now live, newspapers again shout the words on every corner. My sons glance at the headline and walk on. It means almost nothing in their lives. It was my birthday. I was four. It was two centuries after Culloden.

And farther west, across another ocean, the sun is rising. Already August 7th. The dead remain silent. We cannot imagine what it is to cease to exist. The body knows only its own watery weight, its heaviness. It burrows into the amorphous mound on the hilltop where it is at home. Memory makes it all one silken thread. Tie the knot anywhere: tie it in 1774. Then thread the needle and pull it across water. Let America begin. Let the crofters find themselves a farm they call their own. Let them marry and die. At Culloden, soldiers sank in marsh, struggled up again, thrashing, slashing, a chaos of color and sound and foolhardy pride. Over Hiroshima, the plane burst through a seam in the sky—a glint, and then a blinding flash. The earth has learned to live with us. It accommodates bone, shadows burned in stone.

Afternoon Tea

Tea is the steady companion of the Scottish day, and each hotel, no matter how humble, stocks its rooms with supplies for brew-ups: electric pot for boiling water, ceramic pot for brewing, china cups and small tea-creamers, a raft of teas, honey, fresh milk, and lemons. This is a delight and an astonishment, for not only is there no such thing in American hotels, but room service even in respectable ones, when asked for tea with milk, can deliver a plastic jug of tepid water, this covered by a square of Saran Wrap, and a drinking glass of milk. To request tea in an American office is often to throw the receptionist into a swivet: he or she believes that there is tea somewhere in the corporate pantry, but where? One prefers not to ask rather than to send this person on a scavenger mission, especially because the tea, if found, is a grim bag-tea like Red Rose. Naturally, one might as well ask for a trip to Bombay as to ask for looseleaf Earl Grey, or first-flush Darjeeling, or Assam tips. Home is a fluid place; each day at four o'clock, I could easily be an expatriate.

One afternoon we are poking up the rocky coastline from Black Craig near Stromness north past Skara Brae to Brough

Head; this western end of the island is folded and fissured in a steady cascade of bays, headlands, gloups, caves, and the handsome invasions of ocean into the land that are called geos. These places are named Lyre, Nebo, Axna, Saed, Sand, and Skipi, in a succession of sounds as quirky and original as the land. We wind slowly north toward Skipi Geo just around the Brough of Birsay, stopping to walk Marwick Head. The wide plateau at the summit of the cliff tilts at a precipitous angle toward the sea, covered with great, loose, cracked plates of flagstone in thin layers: orange, grey, ochraceous rocks that will weather into fertile soil or be pried up for roofing flags if they do not first slide into the sea. The bluff is perpetually wet and glistening, and cold water pools dot the depressions and rectangular fissures in the rock. Over the exposed plateau, wind blows in steadily and coldly from the sea. This is the home of the largest and most spectacular seabird colony on Mainland; some thirty-five thousand guillemots, ten thousand kittiwakes, as well as fulmars and razorbills, who favor the eroded flagstone ledges for nesting and the abundance of shoaling fish for eating. But in this stormy weather, only a few guillemots—auks, and clumsy on land—bumble along the slabs of pitted rock cliff. For miles to the west, there is flat, grey, choppy ocean; for miles to the east, a grey, clouded sky under which low, treeless fields roll smoothly into the moors.

It is nearing four o'clock in the afternoon, and sure enough, parked just off the road, overlooking the pungent tidal flats, we come upon a small caravan camper with its aluminum door open to a late-middle-aged Scottish couple, sitting at a folding table, taking tea and biscuits. Passing by, one only has a glimpse: his thick, white socks and heavy black shoes; her plump pear form and print dress; the electric kettle on the table. The archaeologists are puzzled as to why the people of ancient Skara Brae would locate their huts so close to the sea, and have surmised that in fact the settlement was originally located in a protected hollow, that time has eroded the shoreline inland toward the huts. That would make sense. Indeed, when presented at Skara Brae with the lure of a sparkling sea and the howling wind, we ourselves tucked into the hollow of a dune for lunch, eating cheese and apples in the sun with wind skimming our heads, blowing the sand into rippling ridges, flattening the beach grasses. Probably the archaeologists are right, but this utterly typical sense of Scottish domesticity blithely planted at the edge of harsh cliffs, afternoon tea conducted in the wind and cold, suggests another possibility.

CYNTHIA OZICK
The Shock of Teapots

One morning in Stockholm, after rain and just before November, a mysteriously translucent shadow began to paint itself across the top of the city. It skimmed high over people's heads, a gauzy brass net, keeping well above the streets, skirting everything fabricated by human arts—though one or two steeples were allowed to dip into it, like pens filling their nibs with palest ink. It made a sort of watermark over Stockholm, as if a faintly luminous river ran overhead, yet with no more weight or gravity than a vapor.

This glorious strangeness—a kind of crystalline wash—was the sunlight of a Swedish autumn. The sun looked *new:* it had a lucidity, a texture, a tincture, a position across the sky that my New York gape had never before taken in. The horizontal ladder of light hung high up, higher than any sunlight I had ever seen, and the quality of its glow seemed thinner, wanner, more tentatively morning-brushed; or else like gold leaf beaten gossamer as tissue—a lambent skin laid over the spired marrow of the town.

"Ah, yes, the sun *does* look a bit different this time of year," say the Stockholmers in their perfect English (English as a second first language), but with a touch of ennui. Whereas I, under the electrified rays of my whitening hair, stand drawn upward to the startling sky, restored to the clarity of childhood. The Swedes have known a Swedish autumn before; I have not.

Travel returns us in just this way to sharpness of notice; and to be saturated in the sight of what is entirely new—the sun at an unaccustomed slope, stretched across the northland, separate from the infiltrating dusk that always seems about to fall through clear gray Stockholm—is to revisit the enigmatically lit puppet-stage outlines of childhood: those mental photographs and dreaming woodcuts or engravings that we retain from our earliest years. What we remember from childhood we remember forever—permanent ghosts, stamped, imprinted, eternally seen. Travelers regain this ghost-seizing brightness, eeriness, firstness.

They regain it because they have cut themselves loose from their own society, from every society; they are, for a while, floating vagabonds, like astronauts out for a space walk on a long free line. They are subject to preternatural exhilarations, absurd horizons, unexpected forms and transmutations: the matter-of-fact (a battered old stoop, say, or the shape of a door) appears beautiful; or a stone that at home would not merit the blink of your eye here arrests you with its absolute particularity—just because it is what your hand already intimately knows. You think: a stone, a stone! They have stones here too! And you think: how uncannily the planet is girdled, as stone-speckled in Sweden as in New York. For the vagabond-voyeur (and for travelers voyeurism is irresistible), nothing is not for notice, nothing is banal, nothing is ordinary: not a rock, not the shoulder of a passer-by, not a teapot.

Plenitude assaults; replication invades. Everything known has its spooky shadow and Doppelgänger. On my first trip anywhere—it was 1957 and I landed in Edinburgh with the roaring of the plane's four mammoth propellers for days afterward embedded in my ears—I rode in a red airport bus to the middle of the city, out of which ascended its great castle. It is a fairy-book castle, dreamlike, Arthurian, secured in the long-ago. But the shuddery red bus—hadn't I been bounced along in an old bus before, perhaps not so terrifically red as this one?—the red bus was not within reach of plain sense. Every inch of its interior streamed with unearthliness, with an undivulged and consummate witchery. It put me in the grip of a wild Elsewhere. This unexceptional vehicle, with its bright forward snout, was all at once eclipsed by a rush of the abnormal, the unfathomably Martian. It was the bus, not the phantasmagorical castle, that clouded over and bewildered our reasoned humanity. The red bus was what I intimately knew: only I had never seen it before. A reflected flicker of the actual. A looking-glass bus. A Scottish ghost.

This is what travelers discover: that when you sever the links of normality and its claims, when you break off from the quotidian, it is the teapots that truly shock. Nothing is so awesomely unfamiliar as the familiar that discloses itself at the end of a journey. Nothing shakes the heart so much as meeting—far, far away—what you last met at home. Some say that travelers are informal anthropologists. But it is ontology—the investigation of the nature of being—that travelers do. Call it the flooding-in of the real.

There is, besides, the flooding-in of character. Here one enters not landscapes or streetlit night scenes, but fragments of drama: splinters of euphoria that catch you up when you are least deserving. Sometimes it is a jump into a pop-up book, as when a cockney cabdriver, of whom you have asked directions while leaning out from the curb, gives his native wink of blithe goodwill. Sometimes it is a mazy stroll into a toy theater, as when, in a museum, you suddenly come on the intense little band following the lecturer on Mesopotamia, or the lecturer on genre painting, and the muse of civilization alights on these rapt few. What you are struck with then—one of those mental photographs that go on sticking to the retina—is not what lies somnolently in the glass case or hangs romantically on the wall, but the enchantment of a minutely idiosyncratic face shot into your vision with indelible singularity, delivered over forever by your own fertile gaze. When travelers stare at heads and ears and necks and beads and mustaches, they are—in the encapsuled force of the selection—making art: portraits, voice sonatinas, the quick haiku of a strictly triangular nostril.

Traveling is seeing; it is the implicit that we travel by. Travelers are fantasists, conjurers, seers—and what they finally discover is that every round object everywhere is a crystal ball: stone, teapot, the marvelous globe of the human eye.

MICHAEL ONDAATJE
Harbour

I arrived in a plane but love the harbour. Dusk. And the turning on of electricity in ships, portholes of moon, the blue glide of a tug, the harbour road and its ship chandlers, soap makers, ice on bicycles, the hidden anonymous barber shops behind the pink dirt walls of Reclamation Street.

One frail memory dragged up out of the past—going to the harbour to say goodbye to a sister or mother, dusk. For years I loved the song, "Harbour Lights," and later in my teens danced disgracefully with girls, humming "Sea of Heartbreak."

There is nothing wise about a harbour, but it is real life. It is as sincere as a Singapore cassette. Infinite waters cohabit with flotsam on this side of the breakwater and the luxury liners and Maldive fishing vessels steam out to erase calm sea. Who was I saying goodbye to? Automatically as I travel on the tug with my brother-in-law, a pilot in the harbour, I sing "the lights in the harbour don't shine for me . . ." but I love it here, skimming out into the night anonymous among the lazy commerce, my nieces dancing on the breakwater as they wait, the lovely swallowing of thick night air as it carves around my brain, blunt, cleaning itself with nothing but this anonymity, with the magic words. *Harbour. Lost ship. Chandler. Estuary.*

MARY PAUMIER JONES
The Opposite of Saffron

MINNEAPOLIS, MINNESOTA

I don't remember this. I was too young. But my mother and father told of my childhood habit time and again. From their point of view: their first child wakes in the middle of the night, wakes them up too, not with cries but with giggles. She laughs and recites all the words they have taught her, her litany. I picture Mom getting back in bed after the first time. "What's the matter?" "Nothing, she's laughing and reciting her words." "Now?" "Yes, now." Night after night I did the same.

One day Dad taught me to say Minneapolis, Minnesota, a triumph of such magnitude it became my permanent finale, new words inserted before its resonance. When they heard "Minneapolis, Minnesota," my parents knew they could go back to sleep.

DICTIONARIES

One grade school summer I set myself a daily regime. In the room I shared with my sister at a small desk, I—what should I call it, played school? studied? Nothing sounds exactly right. But I allotted time for this and that, and day after day found satisfaction there alone.

Praying was one thing I did, or my version of it, which had a lot in common with daydreaming, a blue and white statue of the Virgin Mary with the snake under her foot there to inspire me to fantasies of sainthood in which I was beloved and admired by millions.

And I read the dictionary—yes, read the dictionary. My goal was to get through it in the course of the summer—which I'm sure I didn't do, but no matter. The column of words were an endless feast.

Some forty years later I bought a used set of the tiny print edition of the Oxford English Dictionary. I had to find a stand magnifier for it because using the hand-held one that comes with it makes me nauseous. So now I can look up any English word and get its entire history complete with examples of use through the centuries, right in the comfort of my own home.

I lust after the large print edition—or the regular size print edition, I should say—the new updated twenty-four volume $2500.00 one. A set sits proudly on the ledge behind the cash registers in a bookstore I frequent. Whenever I buy anything—which is appallingly often—I look at it and fantasize saying, "Oh, and throw in the OED too."

SYZYGY

A word I looked up: syzygy. (File it away in case you ever have three y's in Scrabble—or can you have three y's in Scrabble?) The morning paper announced that the moon's perigee was falling on its syzygy. The paper called these words "cold and rational," an odd description because syzygy sounds to me as if it sizzles, which indeed it does, coming from the Greek for yoke, pair, conjunction, copulation. (Remember *copulative* verbs? What a shame they've been demoted to *linking*.)

A curious thing has happened to syzygy; time can do strange things to words as well as people. Originally referring to the conjunction of two heavenly bodies, since sometime in the 1700's syzygy has included both conjunction and opposition, so the word has become one of those few whose meaning has extended to include its opposite.

I knew there was a full moon coming. The full is the opposition, the syzygy when the sun and the moon are aligned on opposite sides of the earth. The moon's perigee is the point in its orbit where it is closest to earth. About once a year or so, the full moon occurs at the point when the moon is closest, the perigee and syzygy together. If the clouds clear off, we'll see a big moon tonight.

THE POSSIBLE SUNSHINE

All February the clouds refused to clear off. "Cold air moving over Lake Ontario formed the clouds that blocked the sun," the paper said. "The city got only twenty percent of the possible sunshine."

Then one morning it is over. Objects have volume in space, reflect light, take up room. We have been looking at the world with one eye closed, thinking it flat, circle outlined on a two-dimensional page instead of crosshatched sphere bulging forward, casting shadow.

Telephone wires scallop the road. Cars trail bulbous gray shapes. I'll need my sunglasses—where might they be? Porch railings stripe porch and wall. My old dog feels a rush of youth, pulls against the double leash. And I—even I—am here, my being unmistakable. I cast a shadow, therefore I am.

Odd, but we don't think about it, how the absence of sun is also the absence of shadow.

JUST THE OPPOSITE

In T'ai Chi class Dr. Young talked about yin and yang. In the beginning square form, each movement is followed by a pause: the movement is yin, the pause yang. To my Western ears this smacks of sexism; the masculine principle acting, the feminine doing nothing. But I eventually begin to learn the pause is not nothing. Given its proper weight, gravity, and time, the pause does its work, its stretch, its subtle modification of the quality of the move before and the one to come. Later in the round form, the movement is continuous. Yin and yang, though still opposite, are inscrutably simultaneous, engaged in an ancient abstract intercourse.

In Sunday's *New York Times* David Richards reviews a stage performance by George C. Scott. To encompass it he proposes what he calls a "theory of contradictory impulses." Scott excels in a mediocre role, Richards says, because before giving the audience one emotion, he gives a hint of its opposite: laughter before tears, hate before love. This works because it reflects how life is, each emotion closer to its opposite than to anything like itself.

As a child in Eastern Europe, fiber artist Neda Al-Hilali knit a lot of gray socks for the family, always gray. She lusted for color and when she once managed to get some bright yarn, she hid it as an American boy might his copy of *Playboy,* looking at it, touching, working in secret ecstasy under her bedcovers.

Now she is internationally known for her mastery of color. And personally known as a wonderful cook—her classes usually end with festive party meals. When asked how she gets her colors so vibrant, she replies that she always puts a dash of the opposite color dye in the pot. "You know," she says, as if everyone does, "just like you put in a bit of an opposite spice when you cook."

PICO IYER
In Praise of the Humble Comma

The gods, they say, give breath, and they take it away. But the same could be said—could it not?—of the humble comma. Add it to the present clause, and, of a sudden, the mind is, quite literally, given pause to think; take it out if you wish or forget it and the mind is deprived of a resting place. Yet still the comma gets no respect. It seems just a slip of a thing, a pedant's tick, a blip on the edge of our consciousness, a kind of printer's smudge almost. Small, we claim, is beautiful (especially in the age of the microchip). Yet what is so often used, and so rarely recalled, as the comma—unless it be breath itself?

Punctuation, one is taught, has a point: to keep up law and order. Punctuation marks are the road signs placed along the highway of our communications—to control speeds, provide directions and prevent head-on collisions. A period has the unblinking finality of a red light; the comma is a flashing yellow light that asks us only to slow down; and the semicolon is a stop sign that tells us to ease gradually to a halt, before gradually starting up again. By establishing the relations between words, punctuation establishes the relations between the people using words.

That may be one reason why schoolteachers exalt it and lovers defy it ("We love each other and belong to each other let's don't ever hurt each other Nicole let's don't ever hurt each other," wrote Gary Gilmore to his girlfriend). A comma, he must have known, "separates inseparables," in the clinching words of H. W. Fowler, King of English Usage.

Punctuation, then, is a civic prop, a pillar that holds society upright. (A run-on sentence, its phrases piling up without division, is as unsightly as a sink piled high with dirty dishes.) Small wonder, then, that punctuation was one of the first proprieties of the Victorian age, the age of the corset, that the modernists threw off: the sexual revolution might be said to have begun when Joyce's Molly Bloom spilled out all her private thoughts in 36 pages of unbridled, almost unperioded and officially censored prose; and another rebellion was surely marked when E. E. Cummings first felt free to commit "God" to the lower case.

Punctuation thus becomes the signature of cultures. The hot-blooded Spaniard seems to be revealed in the passion and urgency of his doubled exclamation points and question marks ("¡Caramba! ¿Quien sabe?"), while the impassive Chinese traditionally added to his so-called inscrutability by omitting directions from his ideograms. The anarchy and commotion of the '60s were given voice in the exploding exclamation marks, riotous capital letters and Day-Glo italics of Tom Wolfe's spray-paint prose; and in Communist societies, where the State is absolute, the dignity—and divinity—of capital letters is reserved for Ministries, Sub-Committees and Secretariats.

Yet punctuation is something more than a culture's birthmark; it scores the music in our minds, gets our thoughts moving to the rhythm of our hearts. Punctuation is the notation in the sheet music of our words, telling us where to rest, or when to raise our voices; it acknowledges that the meaning of our discourse, as of any symphonic composition, lies not in the units but in the pauses, the pacing and the phrasing. Punctuation is the way one bats one's eyes, lowers one's voice or blushes demurely. Punctuation adjusts the tone and color and volume till the feeling comes into perfect focus, not disgust exactly, but distaste; not lust, or like, but love.

Punctuation, in short, gives us the human voice, and all the meanings that lie between the words. "You aren't young, are you?" loses its innocence when it loses the question mark. Every child knows the menace of a dropped apostrophe (the parent's "Don't do that" shifting into the more slowly enunciated "Do not do that"), and every believer, the ignominy of having his faith reduced to "faith." Add an exclamation point to "To be or not to be . . ." and the gloomy Dane has all the resolve he needs; add a comma, and the noble sobriety of "God save the Queen" becomes a cry of desperation bordering on double sacrilege.

Sometimes, of course, our markings may be simply a matter of aesthetics. Popping in a comma can be like slipping on the necklace that gives an outfit quiet elegance, or like catching the sound of running water that complements, as it completes, the silence of a Japanese landscape. When V. S. Naipaul, in his latest novel, writes, "He was a middle-aged man, with glasses," the first comma can seem a little precious. Yet it gives the description a spin, as well as a subtlety, that it otherwise lacks, and it shows that the glasses are not part of the middle-agedness, but something else.

Thus all these tiny scratches give us breadth and heft and depth. A world that has only periods is a world without inflections. It is a world without shade. It has a music without sharps and flats. It is a martial music. It has a jackboot rhythm. Words cannot bend and curve. A comma, by comparison, catches the gentle drift of the mind in thought, turning in on itself and back on itself, reversing, redoubling and returning along the course of its own sweet river music; while the semicolon brings clauses and thoughts together with all the silent discretion of a hostess arranging guests around her dinner table.

Punctuation, then, is a matter of care. Care for words, yes, but also, and more important, for what the words imply. Only a lover notices the small things: the way the afternoon light catches the nape of a neck, or how a strand of hair slips out from behind an ear, or the way a finger curls around a cup. And no one scans a letter so closely as a lover, searching for its small print, straining to hear its nuances, its gasps, its sighs and hesitations, poring over the secret messages that lie in every cadence. The difference between "Jane (whom I adore)" and "Jane, whom I adore," and the difference between them both and "Jane—whom I adore—" marks all the distance between ecstasy and heartache. "No iron can pierce the heart with such force as a period put at just the right place," in Isaac Babel's lovely words: a comma can let us hear a voice break, or a heart. Punctuation, in fact, is a labor of love. Which brings us back, in a way, to gods.

JOY HARJO
Suspended

Once I was so small that I could barely peer over the top of the backseat of the black Cadillac my father polished and tuned daily; I wanted to see everything. It was around the time I acquired language, or even before that time, when something happened that changed my relationship to the spin of the world. My concept of language, of what was possible with music was changed by this revelatory moment. It changed even the way I looked at the sun. This suspended integer of time probably escaped ordinary notice in my parents' universe, which informed most of my vision in the ordinary world. They were still omnipresent gods. We were driving somewhere in Tulsa, the northern border of the Creek Nation. I don't know where we were going or where we had been, but I know the sun was boiling the asphalt, the car windows open for any breeze as I stood on tiptoes on the floorboard behind my father, a handsome god who smelled of Old Spice, whose slick black hair was always impeccably groomed, his clothes perfectly creased and ironed. The radio was on. I loved the radio, jukeboxes or any magic thing containing music even then.

I wonder now what signaled this moment, a loop of time that

on first glance could be any place in time. I became acutely aware of the line the jazz trumpeter was playing (a sound I later associated with Miles Davis). I didn't know the word jazz or trumpet, or the concepts. I don't know how to say it, with what sounds or words, but in that confluence of hot southern afternoon, in the breeze of aftershave and humidity, I followed that sound to the beginning, to the place of the birth of sound. I was suspended in whirling stars, a moon to which I'd traveled often by then. I grieved my parents' failings, my own life which I saw stretched the length of that rhapsody.

My rite of passage into the world of humanity occurred then, via jazz. The music made a startling bridge between familiar and strange lands, an appropriate vehicle, for though the music is predominantly west African in concept, with European associations, jazz was influenced by the Creek (or Muscogee) people, for we were there when jazz was born. I recognized it, that humid afternoon in my formative years, as a way to speak beyond the confines of ordinary language. I still hear it.

The Blues Merchant

Long Tongue, The Blues Merchant, strolls on stage. His guitar rides sidesaddle against his hip. The drummer slides onto the tripod seat behind the drums, adjusts the high-hat cymbal, and runs a quick, off-beat tattoo on the tom-tom, then relaxes. The bass player plugs into the amplifier, checks the settings on the control panel and nods his okay. Three horn players stand off to one side, clustered, lurking like brilliant sorcerer-wizards waiting to do magic with their musical instruments.

The auditorium is packed. A thousand inmates face the stage; all anticipate a few minutes of musical escape. The tear gas canisters recessed in the ceiling remind us that everything is for real.

The house lights go down and the stage lights come up. Reds and greens and blues slide into pinks and ambers and yellows and play over the six poised musicians.

The Blues Merchant leans forward and mumbles, "Listen. Listen here, you all," into the microphone. "I want to tell you about Fancy Foxy Brown and Mean Lean Green. They is the slickest couple in the East Coast scene."

Thump. Thump. The drummer plays. Boom-chicka-chicka-boom. He slams his tubs. The show is on. Toes tap. Hands clap. Fingers pop. The audience vibrates. Long Tongue finds his groove. He leans back. He moans. He shouts. His message is picked up, translated and understood. With his soul he releases us from bondage, puts us in tune with tomorrow, and the memories of the cold steel cells—our iron houses—evaporate.

Off to one side, a blue coated guard nods to the rhythm. On the up-beat his eyes meet the guard sergeant's frown. The message is clear: "You are not supposed to enjoy the blues. You get paid to watch, not be human." The message is instantaneously received. The guard jerks himself still and looks meaner than ever.

Long Tongue, The Blues Merchant, wails on. He gets funky. He gets rough. He gets raunchy. His blues are primeval. He takes everybody, except the guards, on a trip. The guards remain trapped behind the prison's walls while, if only for a short time, we are free.

FRED SETTERBERG
The Usual Story

I ambled through the Quarter, down Dumaine Street, up Bourbon, along Chartres, heading no place in particular. The narrow streets thronged with drunks and musicians. In Jackson Square, I rested on the cement steps to finish a bottle of beer I had carried out of a dark, noisy joint near Patout's. The moon arched above the statue of General Jackson saddled upon his horse, his hat doffed in one hand to hail the light. A boy with a trumpet stood at the foot of the invader's statue. He bleated and blahed his way through Miles Davis's "All Blues."

I slipped back into the alleyways and zigzagged for another half-hour until I found myself standing in front of Preservation Hall.

I have never been a fan of traditional jazz. Worse, I have always imagined that the traditional jazz featured inside Preservation Hall would be a shuck, like Disneyland Dixieland—an artifice, unfelt, an impersonation for the tourists. The line in front of Preservation Hall was very long, but a good tenor sax player was wandering up and down the street, playing for free, and so I took my place at the end of the line, as much to rest and listen to the sax man as gain entry. When we were finally ushered into the building, I saw that a lack of artifice was Preservation Hall's greatest asset. The hall looked about twice the size of my hotel room, dimly lit like the gloomy altar of some small country church where a few candles sputtered bravely. Six musicians sat upon wooden chairs atop a small stage raised about eighteen inches from the floor. A half-dozen wooden bench pews filed back from the stage; everybody else—maybe seventy-five people— crowded together in the darkness, shoulder to shoulder.

I didn't recognize the band's first tune, but when the trumpet player took the lead, he shaved the melody close, in the style of King Oliver. After the clarinet solo, he stood up once again and sang out to the audience. His woman had left him, giving him the blues; it was the usual story.

Traditional jazz has never seemed risky enough to me. But as the band inside Preservation Hall continued to bang out one number after another, the piano, bass, drums, banjo, clarinet, and trumpet swelling into a sea of collective fakery with sufficient spirit and peculiarity to challenge all the conventional harmonies, I caught for an inspired instant how truly daring the music must have felt at its inception. Even now the friction of creation showed sparks—the painful *hilarity* of squeezing something unheard before from a motley collection of instruments only recently transported to these shores. The band rambled on, and I realized there was nothing at all quaint about this music; it had always been full of risk, unstable, and liable to combust.

"Everyone is familiar with the Negro's modification of the whites' musical instruments," wrote Zora Neale Hurston in a 1911 essay, "Characteristics of Negro Expression," "so that his interpretation has been adopted by the white man himself and then reinterpreted. In so many words, Paul Whiteman is giving an imitation of a Negro orchestra making use of white-invented musical instruments in a Negro way. Thus has arisen a new art in the civilized world, and thus has our so-called civilization come. The exchange and re-exchange of ideas between groups."

The bass player at Preservation Hall seemed determined to prove this point. He launched into a flutter of notes that were both too rapid and dissonant for New Orleans vintage jazz, playing more like Charles Mingus than Pops Foster. He scurried up the instrument's neck from the bridge to the scroll, shattering the tune. The other players grunted encouragement. Together they were demonstrating how music—culture—argues, blends, dissolves, mutates, advances. The odd bird who hears something different plucks his strings too quickly or queerly or flat out plunks the *wrong* note, but he does it over and over until it sounds right. He finds his own groove and fashions new music from the old.

And that's exactly what American music—American culture—has managed to do. As Hurston understood, as the bass player was now showing, our nation's truest anthem contains the funeral dirge of the New Orleans street band combined with the whore-house piano and the last slave's work song and the bickering melodies of two hundred disparate points of origin, from Marseilles to Dakar, from Manaus to Guangzhou, now stretched out over the American plains like the hide of some mythical beast: the confluence of influences that nobody will ever be able to pick apart note-for-note. It has long been a sophisticated complaint to jeer that America has "no culture," but there couldn't be a sillier idea. We have more culture than one people will ever be able to digest. And that helps explain why the melting pot some-times bubbles up—and when we least expect it, explodes.

Joe Turner's Come and Gone: The Play

It is August in Pittsburgh, 1911. The sun falls out of heaven like a stone. The fires of the steel mill rage with a combined sense of industry and progress. Barges loaded with coal and iron ore trudge up the river to the mill towns that dot the Monongahela and return with fresh, hard, gleaming steel. The city flexes its muscles. Men throw countless bridges across the rivers, lay roads and carve tunnels through the hills sprouting with houses.

From the deep and the near South the sons and daughters of newly freed African slaves wander into the city. Isolated, cut off from memory, having forgotten the names of the gods and only guessing at their faces, they arrive dazed and stunned, their heart kicking in their chest with a song worth singing. They arrive carrying Bibles and guitars, their pockets lined with dust and fresh hope, marked men and women seeking to scrape from the narrow, crooked cobbles and the fiery blasts of the coke furnace a way of bludgeoning and shaping the malleable parts of themselves into a new identity as free men of definite and sincere worth.

Foreigners in a strange land, they carry as part and parcel of their baggage a long line of separation and dispersement which informs their sensibilities and marks their conduct as they search for ways to reconnect, to reassemble, to give clear and luminous meaning to the song which is both a wail and a whelp of joy.

Sunday

White people couldn't cook; everybody knew that. Which made it a puzzle why such an important part of the civil rights movement had to do with integrating restaurants and lunch counters. The food wasn't any good anyway. Principle of the thing, Daddy's buddy Mr. Ozzie Washington would assert. They don't know nothin' about seasoning, my aunt Marguerite would say. I like my food seasoned, she'd add.

If there is a key to unlocking the culinary secrets of the Coleman family, it is that a slab of fatback or a cupful of bacon drippings or a couple of ham hocks and a long simmering time are absolutely essential to a well-cooked vegetable. Cook it till it's *done*, Mama would say. Cook it till it's dead, we'd learn to say much later. When I first tasted a steamed vegetable, I thought it was raw. The Colemans were serious about their cooking and their eating. There was none of this eating on the run; meals lasted for hours, with lots of good conversation thrown in. The happiest I ever saw my aunts and uncles in the Coleman family was when they'd slowly eat their savory meals, washing everything down with several glasses of iced tea. Especially at the Family

Reunion, or on Christmas Day up at Big Mom's house. "Eating good"—with plenty of fat and cholesterol—was held to be essential to proper health and peace of mind.

There were plenty of Colemans: nine brothers—known as "the boys"—and four sisters, the youngest of whom had died when she was a day or two old. (There's enough niggers in your mother's family, Daddy would remark, to cast a Tarzan movie.)

Sunday in Piedmont was everybody's favorite day, because you could eat yourself silly, starting just after church. Mama didn't go to church on Sundays, except to read out her obituaries. She'd cook while we were at Sunday school. Rarely did the menu vary: fried chicken, mashed potatoes, baked corn (corn pudding), green beans and potatoes (with lots of onions and bacon drippings and a hunk of ham), gravy, rolls, and a salad of iceberg lettuce, fresh tomatoes (grown in Uncle Jim's garden), a sliced boiled egg, scallions, and Wishbone's Italian dressing. We'd eat Mama's Sunday dinners in the middle of the day and keep nibbling for the rest of the afternoon and evening. White people just can't cook good, Aunt Marguerite used to say; that's why they need to hire us.

NAOMI SHIHAB NYE
Mint Snowball

My great-grandfather on my mother's side ran a drug-store in a small town in central Illinois. He sold pills and rubbing alcohol from behind the big cash register and creamy ice cream from the soda fountain. My mother remembers the counter's long polished sweep, its shining face. She twirled on the stools. Dreamy fans. Wide summer afternoons. Clink of nickels in anybody's hand. He sold milkshakes, cherry cokes, old fashioned sand-wiches. What did an old fashioned sandwich look like? Dark wooden shelves. Silver spigots on chocolate dispensers.

My great-grandfather had one specialty: a Mint Snowball which he invented. Some people drove all the way in from Decatur just to taste it. First he stirred fresh mint leaves with sugar and secret ingredients in a small pot on the stove for a very long time. He concocted a flamboyant elixir of mint. Its scent clung to his fingers even after he washed his hands. Then he shaved ice into tiny particles and served it mounded in a glass dish. Perm-eated with mint syrup. Scoops of rich vanilla ice cream to each side. My mother took a bite of minty ice and ice cream mixed to-gether. The Mint Snowball tasted like winter. She closed her eyes to see the Swiss village my great-grandfather's parents came from. Snow frosting the roofs. Glistening, dangling spokes of ice.

Before my great-grandfather died, he sold the recipe for the mint syrup to someone in town for one hundred dollars. This hurt my grandfather's feelings. My grandfather thought he should have inherited it to carry on the tradition. As far as the family knew, the person who bought the recipe never used it. At least not in public. My mother had watched my grandfather make the syrup so often she thought she could replicate it. But what did he have in those little unmarked bottles? She experimented. Once she came close. She wrote down what she did. Now she has lost the paper.

Perhaps the clue to my entire personality connects to the lost Mint Snowball. I have always felt out-of-step with my environment, disjointed in the modern world. The crisp flush of cities makes me weep. Strip centers, Poodle grooming and Take-out Thai. I am angry over lost department stores, wistful for something I have never tasted or seen.

Although I know how to do everything one needs to know—change airplanes, find my exit off the interstate, charge gas, send a fax—there is something missing. Perhaps the stoop of my great-grandfather over the pan, the slow patient swish of his spoon. The spin of my mother on the high stool with her whole life in front of her, something fine and fragrant still to happen. When I breathe a handful of mint, even pathetic sprigs from my sunbaked Texas earth, I close my eyes. Little chips of ice on the tongue, their cool slide down. Can we follow the long river of the word "refreshment" back to its spring? Is there another land for me? Can I find any lasting solace in the color green?

Borrowed Time

Ten years ago, several bad things happened to me, all cardiac, and it seemed for a while I had no future at all, not beyond a few weeks. As it panned out, I didn't go rustling off the gurney down the chute, like some of my fellow-patients in Intensive Care. So my future shrank to this instant, this day, this week (if I was feeling sound and bold). Looking back on that time, having had the future I never thought I would have, I still have the sense of living on borrowed time and am reluctant even to ponder whatever future is left. Time for me has become concentric, really a matter of depth and simultaneity. Perhaps this is why numbers all look alike to me, and my way of reading a book is to fix on a phrase or a line and plunge away into and behind it, acknowledging time only in an etymological way. When I hear the phrase *cogito, ergo sum,* I worry that the *"o"* on *cogit* has no right to be there until *ergo sum* has taken place. M. Descartes has no right to presuppose his own conclusion, even if only to suffix a verb. Such is my notion of futurity.

Thus handicapped, I shuffle the futurology cards and stop my mouth with clear answers. The hole in the ozone layer is already repairing itself. There will soon be altogether too much visually sharp television in the world. Already, few know how to read a serious book. Television, essentially a medium of redundant illustration (someone says menu of ideas and a groaning board of smorgasbord appears onscreen), has just about killed the initiative people used to put into metaphor. One side of me, very American, believes in progress: selfishly craving inhalable insulin and better cardiology; another side of me overestimates how much we belong to nature to begin with, and is appropriately fatalistic. I had my true future almost ten years ago, lived symbolically in one month, and all else is trappings on that. I see my life swelling outward like a stain, or an algae patch in a pool, needing only sunlight. I reassure myself that the word future descended from the Indo-European base *bhau-, which gave us not only *fut* but also *fui,* the perfect tense of *esse:* to be. The future is only a matter of emphasis, a better equipped past.

How, then, do I communicate with people to whom the future is a *thing* to come? Like a thriller reader, I believe in the shapeliness of things to come, hoping we have really done our worst, plumbed our nadir, in the 20th century, and that, while cramming the planet with ourselves and our progeny (meaning it no harm), we will get less vicious. I say *hope;* the swarming cannibalism of mice in the overpopulation experiments at Rockefeller University chastens me. The future is a repercussion, not a plan. The future is a novel that ends before you intend it to, or that goes on after you have lost interest. The future is a tesseract for babies to play with.

Loose Ends

For years the following scene would play daily at our house: Home from school, my daughter would heave her backpack off her shoulder and let it thud to the hall floor, then dump her jacket on top of the pile. My husband would tell her to pick it up—as he did every day—and hang it in the closet. Begrudgingly with a snort and a hrrumph, she would comply. The ritual interrogation began:

"Hi, Aviva. How was school?"

"Fine."

"What did you do today?"

"Nothing."

And so it went, every day. We cajoled, we pleaded, we threatened with rationed ice cream sandwiches and new healthy vegetable casseroles, we attempted subterfuges such as: "What was Ms. Boyers wearing today?" or: "Any new pets in science class?" but her answer remained the same: I dunno.

Asked, however, about that week's episodes of "MathNet," her favorite series on Public Television's "Square One," or asked for a quick gloss of a segment of "Lois and Clark" that we happened to miss, and she'd spew out the details of a complicated story, complete with character development, gestures, every twist and back-flip of the plot.

Is TV greater than reality? Are we to take as damning evidence the soap opera stars attacked in public by viewers who obstinately believe in the on-screen villainy of Erica or Jeannie's evil twin? Is an estrangement from real life the catalyst behind the escalating violence in our schools, where children imitate the gun-'em-down pyrotechnics of cop-and-robber shows?

Such a conclusion is too easy. Yes, the influence of public media on our perceptions is enormous, but the relationship of projected reality—i.e., TV—to imagined reality—i.e., an existential moment—is much more complex. It is not that we confuse TV with reality, but that we prefer it to reality—the manageable struggle resolved in twenty-six minutes, the witty repartee within the family circle instead of the grunts and silence common to most real families; the sharpened conflict and defined despair instead of vague anxiety and invisible enemies. "Life, my friends, is boring. We must not say so," wrote John Berryman, and many years and "Dream Songs" later he leapt from a bridge in Minneapolis. But there is a devastating corollary to that statement: Life, friends, is ragged. Loose ends are the rule.

What happens when my daughter tells the television's story better than her own is simply this: the TV offers an easier tale to tell. The salient points are there for the plucking—indeed, they're the only points presented—and all she has to do is to recall them. Instant Nostalgia! Life, on the other hand, slithers about and runs down blind alleys and sometimes just fizzles at the climax. "The world is ugly, / And the people are sad," sings the country bumpkin in Wallace Stevens's "Gubinnal." Who isn't tempted to ignore the inexorable fact of our insignificance on a dying planet? We all yearn for our private patch of blue.

Nostalgia

Whatever happened to the crepuscular? It's never mentioned anymore. Years since I heard any reference to the crepuscular. I wonder if anybody notices it now as we once did, creeping
in and out with silent majesty, leaving some of us with lumps in
our throats. It would be a relief from the carnage and mayhem.
I remember sometimes at that time of day in the autumn when
there was a chill in the air and somebody was burning leaves somewhere, I could nearly die of happiness. But I am older now and
it's illegal to burn leaves. So I guess nobody notices the crepuscular anymore. Or the bucolic. Nobody ever says, "Let's go spend
a bucolic weekend in the country." And nobody calls anything
idyllic. Whatever became of idyllic afternoons beside the river?
And grand passions? Passions don't seem to be grand anymore,
just sort of everyday affairs. I guess it's hard to have a grand
passion without idyllic afternoons and crepuscular evenings, and
we are just too busy to take the time for such things. And nightin-
gales? I never heard one myself, but I certainly read about them,
and they seemed to be almost everywhere at one time. Perhaps
they were no longer needed and they died out or somebody shot

them. Might be a few left in a zoo somewhere, I wouldn't know about that. But surely gentility has survived. You mean gentility is gone too? Lord! But whatever happened to peace and quiet? Somewhere there still must be some peace and quiet. And whatever happened to kindness. . . ?

Across the Street

The man in the house across the street is dying. I began to notice it two years ago in the form of little mishaps: grocery bags standing in the gape of the front door for hours, and the window cat who never went out, soon scratching in everyone's yard. Next, the steaming Buick was jacked on a mash of shrubbery, missing the garage by a mile, while his wife's voice rang with a marriage of exasperation and fear, "Frank? Frank! What's wrong with you?"

He began to study his feet as he walked, and watched his steps grow smaller. Eventually he had to rely on a cane, and that soon gave way to a walker.

I assumed all this was the onset of old age, or of senility—the nerves tangled inside the skull like the knot of a root-bound plant. But one day when I was out watering, she came over and told me it was something about his balance: he kept falling over. She shook her head back and forth. "He used to be an athlete . . ."

Then every day the elderly homosexual man in a blue car took him away and brought him back hours later. The distance between the car and the house seemed interminable to me, watching Frank who was now always too unsure, even with the walker, to step just an inch; and the old man who must have loved him, reassuring him in the soft shuffling sounds of German. Now the man in the blue car pulls up to the house and goes inside and doesn't come out until late at night.

Of course I can't say for sure Frank is dying, maybe I should just say that his health has obviously grown worse. Who can say at what point dying begins? Was he dying the day he ran over the bushes? Or the day the cat traveled into the world for the first time? Or did it start before then, before any noticeable symptoms appeared? Perhaps he was already failing the day I watched him stride back up the hill from the cleaners, his pressed shirts slung over his shoulder, his hips cocked to one side like a kid's as he paused to chat with me. Perhaps even then, with the breeze between us and his smile as easy as any certain thing, that polyethylene sack billowing out behind him was really a kind of phantom.

And what of me? Is there a vantage point, say, from a neighbor's window, where my descent can be witnessed? Would a neighbor's hindsight pinpoint my demise at the unremarkable instant I once turned off the water to catch the phone? If I could stand outside myself enough to see the spectral film uncurling in the air behind me, could I change the scene, fasten my seat belt, take more vitamins and miraculously sidestep the siege?

But if it's already too late, if my number's up and death has begun to grow inside me like a root-bound silence, and I soon can't stand or walk even an inch without someone at my side, will there be someone who loves me, come to take me out into the world for a ride, talking in a language I understand?

BILL CAPOSSERE
A Wind from the North

When three days had passed and the snow still lay in smooth unbrushed drifts across the cold glass and silvery metal of the car, the neighbors, curious or concerned, began a trail of telephone calls that led, eventually, to my own heated home. Later that night, inside a sky of utter clarity and simplicity, it began once more to snow.

The coroner said my uncle had been dead five or six days, dead of a heart attack sometime earlier in the week, dead perhaps in his sleep, or perhaps not, but dead at least quickly, and certainly quietly. It is the quiet part I often wonder about. Five or six days of lying there in his chair while outside the snow piled softly atop his car like all the pale moments of his life gathered together in a cold and singular space. Five or six days gone by, the snow filling in the gaps between the stiff branches of the pine bushes outside the apartment, filling in the hollow between the wheel and the chassis, filling in, even, at last, the cavity formed by his own absence, an absence gone unmarked under the glare of a stark midwinter sun.

What sort of life creates this sort of death? Where after six days, a week, no one turns and says, "Hey, have you seen Louie lately?" Where no one pours an eight a.m. coffee-to-go, then watches it sit atop the counter growing colder by the minute, wondering at least a little before pouring it out into the stainless steel sink. Where no one rings once, twice, many times, before knocking then pounding against an unyielding door. How do sixty years of a man's tracks disappear so completely under a blanket of snow that the world seems a cold and pathless place?

My own memories of him are dim. I seldom saw him off the couch at home, and remember few conversations. Usually the ones we had were brief and one-sided and came about because I had wandered between him and the golf game on television or had strayed too close to his new car—always the same: sleek and sporty and untouchable. I never rode in one.

When he and my aunt divorced, I remember little feeling of loss, inured, perhaps, to such annual occurrence in our lives, or simple acknowledgment maybe of a presence never felt, a connection never made. When he moved back in with my aunt for a while due to finances, I recall only a sense of awkwardness. The two of them did not speak to one another; he moved through the house like the family madman, let out this time from the attic, but still unseen, not to be spoken to. He would come down the stairs when I visited and grasp my hand firmly as if to hold me there until, forced by the pressure of our palms, I would at last acknowledge his existence.

That was perhaps as far as I could go. His hands were thin and dry and bloodless; cool to the touch, they held no history for me. We would stand that way for a moment as he asked a question or two, the right questions, I suppose, the ones he had finally learned one cannot get along without, but we were two strangers by then, and it was all the conversation one might expect to have while waiting in line someplace wide and empty.

I think he began to realize even then the fort he had built round himself, began then to notice the metallic taste of loneliness, like an old coin held too long in the mouth. As he sat in that chair and the snow began to pile up outside, I wonder if he saw in its slow accumulation the heavy weight of a lifetime's chances gone by and felt in its cool accusation the smothering force that pressed him back into his seat and finally crowded out the untethered motions of his heart.

The Eskimo, it is said, have many words for snow, different words for snow falling and snow already fallen. They use *muruaneq* for soft deep snow, *natquik* for the snow which covers the ground and clings to the feet, *kanevvluk* for fine snow, and *quaniisqineq* for snow floating on water. But, as far as I can find, they have no word for the snow that covers a man's death so that even the wake of his passage is obliterated. Unless it be *natquigte,* snow that drifts perpetually along the ground, resting nowhere, holding to nothing, ever-moving particles aloft on the wind.

Snow

To one who lives in the snow and watches it day by day, it is a book to be read. The pages turn as the wind blows; the characters shift and the images formed by their combinations change in meaning, but the language remains the same. It is a shadow language, spoken by things that have gone by and will come again. The same text has been written there for thousands of years, though I was not here, and will not be here in winters to come, to read it. These seemingly random ways, these paths, these beds, these footprints, these hard, round pellets in the snow: they all have meaning. Dark things may be written there, news of other lives, their sorties and excursions, their terrors and deaths. The tiny feet of a shrew or a vole make a brief, erratic pattern across the snow, and here is a hole down which the animal goes. And now the track of an ermine comes this way, swift and searching, and he too goes down that white-shadow of a hole.

A wolverine, and the loping, toed-in track I followed uphill for two miles one spring morning, until it finally dropped away into another watershed and I gave up following it. I wanted to see where he would go and what he would do. But he just went on, certain of where he was going, and nothing came of it for me to see but that sure and steady track in the snowcrust, and the sunlight strong in my eyes.

Snow blows across the highway before me as I walk—little, wavering trails of it swept along like a people dispersed. The snow people—where are they going? Some great danger must pursue them. They hurry and fall, the wind gives them a push, they get up and go on again.

     •

I was walking home from Redmond Creek one morning late in January. On a divide between two watersheds I came upon the scene of a battle between a moose and three wolves. The story was written plainly in the snow at my feet. The wolves had come in from the west, following an old trail from the Salcha River, and had found the moose feeding in an open stretch of the overgrown road I was walking.

The sign was fresh, it must have happened the night before. The snow was torn up, with chunks of frozen moss and broken sticks scattered about; here and there, swatches of moose hair. A confusion of tracks in the trampled snow—the splayed, stabbing feet of the moose, the big, furred pads and spread toenails of the wolves.

I walked on, watching the snow. The moose was large and alone, almost certainly a bull. In one place he backed himself into a low, brush-hung bank to protect his rear. The wolves moved away from him—those moose feet are dangerous. The moose turned, ran on for fifty yards, and the fight began again. It became a running, broken flight that went on for nearly half a mile in the changing, rutted terrain, the red morning light coming across the hills from the sun low in the south. A pattern shifting and uncertain; the wolves relenting, running out into the brush in a wide circle, and closing again: another patch of moose hair in the trodden snow.

I felt that I knew those wolves. I had seen their tracks several times before during that winter, and once they had taken a marten from one of my traps. I believed them to be a female and two nearly grown pups. If I was right, she may have been teaching them how to hunt, and all that turmoil in the snow may have been the serious play of things that must kill to live. But I saw no blood sign that morning, and the moose seemed to have gotten the better of the fight. At the end of it he plunged away into thick alder brush. I saw his tracks, moving more slowly now, as he climbed through a low saddle, going north in the shallow, unbroken snow. The three wolves trotted east toward Banner Creek.

What might have been silence, an unwritten page, an absence, spoke to me as clearly as if I had been there to see it. I have imagined a man who might live as the coldest scholar on earth, who followed each clue in the snow, writing a book as he went. It would be the history of snow, the book of winter. A thousand-year text to be read by a people hunting these hills in a distant time. Who was here, and who has gone? What were their names? What did they kill and eat? Whom did they leave behind?

Decoy

Late in one stubborn, unyielding winter a good many years ago, I undertook to make some decoys for myself, using spruce two-by-eights that were lying around in the barn, and working with a hatchet, pocket-knife, and rasp. They came out looking crude and blocky—a friend picked one up, scrutinized it from several angles, and said it betrayed an imperfectly assimilated Cubist influence—yet they have always done the job. Ducks don't seem to have much of an eye for detail. But I don't take any satisfaction in these merely workmanlike effigies. In the fashioning of them, I had begun to realize that my motives were not practical. Cheap and perfectly serviceable plastic ones were available. The motive was more Pygmalion-like—to give shape to a longing.

When you try to make almost anything, you are probably working in a tradition, whether you know it or not. It is almost more interesting not to know it, and only belatedly come to see that the tradition was working in you before you were conscious of yourself working in it. A considerable time after I had completed my clunky specimens, I began looking a little bit into decoy-making and found that its Golden Age had been from about 1880 to 1920. In the past quarter-century or so, the classifying, authenticating, and collecting of decoys of this vintage has become a big business, very far removed from the salt marshes and tide flats. Recently, the market seems to have declined slightly, but a local dealer tells me that plenty of wooden ducks out there are still bringing what he called "serious money"— $10,000 and upward. And he told me that in 1986, at an auction in Kennebunk, Maine, a pintail made of white pine sold for $319,000, which is the highest price ever paid for a piece of American folk art.

The prices are incidental, and even accidental. The decoys were made to fool ducks, and to cost two or three dollars apiece. You need to look at them that way, as things of use, almost always made by men who gave them that use, and plenty of it. These old decoys vary in style, but they all have in common a precision that is far in excess of a duck's apparent powers of discrimination. Even with all the paint worn off, a redhead decoy is recognizable by its high forehead, a widgeon by its slightly undersized bill. Regardless of species, and somewhat at odds with strict verisimilitude, there is an exaggerated shapeliness usually evident in the curve of the neck and the arch of the back. A good decoy has fine lines in the same way that a good boat does. It looks as though it had been smoothed and molded into existence by a potter, and invites handling.

The $319,000 pintail was made by Elmer Crowell, of East Harwich, Massachusetts. I am not myself convinced that it represents the finest of his work. Although I have only seen his decoys in photographs, the most remarkable to me is of a black duck. It is reaching its head back to preen itself. One wing-tip is slightly elevated, and it gives the bird the asymmetrical tension and poised imbalance of a cantilevered building. You would not think of it as folk art, you would think of it as something that was made to be exhibited on its own small pedestal, in the shadowless light of a bare, silent room. But Crowell was a guide, decoys were his side-line. And even the guiding was a secondary and subsidiary activity—he had become a pusher purely in order to support his habit, which was duck-hunting. He shot ducks commercially until Federal regulation put him out of business, and hunted for sport thereafter, although he preferred the old days of unrestricted slaughter—the sink-box, the swivel gun, the night hunting. You would expect his decoys to be simple, sturdy, and inexpensive, given his businesslike approach to waterfowling. They never were, and in fact had a poor reputation among hunters. He seems often to have used imperfectly cured pine and many of his birds split or checked when subjected to the constant wetting and drying, freezing and thawing of field conditions. The fineness of carving that characterized even his earliest birds meant that the heads, necks, and bills broke too easily, given the rough, offhand treatment that decoys inevitably get.

Crowell looks to me like an extreme case, but not an atypical one. The art of the decoy began to flourish during the final decades of a massacre of migratory birds that was without precedent, and that can never be repeated. The flocks that flowed north and south, spring and fall, will not be seen on this planet again. What you see instead is a dusty, eyeless scaup or scoter sitting in a dealer's showroom, wearing a price that makes you flinch. It was made by and for the men who participated enthusiastically, and often professionally, in the massacre. The astonishing thing is that the men had such an accurate appreciation for the individual grace, beauty, and proportion of the birds they slaughtered so wantonly. They became artists without intending to. The ducks, on their way out, decoyed the hunters.

Duck art and duck kitsch—mallard-headed door knockers, coat hangers, umbrella handles, faucets, canvasback-embossed door mats, bath mats, hearth rugs, lampshades, platters, saucers, ice buckets—are everywhere. No other animal has such a broad-based totemic potency. Eighty or a hundred years ago, all up and down the Atlantic coast, you would have found men who were, socio-economically if not artistically, the equivalents of Elmer Crowell. They no doubt did all kinds of seasonal work—crabbed, clammed, lobstered, oystered, seined, fished—but what they lived for, whether as market hunters or as guides, was the arrival of cold weather and the first waves of ducks. They were not men of property. Their tradition of hunting, to the extent that it owed anything to England, derived from the unlanded underclass of rural society—men who were poachers, practical and sly, handy with boats, nets, guns, dogs, traps, and snares. They were excluded from the English tradition of hunting, which was restricted by law to men of substantial property. In the unbounded space of the New World, they founded the American tradition. Their own range was gradually squeezed and shrunken; one of their last habitats was one of the stubbornest frontiers of all—the intertidal zone of marshes, mudflats, and swamps that were legally and literally no man's land.

When I sit in a den that is all gussied up in the rustic-elegiac, pseudo-outdoorsy Ralph Lauren manner, and see over the mantelpiece a limited edition print, signed by the artist, of black ducks dropping into a tawny salt marsh ("Winter Wings"), I feel something complicated. Duck-hunting has become a rich man's sport, and the print probably hangs there chiefly as an assertion of status. In that respect, it means about what a fox-hunting print would mean in an equivalent English household. But there is a difference. In the fox-hunting print, we see, in the foreground, the human pageant and drama: crop-tailed horses and red-coated riders clearing a hedge or sunken lane in impeccable style. We contemplate their skill, their equipage, and especially the majestic, wooden-faced, definitively British imperturbability with which the hunters pursue their quarry, as though they did not so much intend to kill the fox as to *cut him dead*. Off in the middle distance, we see what they are riding toward—a horse standing quietly, a circle of hounds, a man in the center of it, holding up something scruffy. It could as well be a squirrel or cat. The duck painting, by contrast, focuses on the birds themselves. The perspective is like that of a formal portrait: the ducks, filling the foreground, exceed the dimension of biology. The landscape behind them—the marshes, water, and sky—implies and subserves their power. While the painting may be no more than a status object, it nevertheless removes you completely from your human context. The image celebrates space, freedom, and wildness—the heritage of the unclaimed continent. Pretension is a kind of hypocrisy and hypocrisy is a kind of homage. If you even want to pose as a duck hunter, you must at least pretend to still see the beauty and potency of the birds. And, whether you know it or not, that is a way of claiming kinship with the old guides and decoy-makers, who chose to live marginally—at the margins of a society and in the margin of unpossessed earth that still existed between the tides.

BRENDA PETERSON
Growing Up Game

When I went off to college, my father gave me, as part of my tuition, fifty pounds of moose meat. In 1969, eating moose meat at the University of California was a contradiction in terms. Hippies didn't hunt. I lived in a rambling Victorian house that boasted sweeping circular staircases, built-in lofts, and a landlady who dreamed of opening her own health food restaurant. I told my housemates that my moose meat in its nondescript white butcher paper was from a side of beef my father had bought. The carnivores in the house helped me finish off such suppers as sweet-and-sour moose meatballs, mooseburgers (garnished with the obligatory avocado and sprouts), and mooseghetti. The same dinner guests who remarked upon the lean sweetness of the meat would have recoiled if I'd told them the not-so-simple truth: that I grew up on game, and the moose they were eating had been brought down, with one shot through his magnificent heart, by my father—a man who had hunted all his life and all of mine.

One of my earliest memories is of crawling across the vast continent of crinkled linoleum in our Forest Service cabin kitchen down splintered back steps, through wildflowers growing wheat-high. I was eye-level with grasshoppers who scolded me on my first solo trip outside. I made it to the shed, a cool and comfortingly square shelter that held phantasmagoric metal parts; they smelled good, like dirt and grease. I had played a long time in this shed before some maternal shriek made me lift up on my haunches to listen to those urgent, possessive sounds that were my name. Rearing up, my head bumped into something hanging in the dark; gleaming white, it felt sleek and cold against my cheek. Its smell was dense and musty and not unlike the slabs of my grandmother's great arms after her cool, evening sponge baths. In that shed I looked up and saw the flensed body of a doe; it swung gently, slapping my face. I felt then as I do even now when eating game: horror and awe and kinship.

Growing up those first years on a Plumas National Forest station high in the Sierra Nevada near Oregon was somewhat like belonging to a white tribe. The men hiked off every day into their forest and the women stayed behind in the circle of official cabins, breeding. So far away from a store, we ate venison and squirrel, rattlesnake and duck. My first rattle, in fact, was from a diamondback rattler my father killed as we watched, by snatching it up with a stick and winding it, whiplike, around a redwood sapling. Rattlesnake tastes just like chicken, but has many fragile bones to slither one's way through. We also ate rainbow trout, rabbit, and geese galore. The game was accompanied by such daily garden dainties as fried okra, mustard greens, corn fritters, wilted lettuce (our favorite because of that rare, blackened bacon), new potatoes and peas, stewed tomatoes, barbecued butter beans.

I was four before I ever had a beef hamburger, and I remember being disappointed by its fatty, nothing taste and the way it fell apart at the seams whenever my teeth sank into it. Smoked pork shoulder came much later, in the South; and I was twenty-one, living in New York City, before I ever tasted leg of lamb. I approached that glazed rack of meat with a certain guilty self-consciousness, as if I unfairly stalked those sweet-tempered white creatures myself. But how would I explain my squeamishness to those urban sophisticates? How explain that I was shy with mutton when I had been bred on wild things?

Part of it, I suspect, had to do with the belief I'd also been bred on: we become the spirit and body of animals we eat. As a child eating venison, I liked to think of myself as lean and lovely just like the deer. I would never be caught dead just grazing while some man who wasn't even a skillful hunter crept up and conked me over the head. If someone wanted to hunt me, he must be wily and outwitting. He must earn me.

My father had also taught us as children that animals were our brothers and sisters under their skin. They died so that we might live. And of this sacrifice we must be mindful. "God make us grateful for what we are about to receive," took on new meaning when we imagined the animal's surrender to our own appetites. We also used all the animal, so that an elk became elk steaks, stew, salami, and sausage. His head and horns went on the wall to watch us more earnestly than any baby-sitter, and every Christmas Eve we had a ceremony of making our own moccasins for the new year out of whatever Father had tanned. "Nothing wasted," my father would always say, or, as we munched on sausage cookies made from moosemeat or venison, "Think about who you're eating." We thought of ourselves as intricately linked to the food chain. We knew, for example, that a forest fire meant, at the end of the line, we'd suffer too. We'd have buck stew instead of venison steak, and the meat would be stringy, withered-tasting, because in the animal kingdom, as it seemed with humans, only the meanest and leanest and orneriest survived losing their forests.

Once when I was in my early teens, I went along on a hunting trip as the "main cook and bottle-washer," though I don't remember any bottles; none of these hunters drank alcohol. There was something else coursing through their veins as they rose long before dawn and disappeared, returning to my little camp most often dragging a doe or pheasant or rabbit. We ate innumerable cornmeal-fried fish, had rabbit stew seasoned only with blood and black pepper.

This hunting trip was the first time I remember eating game as a conscious act. My father and Buddy Earl shot a big doe and she lay with me in the back of the tarp-draped station wagon all the way home. It was not the smell I minded, it was the glazed great, dark eyes and the way that head flopped around crazily on what I knew was once a graceful neck. I found myself petting this doe, murmuring all those graces we'd been taught long ago as children. Thank you for the sacrifice, thank you for letting us be like you so that we can grow up strong as game. But there was an uneasiness in me that night as I bounced along in the back of the car with the deer.

What was uneasy is still uneasy—perhaps it always will be. It's not easy when one really starts thinking about all this: the eating game, the food chain, the sacrifice of one for the other. It's never easy when one begins to think about one's most basic actions, like eating. Like becoming what one eats: lean and lovely and mortal.

Why should it be that the purchase of meat at a butcher shop is somehow more righteous than eating something wild? Perhaps it has to do with our collective unconscious that sees the animal bred for slaughter as doomed. But that wild doe or moose might make it without the hunter. Perhaps on this primitive level of archetype and unconscious knowing we even believe that what's wild lives forever.

My father once told this story around a hunting campfire. His own father, who raised cattle during the Great Depression on a dirt farm in the Ozarks, once fell on such hard times that he had to butcher the pet lamb for supper. My father, bred on game or their own hogs all his life, took one look at the family pet on that meat platter and pushed his plate away. His siblings followed suit. To hear my grandfather tell it, it was the funniest thing he'd ever seen. "They just couldn't eat Bo-Peep," Grandfather said. And to hear my father tell it years later around that campfire, it was funny, but I saw for the first time his sadness. And I realized that eating had become a conscious act for him that day at the dinner table when Bo-Peep offered herself up.

Now when someone offers me game, I will eat it with all the qualms and memories and reverence with which I grew up eating it. And I think I will always have this feeling of horror and awe and kinship. And something else—full knowledge of what I do, what I become.

Rose Vegetables

In 1960, on one of the hottest June days on record, I went with my family to watch the Grand Floral Parade of Portland's annual Rose Festival. "Rose Vegetable," hippie friends would later dub it, with no argument from me. At age eight, though, one assumes that when a billion flowers get beheaded and thrust on public display, they've died for some noble purpose. So there I hunched, front-row-seated on the curb, watching the edible-looking floats and neurotic clowns; the gymnasts, marching bands and National Guard rockets, the stuntmen, stilt men and sequined majorettes; unicyclists, Indian chiefs, rope-trick artists. White-gloved, admiration-stoned princesses reached toward us through the air, slowly unscrewing invisible jar lids. Beefy Rosarians glad-handed us. Rows of robotic soldiers disdained us. Peanut, ice-cream and bauble vendors hustled us. Magicians and jugglers regaled us. And none of them stuck around long enough to bore us. I grew mesmerized. I can't say for certain that I was having fun, but I was definitely an enthralled little Rose Vegetable, pleased as Pepsi to be a Portlander, wishing I'd a flag, gun or red rose to wave.

The Meadowland Dairy wagon came clomping toward us—a huge, turn-of-the-century bandwagon, drawn by eight enormous black Clydesdales, with a uniformed brass band aboard. The parade abruptly halted, in that inexplicable way parades do, placing the wagon right in front of us. The band lit into some better-than-average Sousa. Parade-goers began bobbing to it like hundreds of happy toilet plungers. Then—in sudden, shocking disagreement with the reigning Rose Vegetable mood—one of the Clydesdales shrieked, and began to rear in its traces. All seven of the other horses began doing the same. The brass band was jerked so violently the Sousa was yanked into silence. And we suddenly knew—as the wagon driver roared his puny "Whoa's," jerked futile reins, and mothers began gripping kids—that those horses could drag their wagon anywhere they chose, including straight through the marching band in front of them, or into the crowd on either side.

That was when I first noticed a man who'd been trudging along by the Clydesdales from the beginning. Just this bland-faced, pale old bald guy wearing black slacks and a short-sleeved shirt so boring he looked more like a lost salesman than part of a gala parade. Definitely not the guy you'd choose to save a day. But he was holding a riding crop in one hand. And he shuffled back along the rearing team, applied his crop to the trouble horse and managed, in no time, to quell all eight of them. No sooner had he calmed the horses, though, than he fell facedown on the asphalt. And didn't move, though the pavement was blistering hot. Seeing this odd behavior, the horses took a few nervous steps forward, and the wagon's huge wooden-spoked, steel-rimmed wheels turned just once. But once was enough: while we stared as if at another clown stunt or magician's trick, the right front wheel of the Meadowland Dairy wagon rolled, with majestic slowness, not so much over as *through* the old man's head.

The smell of a hospital, the air in a full church—normally these are all it takes to make me faint. But the sense of unreality the parade had engendered in me was so complete that not even the sound of crunching skull or the widening pool of brain made me queasy. When easily twenty-five people, including my father, flopped to the ground as if playing Simon Says with the dead man, the unreality only thickened: I didn't understand till my father recovered and told me, later, that it had been a mass faint.

It betrays my slant on civic pride that I consider this, by far, the most edifying Rose Festival event I've ever witnessed. When I try to this day to grasp the driving force behind words like *karma, destiny* or *fate,* I picture those eight enormous black Clydesdales. And when I first read of the Buddhist symbol of the Great Wheel, you can imagine which wheel's slow turning sprang to mind.

So what a comedown, what a piffle-ization the next morning, to watch my parents paw the daily *Oregonian* from end to end and find that the only mention of this soul-shaking event was a three-sentence piece of denial on the obituary page. The old guy had died a hero; he'd gone down for the Rose Vegetable cause; his actions were the first I'd seen outside a boob tube or movie theater that bore even faint resemblance to Christ's line: "He that loseth his life shall save it." And the paper stated his name, age and ex-address; stated the time and place of his death; called the cause of his death "heat stroke"; and that was that.

The Lord can only giveth. The media account is free to sweep what the Lord giveth away. This was my first exposure to this gruesome kind of clean-up operation. I have distrusted newspapers and civic celebrations ever since. I have also believed, ever since, that we live among quiet heroes.

WILLIAM KITTREDGE
Interlude

At a very proper New English sort of Thanksgiving dinner, at my grandmother's table, I was seated on a couple of books in a straight-backed chair beside my great-uncle Hank, a dim, lank old alcoholic bachelor with a whiskery beard.

Uncle Hank was munching along in his silent way when he muttered some unintelligible thing and pulled his complete set of false teeth from his mouth, setting them out to dry on the fine white linen tablecloth. Hank's teeth were inextricably tangled with long strings of bright green spinach. They sat there damp and alive, staining the linen cloth, while he went on eating. I began whimpering—what a fool of a child I must have been— and there was a scene. I wish I could remember how it came out. I wish I knew if Uncle Hank was drunk that late afternoon; I wish he was here now.

Uncle Hank used to lie on the lawn in front of the old white-painted ranch house where my grandparents lived when they came to visit their properties in Warner Valley, an aged man flat on his back, watching the birds as they nested. I like to think about Uncle Hank, and what he thought about as he gazed up into the poplars. He was the prime figure of failure in my family: a stranger, the official eccentric, a drunk, a cautionary figure to frighten boys when they were lazy. Hank, it was said, was like a turkey. "He just pecks where he pecks." Which was as much as anybody could make of him. I like to imagine that Uncle Hank was intimate with the habits of birds. I want to tell myself he led a considered life, and knew it was worthwhile to spend his time utterly absorbed in the look of light through the poplar leaves.

I value his indifference to the ambitions which drove my family. He refused to join their scramble to fence the world. I want to believe he was correct, and not just lazy or drunk all the time. I want to think Uncle Hank loved to ride the nesting-ground swamplands in Warner, and thought grid-map plans for reclamation were an abomination, a bad thing in the long run, for us and not just the muskrats and waterbirds. If someone asked, "Who was your model of conduct when you were a child?" I might lie and say Uncle Hank. His is the great-hearted tradition in my family, at least in this version of things.

GWENDOLYN NELSON
Orange Who?

My father was a short man who didn't know it. On hurricane energy he flirted and joked women out of cars, money, and filet mignon. He knew how to decorate a promise indiscriminately—for waitresses, salesclerks, dental hygienists, and Seventh Day Adventists—with a social director's forcible cheer. Never a drinker, his only vices were women and an excessive use of pepper. He finished showers with an unshaken faith in closed pores and praised the benefits of sprinting.

He should have been a dancer. Instead, he shuffled and bounced in a boxing ring to no music, scrambling leap-frog brains in exchange for a bantamweight title. At eighty-five, he rejected a walker when his legs betrayed him. Not for him, not after ice skating an 18-barrel jump at Lake George, not after the cover of *Ring* magazine, and surely not after bulleting the length of Duquesne Gardens in professional hockey, a spray of ice following long blades, his speed-bent torso parallel to the ice. He played sports when all you had to do was love games and moving, be good, and believe you were great. He played when it was enough to give your heart-pumping all, before lessons had to start as early as toilet training with parents in hock for expenses, before sports were hard business.

In between, he worked in steel mills, and after the high times sold Hoover vacuums and Knapp shoes. Once he sold enough vacuums to win a choice of luggage or an oil paint set. The rows of neat paint tubes were cited often as proof of a father's priorities. In the car, he told knock-knock jokes when he wasn't cursing flawed drivers, his red head straining out a window in Scotch-Irish fury. I remember waiting in the car drinking milk from a quart carton while he demonstrated a vacuum's suction power: the car rolled backward, stopped at a tree, and he came running, arms out as if he were on fire.

Once my father ejected a woman from her own car and drove off. I could see her grow small in the distance, screaming in the street and jabbing the air with an umbrella. Eventually he did some hard time for trouble with women, and he was perplexed and hurt, as if there had been some misunderstanding. In an untypical search for reason, he attributed the sorry business to boxing: "It must have messed up my head—worse than I thought."

Youngest of five brothers, he was, by the time I knew him, trying to grab hold again of glory days, the big break always just about to find him. Two brothers were rich; a third preferred the woods, and the fourth hung out in Atlantic City's beach life. We always visited the rich brothers at dinner time. One of these, a chemical magnate, went to Monaco for Princess Grace's wedding. My father felt directly connected and satisfied by his brother's invitation, and this social triumph was cited as frequently as closed pores and the paint set.

As the grand success eluded him, he relied more on dreams. To a feasible plan, he would say, "Let's not and say we did," with his own robust version of reality. He never gave up the conviction that my mother, too, would come looking for him.

They met on vacation at Rehobeth Beach, where he was play-ing knock-knock jokes in high spirits, going door-to-door. Tall and realistic, she opened hers. Before long the Women's Army Corps and World War II looked safer, so she joined up, shipped out, and counted on change. Over the years, she acquired in his mind a mythic beauty and the attraction of a lost paradise. Some men cry quietly; my father was given to commotion and waving fists, but not for this loss that made others lighter by comparison and marked a downturn for everything afterward. In him, Gatsby met Willy Loman, a doubled formula for the dream doomed.

Crushed by an air compressor at sixty-five, he was hospitalized with tubes in his nostrils, arms, and abdomen—too many to count at a glance. Strange to see him holding still. The nurse said, "This man can't be sixty-five." I think rearranging and losing facts spared him some of their stress and natural toll. At eighty-five, without the walker, he refused to sell his piece of land, the top of Brown's Mountain, though developers snaked up there touching their wallets, fingering surveys. He stood his ground, a goalie in front of a hybrid house. He shouted over promises of paved road and regularly rang up the governor with a confused and obscure agenda. But he hung onto the mountain top, a salesman with goods too right to sell.

Once in a while he called to warn me that the government was not leveling with us about Alaska's coldest temperature. Once in a great while he wanted to know, "What went wrong?" and the receiver felt heavy.

Knock-knock.

Who's there?

Orange.

Orange who?

Orange you glad I'm here?

TED KOOSER
Hands

More and more frequently since I entered my fifties I have begun to see my father's hands out at the ends of my arms. Just now, the left and more awkward one lies curled in my lap while the right one massages the beard on my chin. On the ring finger of the left is the silver wedding band that my wife gave me, not my father's gold ring with its little yellow sapphire. But I am not deceived; this wearing of my ring on his ring finger is a part of my father's respectful accommodation of me and of my life and marriage. Mine have succeeded his, which is, as he would have said, only as it should be.

I recognize his hands despite the ring. They are exactly as I remember them from his own middle age—wrinkled, of course, with a slight sheen to the tiny tilework of the skin; with knotted, branching veins; and with thin dark hair that sets out from beneath the shirtcuffs as if to cover the hand but that within an inch thins and disappears as if there were a kind of glacial timberline there. There is, as we know, a field of coldness just beyond the reaching tips of our fingers and this hair has been discouraged and has fallen back.

As a young man my father had been a drapery salesman in a department store and his hands were ever after at their best when smoothing fabric for display—the left one holding a piece of cloth unrolled from a bolt while the right lovingly eased and teased the wrinkles from it, his fingers spread and their tips lightly touching the cloth as if under them was something grand and alive like the flank of a horse. I can feel the little swirls of brocade beneath the ball of his thumb.

These hands have never done hard physical work, but they are not plump, or soft, or damp and cool. Nor are their nails too carefully clipped or too carefully buffed and polished. They are firm, solid, masculine hands, and other men feel good about shaking them. They have a kind of brotherly warmth and when they pinch the selvage of the drapery fabric and work it just a little between thumb and finger they do it with power and confidence. There are pairs of hands like these—some brown, some black, some white—in every bazaar in the world—hands easing and smoothing, hands flying like doves through the dappled light under time-riddled canvas.

I would like to be held by these hands, held by them as they were when I was a child and I seemed to fall within them wherever I might turn. I would like to feel them warm and broad against my back and would like to be pressed to the breast of this man with his faint perfume of aftershave, with the tiny brown moles on his neck, with the knot of his necktie slightly darkened by perspiration. Now he has taken his glasses off and set them on the mantel and there are small red ovals on the sides of his nose. I reach to touch them and find them wet, as if I were touching something deep inside him. Now I hear him singing, softly singing, the words buzzing deep in his chest.

But these old hands of his are past all that. They lie side by side in my lap, their palms turned up as if to catch this fleeting moment as it falls away. But as I peer down into them they begin to move on their own, to turn and shift. I watch the left hand slowly rise to place its palm against my heart, and watch the right rise swiftly to enfold the other.

The Signature of God

I was feeding my mother her breakfast at Emory Hospital, where we had taken her again for more tests, when she picked up a small piece of plastic torn from the utensil wrapping. She waved away the spoon when I brought it toward her and, holding up the piece of clear trash, she said, "Isn't this a cute thing?" then continued to look at it for a long time. She pointed at the toe of my boot and said, "Whose head is that? Is it a baby's?" She looked at the sunlight coming along the wall and asked me why they had done that, why they hadn't left it the way it was.

After the meal, she appeared to doze, then opened her eyes and said, "What am I supposed to know? Do I know anything? Do I have a name?"

●

And that evening when I drove toward home and stopped for gas at the intersection of two country roads, there were thousands of starlings in the bare oaks lining the road. I paid for the gas and started to drive off, but just then the birds burst from the trees all at once and curved through the sky, throwing darkness over me as they crossed in front of the sun already half hidden by the horizon. I pulled the car away from the gas pumps, cut the engine, rolled down the windows, and sat watching as the giant flock curled and dived and swept across the sky gone hazy blue and deepening. I saw them curving back toward the oaks—a river of birds, a grand black current winding through the heavens. They alighted in the branches squawking and calling, the sound growing louder and louder as they came, thousands of them, burdening the trees, until a roar of squawks, each piercing, filled the dusk.

Another car stopped next to mine, and a young couple got out and leaned against the side of their car, laughing and pointing and shouting to each other.

Then, for no reason I could discern, the birds stopped and lifted off, with the sound of a single wingbeat—silence and then a rush of air with a dampened pop, as though an enormous thick quilt snapped once in the wind.

The young man walked over to me as the birds flew high above the pasture, weaving and turning. "It's like God writing on the sky," he said, "it's like the signature of God."

And I heard myself answer him in a changed voice, though not a new one. "It's something," I said, and I started my car, and I waved to them as I drove away from there, a child heavy with hurt, wanting his mother.

WILL BAKER
My Children Explain
the Big Issues

FEMINISM

I am walking up a long hill toward our water tank and pond. My daughter Montana, 23 months, has decided to accompany me. It is a very warm day, so she wears only diapers, cowboy boots, and a floral-print bonnet. At the outset I offer to carry her but she says "I walk," and then, "You don't have to hold my hand, daddy."

This is the longest walk she has taken, without assistance. I see droplets of sweat on the bridge of her nose. Just before the water tank there is a steep pitch and loose gravel on the path, so I offer again to help.

She pulls away and says, "You don't have to hold me, daddy." A moment later she slips and falls flat. A pause while she rolls into a sitting position and considers, her mouth bent down. But quickly she scrambles up and slaps at the dirty places on her knees, then looks at me sidelong with a broad grin. "See?"

FATE

I first explained to Cole that there was no advantage in dumping the sand from his sandbox onto the patio. He would have more fun bulldozing and trucking inside the two-by-twelve frame. Heavy-equipment guys stayed within the boundaries, part of their job, and the sand would be no good scattered abroad, would get mixed with dead beetles and cat poop.

Next I warned him firmly not to shovel out his patrimony, warned him twice. The third time I physically removed him from the box and underscored my point very emphatically. At this stage, he was in danger of losing important privileges. Reasonable tolerance had already been shown him and there was no further room for negotiation. There was a line in the sand. Did he understand the gravity of the situation? Between whimpers, he nodded.

The last time I lifted him by his ear, held his contorted face close to mine, and posed a furious question to him: *"Why? Why are you doing this?"*

Shaking all over with sobs of deep grief, he tried to answer.

"Eyeadhoo."

"What?"

"Eyeadhoo, eyeadhoo!"

One more second, grinding my teeth, and the translation came to me. I had to. I had to.

EXISTENTIALISM

Cole is almost three and has had a sister now for four months. All his old things have been resurrected. Crib, changing table, car seat, backpack, bassinet. There have been visitors visiting, doctors doctoring, a washer and dryer always washing and drying.

He has taken to following me around when I go to work on a

tractor or pump, cut firewood, or feed the horses. We are out of the house. It doesn't matter if it is raining. In our slickers and rubber boots we stride through a strip of orchard, on our way to some small chore. I am involved with a problem of my own, fooling with a metaphor or calculating if it's time to spray for leaf curl. The rain drumming on the hood of the slicker, wet grass swooshing against the boots, I completely forget my son is there.

"Hey dad," he says suddenly, and I wake up, look down at him, and see that he is in a state of serious wonder, serious delight. "We're *alone* together, aren't we dad?"

EAST AND WEST

My other daughter, Willa, is a Tibetan Buddhist nun on retreat. For three years I cannot see her. She writes me to explain subtle points of the doctrine of emptiness, or the merit in abandoning ego, serving others unselfishly.

I will write back to remind her of a party I took her to in 1970. The apartment was painted entirely in black, and candles were burning. There was loud music and a smell of incense and skunky weed. It was very crowded, some dancing and others talking and laughing. People were wearing ornaments of turquoise, bone, feather, and stained glass.

I glimpsed my six-year-old daughter, at midnight, sitting cross-legged on the floor opposite a young man with very long blond hair. He had no shoes and his shirt was only a painted rag. They were in very deep conversation, eyes locked. I did not hear what the young man had just said, but I overheard my daughter very clearly, her voice definite and assured.

"But," she was saying, "you and I are not the same person."

The Complaint

I don't complain that he has misrepresented me, for the impersonation is skillful. Slander is scarcely the issue: on balance, he has made me seem both a livelier and better person than I fear I am.

People who make the mistake that I am he expect an ironic skepticism, a bruised worldliness, and, maybe, like a caption you wouldn't have thought a picture needed until an exact one got supplied, an apt little tag phrase, maybe in Latin. He is, people say, witty, and also smart. I feel like a widower's bride being told of her brilliant predecessor, and I fill with formless murk.

The people who tell me these things while I stand stiffly mute are not the ones to whom I seem both a livelier and better person than I really am, needless to say.

People I've never met make that mistake, and why would I have met them? Who stands behind a podium and theatrically extracts his reading glasses from a nifty leather case, rocks back on his heels and unreels some genial patter, and then reads, in that cigarette-rasped old-friends voice of his, a poem which the hipper members of the audience applaud by making small, barely but firmly

audible, all-vowel noises, like gerbil orgasms? Who travels to the
Rockefeller Foundation's Study and Conference Center on Lake
Como to write for a month under a cantilevered Tizio lamp, and
then returns with droll instructions to find the best *gelati* in Bel-
lagio? Mr. Travel On Other People's Money, that's who. Mr.
Leisure Of The Theory Class.

Well, I guess you can hear the resentment now. I'm the emotional one, wit be damned, and he's broken my heart. It wasn't
always like this. In the beginning, I wallowed in his attentions.

"Me?" I would think, fluttering at the mirror.

Then: "Me!"

Then, of course, I knew, or thought I knew, what he wanted.
But now? Material? He's not an "autobiographical" writer. I often
recognize my emotions, of course, in his poems. But they're shorn
of the exact details and private references that made them mine.
They have details and references he's made up, but those could
be anyone's. And anyone's is drab.

That's why I resent him. OK, I'm very emotional and easily
filled with formless murk, and sometimes I get weepy like this,
I'm sorry. Yes, thank you. He's glib, he files his tongue before he
brushes his teeth, and he's diligent as a dog. He hasn't called in
two days.

He looks like me, but happier.

I don't suppose this will matter to your investigation, but I stole
the phrase "formless murk" from a rejected draft of one of his
poems. "Stole" is perhaps the wrong word. He'd thrown it away.
I didn't have to uncrumple any paper. It was in plain view. He
owes me a lot.

What? That's not a hard question. Of course it's a domestic
dispute. After all, which of the persons I mentioned is missing?

ALEIDA RODRÍGUEZ

My Mother in Two Photographs, Among Other Things

There she is, standing next to her own mother, behind the symmetrical and somewhat religious arrangement of two Coca-Cola bottles flanking a birthday cake on a small table. If you look closely, it's really the sewing machine shut down, the cake on the slightly raised platform in the center, where the machine part turns upside down into its cabinet: a little altar for an impromptu picture of "just the family."

•

It is December 1962, my cousin María's eighth birthday. My brother, my sister, and I were sent five months earlier to a foreign country, so we are not in the picture. In two days, my grandmother will die, and on the right side of the photograph, directly opposite her, forming a Rorschach double, lurks the dark figure of the guide who came to lead her away. The shadow's hand is on its hip, its face swirls in a smoke that obscures the features. My grandmother is the only one not looking—even the baby held up by Panchito is—into the camera, the eye of the future. She seems distracted, as though she is contemplating an answer. Two days after her party, María and Panchito wake up in bed with our grandmother, who has wet the bed and will not rouse.

•

But what about my mother? Like opposite aspects of the same person: my mother, my grandmother's shadow. Here, she's smiling, though not broadly. Her children are gone, but her mother's there, telling her *aguántate, cálmate,* as they sit over *café.* Or maybe she's relieved. It is, after all, the first time since their marriage that she and my father are alone, like newlyweds. But suddenly a kitchen towel, embroidered with the day of the week, *martes,* and smeared with another woman's lipstick, flies from my mother's hand, lands like an open book by my father's mud-caked boots.

•

In this photograph, a coffee-dark V shows through the collar of her dress, evidence of the enforced labor in the cane fields since the revolution. Above her head is a wall vase filled with plastic flowers, hanging under the framed painting of a saint, who can't be seen above the melted-chocolate folds of a robe, and above that, perhaps, two hands are held palms up, checking the spiritual weather. But the hands are outside the photograph, just like my hands, which can't touch my mother at that brief oasis, or my grandmother, right before she turned and left with the shadow.

•

Grandmother left so abruptly, left my mother in mid-sentence, fingering the legendary length of fabric her mother had once transformed into The Miracle of the Three Dresses. Alone, she collapsed into her mother's absence like a slave into bed at the end of the day.

•

Then one afternoon two years later the air of her kitchen spun like someone whirling toward her, and she knew something had happened to her son: locked in a mental ward at sixteen after chasing his foster mother around the block with a kitchen knife. He had dropped out of high school, washed dishes for a living. Sporting long sideburns, he rewarded himself first with a round-backed two-toned Chevy then a series of garish Mustangs. Married to his fate, he left a trail of cars, each wrapped like a wedding ring around a telephone pole.

•

A vision of her oldest daughter—forever regretting she hadn't been born into a TV family—flashed thin against the white walls of college, her body a blade sharpened to sever the question from the answer. Her face a glossy ad of the ideal American living room.

•

In the newspaper photo above the caption "Family of Cuban Expatriates Reunited Here," I am the only one gazing at the camera, my face twisted into a complex curiosity. Two years on my own among strangers had only taught me how to be one. I stood, my first tongue ripped out, with my mother's wet, round cheek pressed to the top of my head. The dark flag of her mustache. Their sour smell, like clothes trapped in a hamper. Emblems of the exile. While bureaucrats toyed with their time and their fate, my parents had waited, uncomplaining, afraid.

•

But I didn't know that back then. I placed myself instead in the camera lens, looking back at the spectacle we made in the bus station. Under my skin, the rice fields of my hometown were flooding the place of language. Though my mother pulled me toward her with one arm, she scooped up only watery absence; my body had long drifted downriver. My mother's face in this photograph, captured by a stranger, betrays the weight of emptiness in her arms.

SUSANNA KAYSEN
Ice Cream

It was a spring day, the sort that gives people hope: all soft winds and delicate smells of warm earth. Suicide weather. Daisy had killed herself the week before. They probably thought we needed distraction. Without Daisy, the staff-to-patient ratio was higher than usual: five patients, three nurses.

Down the hill, past the magnolia already losing its fleshy blossoms, the pink turning brown and rotten along the edge, past the paper-dry daffodils, past the sticky laurel that could crown you or poison you. The nurses were less nervous on the street that day, spring fever making them careless—or perhaps the staff-to-patient ratio was a more comfortable one for them.

The floor of the ice cream parlor bothered me. It was black-and-white checkerboard tile, bigger than supermarket checkerboard. If I looked only at a white square, I would be all right, but it was hard to ignore the black squares that surrounded the white ones. The contrast got under my skin. I always felt itchy in the ice cream parlor. The floor meant Yes, No, This, That, Up, Down, Day, Night—all the indecisions and opposites that were bad enough in life without having them spelled out for you on the floor.

A new boy was dishing out cones. We approached him in a phalanx.

"We want eight ice cream cones," said one of the nurses.

"Okay," he said. He had a friendly, pimply face.

It took a long time to decide what flavors we wanted. It always did.

"Peppermint stick," said the Martian's girlfriend.

"It's just called 'peppermint,' " said Georgina.

"Peppermint dick."

"Honestly." Georgina was revving up for a complaint.

"Peppermint clit."

The Martian's girlfriend got a nurse nip for that.

There were no other takers for peppermint, chocolate was a big favorite. For spring they had a new flavor, peach melba. I ordered that.

"You gonna want nuts on these?" the new boy asked.

We looked at one another: Should we say it? The nurses held their breath. Outside, the birds were singing.

"I don't think we need them," said Georgina.

VIVIAN GORNICK
On the Street

A writer who lived at the end of my block died. I'd known this woman more than twenty years. She admired my work, shared my politics, liked my face when she saw it coming toward her, I could see that, but she didn't want to spend time with me. We'd run into each other on the street, and it was always big smiles, a wide embrace, kisses on both cheeks, a few minutes of happy unguarded jabber. Inevitably I'd say, Let's get together. She'd nod and say, Call me. I'd call, and she'd make an excuse to call back, then she never would. Next time we'd run into each other: big smile, great hug, kisses on both cheeks, not a word about the unreturned call. She was impenetrable: I could not pierce the mask of smiling politeness. We went on like this for years. Sometimes I'd run into her in other parts of town. I'd always be startled, she too. New York is like a country, the neighborhood is your town, you spot someone from the block or the building in another neighborhood and the first impulse to the brain is, What are *you* doing here? We'd each see the thought on the other's face and start to laugh. Then we'd both give a brief salute and keep walking.

On the Street

Six months after her death I passed her house one day and felt stricken. I realized that never again would I look at her retreating back thinking, Why doesn't she want my friendship? I missed her then. I missed her terribly. She was gone from the landscape of marginal encounters. That landscape against which I measure daily the immutable force of all I connect with only on the street, and only when it sees me coming.

ALEC WILKINSON
Call Guy

Here is a cautionary tale about loneliness and modern appliances. The other night, my wife and I were having dinner at the apartment of friends who have a baby. The child was asleep. Beside the table we were sitting at, our friends had one of those monitors that allow parents to hear their child if he wakes. I have no idea when people began using these devices, but I think that by now everyone is sufficiently familiar with them to know they are just as likely to broadcast a policeman's radio call as a child crying. Once, late at night, over the monitor that my wife and I have for our son, I heard a woman sobbing and a man's voice saying, "If you don't quit drinking, I don't think there's much hope for our marriage."

After dinner, we were talking—there were four of us—and a woman's voice came over the monitor. "Well, what time, then?" she said, peevishly. We could hear a man's deep voice at the other end of the line, but we couldn't hear what he was saying—when he talked we mostly heard static. What we gathered was that he was in a car in New Jersey, heading toward the Lincoln Tunnel.

"Where am I supposed to meet you?" she asked.

"   "

"Port Authority!"

"   "

"You want me to wait in the cold in a doorway?"

"   "

"I can't believe this. All right. Wait a minute. All right. South side of Forty-second Street, between Eighth and Ninth Avenues, halfway down the block. How am I going to recognize your car?"

"   "

"Jesus Christ. I asked for a gentleman, and they sent me you."

I think he offered to pick her up at her building, because she said, "No, I don't want anyone seeing us."

About then, it dawned on us that the woman had called an escort service, and that this was the date they were sending. He must have asked how he would recognize her. "I look like Lady Godiva," she said. "With brown hair."

"   "

"All I can say is, you better not keep me waiting."

"   "

"And you *better* be romantic." Then she hung up.

It can have been only a few seconds before we heard her again. She called a friend, a woman, I'm guessing—we couldn't hear that voice either—who seemed to believe that standing on Forty-second Street late at night to meet a prostitute was an insufficiently considered idea. "Listen, honey," the woman said, "I'm looking for love. I'm old enough. I'm allowed."

I don't remember what she said next. What I remember instead is one of our friends saying, "That's the woman in 7C! The paralegal with the cocker spaniel! I knew I recognized that voice!"

"I'm dressed like a cheap hooker," the woman said, and then she said that it was time for her to leave.

Our friends' apartment is on the fourth floor. I ran down the stairs to the lobby. The building has a self-service elevator, which was in the lobby when I arrived. Nothing happened for what seemed so long that I was about to walk back upstairs. Then the elevator rose. I heard it pause and descend. The lobby is very small. When the elevator doors opened, she walked toward me. She was perhaps fifty. Her face was long and thin and a little tense. She had on a fur coat held tightly closed with one hand at her neck, and she had thin legs and was wearing black stockings and heels. The color in her cheeks and around her eyes had required some time before a mirror. I thought it would be funny to say "Going to Forty-second Street?" and then realized that it wouldn't be. She walked out the door and called a taxi and got in and rode away.

I watched the tail-lights disappear and felt the strange, thrilling (and totally one-sided) sense of intimacy around me dissolve. I imagined the woman stepping out of the cab, wrapping her fur coat more tightly around her, then climbing two steps, turning toward the street, and waiting in the doorway, for a car to pull to the curb. I did this a number of times. Each time her face became more and more difficult to recall, until finally I couldn't picture it anymore, and then I went back upstairs to the party.

STEPHEN DUNN
Locker Room Talk

Having been athletic most of my life, I've spent a fair amount of time in locker rooms and have overheard my share of "locker room talk." For reasons I couldn't understand for many years, I rarely participated in it and certainly never felt smug or superior about my lack of participation. In fact, I felt quite the opposite; I thought something was wrong with me. As a teenager and well into my twenties I'd hear someone recount his latest real or wishful conquest, there'd be a kind of general congratulatory laughter, tacit envy, but what I remember feeling most was wonderment and then embarrassment.

There was of course little or no public information about sex when I was growing up in the forties and fifties. The first time I heard someone talk about having sex was in the school yard (the locker room without walls) when I was twelve or thirteen. Frankie Salvo, a big boy of sixteen. Frankie made it sound dirty, something great you do with a bad girl. It was my first real experience with pornography and it was thrilling, a little terrifying too. My mind conjured its pictures. Wonderment. Not wonderful.

Some years later, after experience, wonderment gave way to embarrassment. I wasn't sure for whom I was embarrassed, the girl spoken about, the story teller, or myself. Nevertheless, I understood the need to tell. I, too, wanted to tell my good friend, Alan, but for some reason I never told him very much. In retrospect, it was my first test with what Robert Frost calls knowing "the delicacy of when to stop short," a delicacy I took no pride in. I felt excessively private, cut off.

I began thinking about all of this recently because in the locker room at college a young man was telling his friend—loud enough for all of us to hear—what he did to this particular young woman the night before, and what she did to him. It was clear how important it was for him to impress his friend, far more important than the intimacy itself, as if the sexual act weren't complete until he had completed it among other men.

This time I knew something about the nature of my embarrassment. It wasn't just that he had cheapened himself in the telling, but like all things which embarrass us it had struck some part of me that was complicitous, to a degree guilty, the kind of guilt you feel every time there's a discrepancy between what you know you're supposed to feel (correct feelings) and what in fact you've thought of, if not done. But more than that, I was embarrassed by the young man's assumption—culturally correct for the most part—that we other men in the locker room were his natural audience. There were five or six of us, and we certainly didn't boo or hiss. Those of us who were silent (all of us except his friend) had given our quiet sanctions.

What did it all mean? That men, more often than not, in a very fundamental way prefer other men? Or was it all about power, an old story, success with women as a kind of badge, an accoutrement of power? Was the young man saying to the rest of us, "I'm powerful"? I thought so for a while, but then I thought that he seemed to be saying something different. He was saying out loud to himself and to the rest of us that he hadn't succumbed to the greatest loss of power, yielding to the attractiveness and power of women, which could mean admitting he felt something or, at the furthest extreme, had fallen in love.

From Samson, to the knight in Keats' poem "La Belle Dame Sans Merci," to countless examples in world literature, the warning is clear: women take away your power. To fall in love with one is to be distracted from the world of accomplishment and acquisitiveness. But to have sex and then to talk about it publicly is a kind of final protection, the ultimate prophylactic against the dangers of feeling.

"Love means always having to say you're sorry," a friend once said to me. The joke had its truth, and it implied—among other things—a mature love, a presumption of mutual respect and equality. On some level the young man in the locker room sensed and feared such a relationship. He had ventured into the dark and strange world of women and had come out unscathed, literally untouched. He was back with us, in the locker room which was the country he understood and lived in, with immunity. He thought we'd be happy for him.

SHERMAN ALEXIE
White Men Can't Drum

Last year on the local television news, I watched a short feature on a meeting of the Confused White Men chapter in Spokane, Washington. They were all wearing war bonnets and beating drums, more or less. A few of the drums looked as if they might have come from K mart, and one or two men just beat their chests.

"It's not just the drum," said the leader of the group. "It's the idea of a drum."

I was amazed at the lack of rhythm and laughed, even though I knew I supported a stereotype. But it's true: White men can't drum. They fail to understand that a drum is more than a heart-beat. Sometimes it is the sound of thunder, and many times it just means some Indians want to dance.

As a Native American, I find it ironic that even the most ordinary moments of our lives take on ceremonial importance when adopted by the men's movement. Since Native American men have become role models for the men's movement, I find it vital to explain more fully some of our traditions to avoid any further misinterpretation by white men.

Peyote is not just an excuse to get high.

A Vision Quest cannot be completed in a convention room rented for that purpose.

Native Americans can be lousy fathers and sons, too.

A warrior does not necessarily have to scream to release the animal that is supposed to reside inside every man. A warrior does not necessarily have an animal inside him at all. If there happens to be an animal, it can be a parakeet or a mouse just as easily as it can be a bear or a wolf.

When a white man adopts an animal, he often chooses the largest animal possible. Whether this is because of possible phallic connotations or a kind of spiritual steroid abuse is debatable. I imagine a friend of mine, John, who is white, telling me that his spirit animal is the Tyrannosaurus rex. "But John," I would reply gently, "those things are all dead."

●

As a "successful" Native American writer, I have been asked to lecture at various men's gatherings. The pay would have been good—just a little more reparation I figured—but I turned down the offers because I couldn't have kept a straight face. The various topics I have been asked to address include "Native Spirituality and Animal Sexuality," "Finding the Inner Child," and "Finding the Lost Father." I figure the next step would be a meeting on "Finding the Inner Hunter When Shopping at the Local Supermarket."

Much of the men's movement focuses on finding things that are lost. I fail to understand how Native American traditions can help in that search, especially considering how much we have lost ourselves. The average life expectancy of a Native American male is about 50 years—middle age for a white man—and that highlights one of the most disturbing aspects of the entire men's movement. It blindly pursues Native solutions to European problems but completely neglects to provide European solutions to

Native problems. Despite the fact that the drum still holds spiritual significance, there is not one Indian man alive who has figured out how to cook or eat a drum.

As Adrian C. Louis, the Paiute poet, writes, "We all have to go back with pain in our fat hearts to the place we grew up to grow out of." In their efforts to find their inner child, lost father, or car keys, white males need to go way back. In fact, they need to travel back to the moment when Christopher Columbus landed in America, fell to his knees on the sand and said, "But my mother never loved me."

That is where the real discovery begins.

Still, I have to love the idea of so many white men searching for answers from the same Native traditions that were considered heathen and savage for so long. Perhaps they are popular among white men precisely because they are heathen and savage. After all, these are the same men who look as if they mean to kill each other over Little League baseball games.

I imagine the possibilities for some good Indian humor and sadness mixed all together.

I imagine that Lester FallsApart, a full-blood Spokane, made a small fortune when he gathered glass fragments from shattered reservation car-wreck windshields and sold them to the new-age store as healing crystals.

I imagine that six white men traveled to a powwow and proceeded to set up shop and drum for the Indian dancers, who were stunned and surprised by how much those white men sounded like clumsy opera singers.

I imagine that white men turn to an old Indian man for answers. I imagine Dustin Hoffman. I imagine Kevin Costner. I imagine Daniel Day Lewis. I imagine Robert Bly.

Oh, these men who do all of the acting and none of the reacting.

●

My friend John and I were sitting in the sweatlodge. No. We were actually sitting in the sauna of the Y.M.C.A. when he turned to me. "Sherman," he said, "considering the chemicals, the stuff we eat, the stuff that hangs in the air, I think the sweatlodge has come to be a purifying ceremony, you know? White men need that, to use an Indian thing to get rid of all the pollution in our bodies. Sort of a spiritual enema."

"That's a lot of bull," I replied savagely.

"What do you mean?"

"I mean that the sweatlodge is a church, not a free clinic."

The men's movement seems designed to appropriate and mutate so many aspects of Native traditions. I worry about the possibilities: men's movement chain stores specializing in portable sweatlodges; the "Indians 'R' Us" commodification of ritual and artifact; white men who continue to show up at powwows in full regalia and dance.

Don't get me wrong. Everyone at a powwow can dance. They all get their chance. Indians have round dances, corn dances, owl dances, intertribal dances, interracial dances, female dances, and yes, even male dances. We all have our places within those dances.

I mean, honestly, no one wants to waltz to a jitterbug song, right?

Perhaps these white men should learn to dance within their own circle before they so rudely jump into other circles. Perhaps white men need to learn more about patience before they can learn what it means to be a man, Indian or otherwise.

Believe me, Arthur Murray was not a Native American.

●

Last week my friend John called me up on the telephone. Late at night. "Sherman," he said, "I'm afraid. I don't know what it means to be a man. Tell me your secrets. Tell me how to be a warrior."

"Well, John," I said, "a warrior did much more than fight, you know? Warriors fed their families and washed the dishes. Warriors went on Vision Quests and listened to their wives when they went on Vision Quests, too. Warriors picked up their dirty clothes and tried not to watch football games all weekend."

"Really?"

"Really," I said. "Now go back to sleep."

I hung up the phone and turned on the television because I knew it would be a long time before sleep came back to me. I flipped through channels rapidly. There was "F Troop" on one channel, "Dances With Wolves" on another, and they were selling authentic New Mexico Indian jewelry on the shopping channel.

What does it mean to be a man? What does it mean to be Indian? What does it mean to be an Indian man? I press the mute button on the remote control so that everyone can hear the answer.

J O H N   H O L M A N

Cat-Like

My brother and his wife got a white persian cat from someplace, a richer friend I guess. They brought it around my parents' house when it was a kitten, a white fluff bounding about my cuffs. Its name was Omar. I was fourteen. Omar grew to be fluffier, delicate and more beautiful, and turned out to be a girl. She got pregnant as soon as she was of age, and had trouble delivering her litter. She had made a nest under a bush in front of the house. My brother, his wife, and I stood around wondering how to help her until Omar in anguish got up from her kittens and started walking around with the job visibly half done, a kitten dangling. Squeamish about the whole birth process, and sick about poor Omar and the sight of her distress, I told them to do something, anything, call a vet why don't you. They had no money, that's why they didn't.

My brother, accepting his responsibility as owner of the cat, caught up with Omar around the corner of the house and gave her the necessary assistance. That kitten was stillborn, but the others survived. Omar, beautiful, proud and exotic, was to me a symbol of their young marriage. It was a marriage of college teenagers with bright expectations, and Omar was as grand as their promise. She represented what I thought was our foreign essence and our exquisite potential. Omar was not supposed to be an outdoor cat, but because we were outdoor boys and my brother's city-bred wife was adventuresome herself, Omar lived her version of our lives—she did what the other cats did; she fought, climbed trees and caught birds. And she liked it. But she was born for something else, and she looked as though she knew it. I don't remember what finally happened to her. My brother and his wife eventually divorced. Maybe Omar was put up for adoption.

Cat-wise, I was not unprepared when the woman I was pursuing finally let me in her house and introduced me to her cat. She lived in Raleigh and I lived in Durham, and I had met her while we taught at St. Augustine's College. No question, she was the glowingest presence on campus, in town. She had a boyfriend but finally got tired of him. He wasn't easy to shake. I got in on a night when he threatened to come over despite her asking him not to. She was afraid, she said to me when I phoned her. He wasn't acting right. I'll tell you what, I said, why don't I be there when he comes. O.K., she said. But, he's a Vietnam vet.

I'd seen him, of course. He was tall, big. Still, I showered and drove to Raleigh. Chances were that he wouldn't make a fuss. Being a trained killer, he was probably choosy about whom he beat up. Besides, he already was looking nearly foolish and I was betting he wouldn't risk being an all-out creep. He had a high-priced sports car and he cared what people thought about him, what he thought of himself, which was why he was being so stubborn in the first place.

I pulled slowly into the parking lot of the apartment complex, scanning for his car. At her door, I thought that he might already be inside, forgetting already that I hadn't seen his car, then remembering, then thinking that he might be skilled in concealment. But it was my own obsession's glowing face before me when the door opened. *She* didn't look worried. She looked happy to see me. She led me inside her small apartment and we sat to wait for the soldier to show up. We listened to her jazz records and drank her beer.

She had antique furniture from a flea market, a good deal, she told me. The chair I sat in was big and green, and when I looked closely I could make out how pretty the fabric must have been before it faded; there were tiny gold flowers threaded into the small triangle patterns, with pink centers. I tried to be calm in that chair while in the kitchen she stirred a pot of spaghetti sauce—my last meal, I told myself, if it got served soon.

About then her cat jumped from nowhere onto my lap. I didn't know she had a cat, hadn't seen it, heard it, or smelled it, but I accepted it as calmly as I did the yellow flowers in the fabric of the chair. It was a tabby-point, my hostess explained to me later, part siamese and part tabby; it looked part alley, its tail and legs subtly grey-striped and its body pale sand. Its eyes were blue and its face was faintly striped beneath the soft-grey ears. While the jazz piano trickled from the stereo speakers, I scratched the cat's head, and when I stopped it nudged my hand for more.

I was in that way occupied when Carmen came from the kitchen with a fresh bottle of beer for me. I was told that I was cuddling Kitty Kat, whom she had found lost and mewing in a littered supermarket parking lot, a kitten filthy with motor oil and dirt. She had brought it home, cleaned it up. While I listened to her story, Kitty Kat purred deeply and pranced, sinking its claws into the cloth of my corduroys—a new pair to look my best— and I was trying to shift and shrink in my clothes to avoid the sharp claw points. It was in my favor that Kitty Kat liked me enough to stay in the chair with me.

I sat like that at least an hour—the cat going to sleep, Carmen changing records—forgetting the menace of the angry boyfriend who never arrived. We talked, finally ate, and I went home, only to visit again and again until two years later we married. With the marriage, the Kitty Kat became mine. She would be inches from my face when I woke up in the mornings. My wife's face and my cat's face were similarly shaped—oval—and they both had cool bright eyes with aspects mysterious lazing and lurking deep behind them. My wife's eyes are light brown, like stream pebbles, and I thought of her as a forest creature. I began to suspect that she was a cat reincarnated as human, that she might have formerly possessed feline eyes that watched glowing from behind forest leaves.

Kitty Kat lived eighteen very dignified years. She moved from Raleigh to Greensboro, to Durham, to Winston-Salem, to Hattiesburg, back to Winston-Salem, to Tampa. She visited Atlanta often. She walked across the pages of books I tried to read. She brushed against my hand as I tried to write, wanting a scratch. She woke me up early mornings when I thought no one but I knew of my plan to wake and work before dawn. She roused me when a pipe burst under the kitchen sink. She brought birds in the house. She caught a bat and struggled with it on our bed in the middle of the night, terrifying us. (A struggle of consonants, still a terror.) She played with chipmunks until they died, tore their hearts out. She ignored the roaches in Mississippi, to our disappointment, but was fond of lizards. One midnight in Mississippi, she hooked a claw in the flesh of my little finger when I fetched her from the roof of a car stereo shop. For several puzzling minutes, we were joined. The wound healed in a day.

When she died, our hearts broke, and we got another cat, rescuing it from a flea-infested house of dogs, a cat that looked like Kitty Kat. Sarafina had one litter when she was seven months old. I feared she would have difficulty, like Omar, but we were fortunate to know some veterinary students whom it was my wife's job to advise. A good student came over, stood vigil. When my children left for school in the morning we had four kittens, and when they came home we had seven. It was my daughter's birthday, too—she was nine years old. *Her* birth had been frightening, difficult and dangerous, just as I had suspected, but we had a good doctor that day, also.

We kept one kitten, a solid grey boy with a wide face. It looked like a tiny bear, so our son named it Bear Cat. Sarafina was killed by a car two weeks before we moved from Tampa. But by then Bear Cat was grown. Once he brought home a bird, let it go in the house, and while it flew through the room he leapt off the arm of a chair and caught it. Most impressive.

I've written a story that has a cat in it, a dirty alley cat with white dry wounds on its haunches and head. That cat might be for all the cats in my life. It is a grand, wounded, striving, lucky animal, an obnoxious object of great generosity. I suspect now that it was the dignifying influence of Carmen's Kitty Kat that caused her angry boyfriend to rethink his threat those years ago. Certainly Omar, Kitty Kat, Sarafina and Bear Cat have forced me to confront their awesome respectability. These cats amaze me. They are beautiful show-offs. They eat other animals raw. They carry their suffering with dignity. They get what they want. They let you love them. Perhaps all my two-legged characters are, as with my fantasy about my wife, cats reincarnated, creatures admirable and disturbing that I'll never understand.

MRI

"Are you claustrophobic?" the nurse asks me.

"Well, more like claustrosensitive," I say.

"We can write you a prescription for Valium if you wish."

"No, I won't need that."

Later, in the Magnetic Resonance Imagery outer office, I watch a videotape narrated by the last astronaut to walk on the moon. He mentions claustrophobia also, dismisses it as no worse than being in a space capsule—a less than comforting comparison and the subject of some rather "claustrosensitive" dreams. The video shows a woman being placed on a board, her face covered by a ventilated helmet, for communication, and shoved headfirst into the tunnel-shaped orgasmatronic MRI. Headfirst, helmeted! I need that Valium. I wonder if these techno-nurses have some.

I change into my one-size-fits-all-Parisian-bell-ringer gown and wait my turn. All I can see of the machine is a man's socks sticking out. We discuss my favorite radio station. I am to be supplied with headphones; the MRI is "rather loud."

The socks emerge and my two assistants prepare the bed for me. I am to go in feet first for some marvelous, unknown reason. Because I am supposed to be as immobile as possible, they strap my arms to my side with an enveloping wrap. They slide me in until the concavity of the machine looms over me. With utmost eye rotation upwards, I can just barely see *out* of the machine and into the room. Panic, heretofore an abstraction, becomes a physical manifestation actually crawling from my stomach to my head.

"Are you okay?" the technician asks. "Yes," I lie, not wanting to embarrass myself and doubting I would ever get this far again.

She leaves. I listen to 90.1—"the station with all the jazz"—before the machine warms up. When it comes on, the noise is somewhere between a jackhammer and a .50 caliber machine gun. No physical sensation except for the ascending panic of being strapped down in a tunnel unable to move anything. Itches set in. My mind drifts to "The Cask of Amontillado." I sweat. I try to outreason my fears—an unfair battle that I lose. I think of "other things," though no other things can dislodge images of being buried alive. I contemplate calling up my trusted sexual fantasies but worry about tumescence's effect on such detailed imagery. Would the technician notice, jump, or laugh?

The technician is an angel of mercy. She comes in after every event to ask how I'm doing. I continue to lie and am amazingly comforted that she hasn't just left me here. She says "we" have two left: one ten minutes long and a short one of about three minutes. I brace and endure the long one though I am truly panicky by now. She doesn't appear between blasts, but I anticipate a short finale. It starts and goes on and on, way past any approximation of three minutes. Has she taken a break? Is she passed out on the console? Eating that calzone she ordered earlier? Where is the slut? I'll kill her. I'll stuff her careless body into this machine. I begin to croon, "Helloooo, helloooo, is anybody there?" No answer over the pounding resonance.

She appears, says, "We're done, how are you?" "Fine," I lie, "though the last one seemed a little long." "Yes, it's because you're tall," she replies. "Yes, I am," I meekly say.

I change, escape to the night and the blissfully open spaces of my car.

On Two Wheels

Air leaked into my rainsuit and inflated me. The rainsuit collar flapped fast in the wind, plastic against plastic, sounding like the propeller of a small airplane. After a while, the rainsuit ripped from the force of the wind, and water soaked the jacket under it. The weight of the wet jacket was heavy on my shoulders. The wetness stuck to my warm skin and I shivered as I rode. Periodically, I wiped water from my face shield, drenching my gloves. The water rolling from the gauntlets of my gloves swept under the shield and soaked my face. My cheeks started to itch and I scratched them with my wet gloves. The rain, blown by the wind, pricked my chin and rolled down my neck. Cold water puddled on the seat, shriveling my crotch. Trucks coming in the opposite direction punched me with mud, while my tires skidded over the pavement on water mixed with oil leaked from hot engines. The brake linings got wet and grabbed dangerously. The water, rolling off the seat, drained down my leg, filling my boot.

Burt and I were riding our motorcycles on Skyline Drive near Staunton, Virginia, and it had been raining for eight straight days.

Three hours out of Pittsburgh, the rain had started. We detoured south into Cumberland, Maryland, then into West Virginia, but the rain kept up. We went northeast back into Pennsylvania, then south into West Virginia and Virginia, but the water dogged us. We stopped at taverns and diners along the way for television weather reports, then headed toward the warm fronts, looking for a dry pocket in which to rest. During the day, rain soaked our gear. We couldn't cook at night. We bought plastic garbage bags to cover everything, but when the wind was strong, it ripped the plastic. Every morning we first found a town with a laundromat, and for twenty-five cents, bought some man-made sun.

On the eighth day, the fog came up in the Shenandoah Mountains. We traveled the whole day through fog that stuck in our eyes and wafted over the road. We followed the road by watching the shapes of the trees that lined the edge of the pavement. I could see the wheels of my motorcycle as we crept through the mountains, but not where they touched the ground. I could see the glowing eyes of cars coming in the opposite direction, but never the exact shape of the cars or the people inside. Sometimes I could see Burt's red taillight in front of me and sometimes I couldn't. It was the thickest fog I have ever seen. Creeping through it the whole day, we could make only fifty miles.

I have never been skydiving, but driving through that fog is how I would imagine it. We floated through the clouds, guided by the way the wheels sounded against the road; we could tell when we neared the edge of the road, because some of the pebbles spilling from the shoulder, swept up by the tires, would clink against our exhaust pipes.

And we relied on our memories of riding in the past. If you think back hard enough to a special day, when the sun was warm and you cruised a long mountain road, if you can remember how it was and can concentrate, then you can duplicate that ride even though you cannot see. Taking the turns just as you have so many times before, leaning just enough, straightening slowly, feeling for the right balance, rolling that way. You don't always need eyes to ride a motorcycle, as long as you have a good memory and the ability to recreate what you know you should see.

The persistence of rain dulls your perceptions, but the fog reactivates them. You can taste the rain in the fog. And since you cannot see trees, grass, and wildflowers, you smell them. There are actually lines in the fog; it is not just a milky haze; streams of fog of different shades come together to make a screen. It feels strangely warm against your face, slightly wet. You push away the fog with your hand and, like water, more flows in to take its place. Floating through the fog seems both prehistoric and futuristic; it is in that gap where earth loses contact with the heavens.

Running Xian

China in my mouth, in my lungs.

Once a week or so I run to Big Goose Pagoda, Xian's tallest landmark. By way of cabbage fields and raucous tree-lined lanes crowded with bikes and mule carts and school kids wearing the bright red scarves of the Communist Youth League, it's maybe five miles round trip from the campus where I teach.

I rush through jumping jacks on the edge of the sports field and watch one of my students rock on a set of parallel bars, his baggy Mao jacket flapping behind. At a concrete Ping-Pong table two girls in pigtails smash forearm shots across a line of bricks that serves as a net. A couple of smiling boys look on, their arms draped around each others' waists and shoulders. I call them boys and girls—most look about sixteen—but they're college seniors, preparing for what are probably life-time job assignments from the government.

I'm speeding through my warm-up because I don't want the boys on the track team to see me. They'd try to make me run with them, and I don't want to feel guilty for holding them back while their chain-smoking coach, overcoat draped over one shoulder, scowls at us. Somehow my slender students see in my sturdy, wide-shouldered frame a talent for running that no stopwatch has ever detected.

I start along the backstretch—and almost step on a tiny, moon-faced child squatting in the middle of the track. His three layers of flowered pants are split open in customary Chinese fashion. Where are his parents? He doesn't seem to care. He just goes about his business, grinning hugely as I jog by.

I loop the field past elderly men and women performing the seamless slow motion of Tai C'hi, coal smoke from heaters and stoves hanging eerily in the air. Last week a team of squatting peasants trimmed the brown infield grass with hand axes.

Out through the school gate, farmers from the countryside hunch behind wicker baskets of potatoes, green beans, onions. A woman in a frayed black coat tilts back her head and sucks on an egg as if it held fine whiskey. A tailor cuts patterns on a card table under a tree, and a bald man who looks about a thousand years old smokes a metal pipe. They all stop what they're doing to watch the dark-bearded foreigner clump by. I draw stares every minute of the day, and not always friendly ones. I smile at the bald man, who is squinting hard at me through his pipe smoke. He makes a fist, sticks up his thumb, and laughs.

Turning onto Changan Street, I pick up my pace—just to stay even with the insanity of the street. Bicycles everywhere, *rivers* of them flowing with tinkling bells past other bikes, motorcycles, hand-cranked trucks that might have rumbled out of 1930s gang-busters movies, handcarts, goats. Now and then a car whooshes by, the white-gloved driver honking like mad, a lace curtain veiling the VIPs in the back. Why aren't there more accidents?

"Hello, Teacher John!"

I turn. Jogging next to me is Flying Dragon, one of my brightest and most eager English students.

"Let us now run together," he says happily.

A lot less happily, I recall the way I've seen him zip around the school track, again and again. "How *far?*" I say.

"Big Goose Pagoda!"

So I'm in for a run at his pace—he's much too polite and charming to turn down. Soon we're bumping elbows as we squeeze between a packed bus and a bike with half a pig draped over the back fender. We split up to avoid a creaking hay wagon on which three men lie snoring. Then we pass the other half of the pig.

Flying Dragon brings up the subject of English grammar—he seems entranced with subordinate clauses—but I try to steer us back to talk of our hometowns, food (like the minced Mongolian camel thighs I just had at a downtown restaurant), the wonders of running. It turns out that he's the school record holder at 1500 meters!

Overworked and far undernourished compared to my students back in Ohio, Flying Dragon and his classmates are nevertheless lucky to be in school at all. Only two percent of their age group attends universities. A lot of my students work like mules when they're home in the countryside, but they also know the luxury of exercise for its own sake. I worry, though, about the people we're jostling past on this street, a boy strapped with a tumpline to a handcart full of bricks, the girls in the fields ladling water from buckets they've hauled there by hand, the peasant in rags nodding off at the reins of his jingling horse cart. What do they think of us?

I feel strong, but the air's a little drier than I expected. After a while, as the thirteen-hundred-year-old pagoda looms into view through a brown haze of dust, I begin to feel like I'm bringing up the rear of a cattle drive. A friend once told me that jogging two miles a day through this stuff is like smoking two packs of cigarettes a week. Half the bicyclists wear surgical masks, and they're not doctors.

Flying Dragon now wants my opinion on adverbial clauses, but by the time we circle the graceful, earth-colored pagoda, I'm down to monosyllables. Another mile and I'm gulping for air, my mouth as dry as sand.

Flying Dragon looks over, smiles, and says, "Teacher John? Would you now please analyze for me the most excellent writing style of Henry James?"

"Uhhn-n-n?"

That's all that comes out. Then I laugh. Finally, with hand signals and much rolling of the eyes, I manage to tell him that I'm merely exhausted. I wave him on. He nods, pats my back, shifts gears, and is gone.

I jog and walk back to school amid crowds and the endless ringing of bicycle bells. Next time I'll wear one of those masks, I tell myself. Next time I'll run farther, and faster. Next time I'll read up on my Henry James.

A Note About Allen Tate

I took Literary Criticism with Allen Tate. My mind was not on the subject, because—I liked to think—I preferred the abstractions of philosophy and the music of poetry to the explication of the obvious. Literary criticism seemed to me to be mostly paraphrase. But I have since learned to love writing about writing, and perhaps the real reason I was distracted, that bright autumn semester so long ago, was that I had fallen in love. I was going to be married over the Christmas break.

Mr. Tate—we called him "Mr." Tate, not "Dr." or "Professor," and never in our wildest dreams "Allen"—began each class by reading the roll. *Present,* I would say, staring out the window and thinking about licenses, announcements, what dress to wear. *Here.* I wasn't, really.

While he went down the list of last names, Mr. Tate played with his cigarette lighter. It was, I'm sure, a gold lighter. It *looked* gold, and I doubt that Mr. Tate would ever have been happy with something that looked gold but was not gold. He flipped the lid open. Twirled, with his thumb, the little wheel that ignited the wick. The lighter flared. He snapped the lid shut. Sometimes he snapped the lid shut with the thumb of the same hand with which he was holding the lighter; sometimes he gently palmed the lid shut with his other hand.

Oddly, I can't remember whether he smoked in class. It's likely that he did; I think that teachers probably were allowed to smoke in class in those days. But in those days everyone I knew smoked. But not everyone I knew—in fact, no one else I knew—had a gold cigarette lighter. It was the lighter, not the smoking, that was interesting. The lighter, and that Mr. Tate played with it nervously all through class.

He was slender, shortish, with a formal bearing. His manners were of a kind seldom encountered today: the enactment of established rituals of courtesy and consideration. To shake his hand was to participate in a small ceremony. To pass him in the hallway and say hi was to play a minor but, one understood, important part in a well-known drama. (And never a melodrama.)

Maybe there were melodramas in his life. I wouldn't know, because I didn't know him outside of class. He was not the kind of teacher a shy student got to know outside the classroom. Maybe *he* was shy. He certainly did fiddle nervously with that cigarette lighter.

He addressed us with a title, too. We were "Mr." or "Miss." (I have to interrupt myself here to say that although "Ms." had, according to the Oxford English Dictionary, been invented, it had not yet arrived in North Carolina, so he can hardly be faulted for not using it.)

Jonathan Silver and I were married at my parents' house in front of a picture window while the worst blizzard in Richmond's history whited out the view. Guests gazed forlornly at their cars being buried under drifts of snow. Jonathan's mother and father had refused to attend; the mood was solemn, more suited to political and religious history than to romance. There was a sense that we were all engaged in a subversive activity, but against our

will, as if we were also surprised, and unsettled, to discover ourselves engaging in anything subversive. People wanted to be in
their own homes, not facing the prospect of digging out, putting
on snow chains, driving down unplowed roads. As soon as the
minister pronounced us husband and wife, coats were grabbed,
and people stood in the foyer, sweating in swathes of scarves, waiting only for Jonathan and me to leave first. We had borrowed my
father's car. As we turned the corner, I looked back to see the
party, which had never quite begun, breaking up. The picture
window framed the scene, and it was like something by Hopper,
beautiful and sad.

There were two weeks remaining in the semester after the hol-
idays. The first day I returned to Literary Criticism, Mr. Tate, as
usual, called the roll, but he did not read my name among the
C's. He read most of the roll without stopping. When he reached
the S's, he stopped to flick his gold lighter open. Then he called,
"Mrs. Silver."

Here, I answered. *Present.*

He flicked his lighter shut and finished the roll call.

That was all. But I knew that this man—this deeply quiet
man—had paid more attention to me than I ever had paid to Literary Criticism. Perhaps contemporary women, who prefer "Ms."
to "Mrs." and who keep their own names instead of changing
them, won't like this story. But I am a contemporary woman, who
has reclaimed her own name, and yet I remember the day Mr.
Tate called me by my married name as the day I learned what literary criticism is all about. Literary criticism is about the inter-
lineation of text and interpretation. It is about locating new
meaning in the words we have been given. It is about knowing
how to call the roll—with respect, that is, and observantly, in a
way that recognizes change in the world.

BRUCE BERGER
Fernando and Marisela

The drawers of nightstands are filled with hexes against the long dark—a small cross, a book of sayings, a bottle of Valium. For reasons unclear to me, I keep a piece of litter I found under a cactus outside Tucson. I was staying in one of those transition zones where fresh houses breach the desert. My hostess was the developer, a woman who built custom homes—living in one while she supervised the next—until she had designed and inhabited all the houses on a little lane named for herself. It was June, 1974, and the temperature was 115. Bored with the air conditioning, stunned outside, I wandered between the lady's constructions poking at the small.

Otherwise I never would have spotted a scrap so bland and so dense. I reached carefully between the barbs of fallen cholla, tweezering it out between thumb and forefinger. I unfolded it once, then again. An inch and a half square unfurled, it was a portrait of a girl against a neutral backdrop, snapped in a cheap studio or perhaps a machine. In her late teens, with full but sad features, she gazed into the lens with moist dark eyes, black lashes, black eyebrows, and dyed blond hair. Though the photo was in black and white, you could tell she had one of those bleach jobs that turns dark hair reddish and leaves it murky at the roots. On the other side, in schoolgirl cursive, she had written in Spanish, "Fernando, though you are far away, don't feel alone, for there is one who remembers and will wait for you always. Marisela, Nogales, Sonora. April 17, 1972."

The desert is known for keeping the most fragile objects intact for years. Dated two years back, the photo might have spent its life under the cholla. But two seasons of winter drizzle and two of summer thundershowers had not turned the paper brittle, nor had two years of burning sun yellowed a corner of the back. The photograph, so charged with unknown lives, had barely preceded me.

But had it been lost or thrown away? The photo gallery in one's pocket seems one more tense of a Spanish verb, and Latin wallets resemble souvenir albums with money in the binding. Marisela's snapshot would have fit neatly in a plastic leaf, and perhaps it had. Yet it had been doubled and quartered so that her face was disfigured by the crosshairs of folds as if by a rifle sight, leaving the tiny quadrangle more unwieldy than before. Marisela hadn't been lost; she had been freshly and consciously discarded.

Though you are far away . . . Were all of Marisela's friends dyeing their hair that year, or did she do it just for Fernando? She presumably gave him her picture before he headed to find work in a land where the girls were blonde and radiant. When he was far away, surrounded by golden Americans, the photo would remind him that he had a blonde girlfriend back home. The Yankified glamor falsified Marisela's own beauty, but her dewy black eyes held their ground with perfect honesty, perfect desperation.

Far away . . . Yet Tucson is not far; it is a quick and cheap bus ride back to Nogales, a day's excursion. Did Fernando go back to see Marisela? Surely at first. But two years is a long time for a young man tasting the novelties of another country. If she tried to hold him with those pleading moist eyes, he would only have felt trapped and resentful, less inclined to bus himself into the past. If he showed up less often, she would turn icy, then accusative. He might easily drop out of her life, not even think of her for months. One hot spring day, working construction for a lady who built custom homes, he weeded through his wallet during a cigarette break, and ran across this embarrassing back number, this phony blonde who was two years and one language late. Perhaps there was a quick stab of regret, but you couldn't be sentimental forever.

Marisela, it is over a decade since a passing gringo, stunned by the heat, rescued your photo from beneath a cactus. You were right to let your hair grow dark, to embark on adulthood, to forget the worthless Fernando. After high school your friends married and began families, or became shopgirls, or sold themselves in the streets to Fernando's new cronies from across the border. Nogales is not a town where jilted girlfriends pine by the casement, nor were you the Lady of Shalott. Fernando has doubtless pursued the construction dollar and begun a family with another person, probably not blonde. He no longer worked for the lady who built custom homes, for she has died, the cactus she left between her constructions has filled with other homes, and her name is kept fresh only by a street sign. The desert is less and less able to keep what we throw away, and your photo barely preceded the bulldozer.

But if you ever feel alone in your new life as a mother, a salesperson, a streetwalker, remember that there is someone far north of Nogales, far north of Tucson, who is unaccountably haunted by your eyes, and who keeps your photograph within reach for solace in the night.

S T E P H E N   C O R E Y
A Voice for the Lonely

The right silence can be a savior, especially in these days
of motorcycles, leaf blowers, and malls that thrum with a thousand voices and dozens of sundry machines. Five or six days a
week, I get up pretty early—generally around 4 a.m.—and one
of the things I like most about those last hours of darkness is their
stillness. The house is quiet, the streets are quiet, and (except on
weekends, when some of the serious drunks are hanging on) the
all-night restaurants are quiet. Reading and writing and thinking
come more easily when you know you won't be interrupted, and
over the past 20 years I've never found a better mental bodyguard
than the hours before dawn.

I got my first serious training as an early riser when I acquired
a newspaper delivery route in seventh grade: three miles of widely
scattered houses on the edge of Jamestown, New York, and
beyond—just me, the moon, darkness, and the various faces of
silence. I recall stopping my brisk walk sometimes, especially
in winter when every step squeaked and crunched on the snow
that nearly always covered the ground, and marveling at how
there were no sounds except those of my own making. But just

as often, that quiet made me nervous, even though my hometown was awfully safe in those days. I learned to offset the urge to look over my shoulder by carrying a pocket-sized transistor radio.

The music helped me to cope with more than just the empty morning streets—I was, as I said, in seventh (and then eighth, and finally ninth) grade during those lone marches. In short, I was just learning something of what much of that music was about: love—lost, found, hoped for, and despaired of.

Most habits die hard, and old ones can seem immortal. Last week, I was up as usual at 4 a.m., and I headed out in the car toward the nearest newspaper box. As always during these quick runs, I flipped on the radio for some wake-up rhythms to jolt my system for the solitary work time soon to come back at the house.

Instead of music, I caught the voice of the all-night deejay just as she was saying, "We have tragic news in over the wire: singer Roy Orbison is dead . . ." She gave a quick flurry of details (heart attack, Hendersonville, North Carolina, hospital), repeated the central fact—"Roy Orbison, dead at 52"—and then (my heart applauds her still for this) said not a word but cut straight into "Only the Lonely."

There I was, cruising down the abandoned city street with the radio now up as loud as I could stand it, mouthing the rising and falling words, rocking side to side as I held the wheel, and riding Orbison's waiting, nearly-cracking voice back 24 years to the passenger seat of Jon Cresanti's Volkswagen beetle.

We're told these days that the hottest and fastest wire into memory is our sense of smell, but music must run a close second. Some songs carry us into a certain mood, some to a general region of our past lives, and some to a very particular moment and situation in time. Jon and I were brought together by chance and loneliness for a couple of months during our sophomore year in high school. The alphabetical seating in our homeroom put us next to each other in the back row, and Jon was a talker. We hadn't known each other before: we came from different parts of town, had different friends, and moved through different sequences of classes. But for a while we found a bond: my girl-friend had recently dropped me after more than a year of going steady, and Jon had eyes for a girl who had none for him.

I had time—all the time I was no longer spending with my girl. John had a car and was old enough to drive it, having failed a grade and thereby become a crucial year older than the typical sophomore. I signed on board, and we cruised day after day, weekend after weekend, killing time and eating at the wondrous new "fast food restaurant" that had just opened. We sat in his car eating 15-cent hamburgers and 12-cent french fries near the real golden arches, the kind that curved up and over the entire little structure (no inside seating, no bathrooms)—and, naturally, lis-tening to the radio. The Four Seasons were with us, as were The Beach Boys, Nat King Cole, The Supremes.

But in those two desperate months of shotgunning for Jon, there was only one song that really mattered, one song we waited for, hoped for, and even called the radio station and asked for: Roy Orbison's "Pretty Woman."

That opening handful of heavy guitar notes (a lovesick teenager's equivalent of Beethoven's Fifth) carried us into a world of possibility, a world where a moment's fancy could generate love, where losers could be winners just by wishing for success. The pretty woman walks on by, and another failure has occurred—but suddenly, the downward sweep of the wheel is reversed as the woman turns to walk back, and there is nothing in the world but fulfillment of one's dreams.

Pop songs are full of such stuff, of course, and have been for as long as the phonograph record and the radio have been with us; we get all kinds of talk about the importance of television in modern life, but I think we need more examination of the ways we have been encompassed by music. I'm not talking about rant-

ing "discussions" of the immorality of certain strains of pop
music, but some real studies of the much wider and deeper
implications of growing up in a world awash with radio waves.

Needless to say, I wasn't concerned about such matters there
in the McDonald's parking lot. I wouldn't even have thought
about what it was in Orbison's singing that made him so important to me. I took the words of the song's story for their relevance
to my own emotional state, and I floated with those words inside
a musical accompaniment that both soothed and roused my
fifteen-year-old body.

When I heard of Orbison's death, I found myself wanting to
figure out just what it was in that strange voice that might have
been so compelling for me and others across the years. I think it
might be in the way the voice itself often seems about to fail: in
Orbison's strange and constant modulations, from gravelly bass-
like sounds to strong tenor-like passages to piercing falsetto cries,
there is the feeling for the listener that the singer is always about
to lose control, about to break down under the weight of what
he is trying to sing. Never mind that this is not true, that Orbison's style was one carefully achieved; what we are talking about
here is emotional effect, the true stuff of pop and country music.

If Roy could make it, we could make it. And if Roy could
stand failing, so could we.

This feeling of camaraderie with the faraway record star in-
creased for me, I think, the first time I saw him. He was so
ordinary-looking—no, he was so *homely,* so very contrary to what
one expects romantic musical heroes to look like. He was *us.*

The right singer, the right sadness, the right silence. The way
I heard the story of the death of Orbison's wife in 1966 (and the
way I'll keep believing it) was that the two of them were out
motorcycling when an errant car or truck hit them from an
angle. She was riding just a few feet to the side of and behind him,
so the other vehicle clipped the back of his cycle but caught hers

full force. I've never gotten over this chilling illustration of the forces of circumstance and the fate of inches, so much so that over the years I have regularly found the story called to mind for retelling in classrooms or at parties.

I graduated from high school the year of the accident, and Orbison disappeared from the national music scene. (It wasn't until recently that I heard how the death of two sons by fire in 1967 compounded Orbison's private tragedies.) Oddly, there is a way in which the disappearance or the death of a singer these days doesn't really matter to his or her listeners, since that person is still present in exactly the same way as before. All the songs take on a slightly new cast, but the singer still lives in a way that one's own deceased relatives and friends cannot.

When my girl wanted me back, I dropped Jon's friendship and never tried to regain it—a not-very-commendable way to be. But we were glued for a while by those banging Orbison notes and those erratic vocals, and maybe that was enough, or at least all that one could hope for.

Music can block out silence, on dark scary roads and in moments of loneliness. But there's also a sense or two in which a song can create silence: when we're "lost in a song" the rest of the world around us makes, for all practical purposes, no sound. And in an even more strange way, a song we love goes silent as we "listen" to it, leaving us in that rather primitive place where all the sounds are interior ones—sounds which can't be distinguished from feelings, from pulsings and shiverings, from that gut need to make life stronger than death for at least a few moments.

When "Only the Lonely" faded, that wonderful deejay still knew enough not to say a word. She threw us straight forward, 4:15 a.m., into "Pretty Woman."

Museum Piece

Jan Vermeer's "The Girl with the Red Hat" always ap-
pealed to you because of that hat. Incredible scarlet aura spinning
around her head like pure energy. Mouth open. Delicate coating
of light that makes you think she's just licked her lips. Got to ap-
preciate the composition. Lively and precise at the same time. The
face of the girl isn't much. You like the look of her hat. You know
it excites her to be wearing that hat. But there's nothing about
the actual person. What she has to say wouldn't be much. Features are crude. Common girl all dressed up.

Another Vermeer here you've gotten to know. "Maiden with
a Flute." Little sister of "The Girl with the Red Hat." Not nearly
as flamboyant, but it's another composition that makes you smile.
They're both paintings that have some wit.

This one day, instead of passing with a quick pause-and-look,
the way you always have before—maybe because the room is
empty, and you have plenty of time—you take one step closer to
the third of those Vermeers: "A Lady Writing." One step closer
to a picture you've seen dozens of times before.

The lady of the picture isn't really writing. She's stopped writing. Her pen—it's a small feather quill—is still in place on the paper. Her other hand is holding the page down. She's just looked up. You've interrupted her. Her face has this expression that is warm and so complex. But that expression is not for you—it's left over from the moment before she saw you. She looks that way because of whatever it was she was writing. It has to be a letter: this lady is writing to her good friend—or maybe to her sister—about something that really pleases her. You wonder what it could be. You can almost sense the pleasure flying away from her as she stops her writing.

She isn't beautiful. The way her hair is fixed, it looks like she's put it up in curlers. But you get her whole life out of this picture. All those art history courses, all these visits to the museum, attending lectures, reading catalogs: nothing teaches you just to look the way you're doing it now! Thousands of days of this lady's living click into this single instant. Across three hundred years of time, she looks you straight in the eyes. *Look,* she says. *Go ahead and look. My life feels to me the same as yours feels to you—so full I could burst with it. Please let me get back to my letter. You go on with whatever you're doing out there in the twentieth century.*

CAROL BLY
An End to the Still Lifes

I was sent South to stay with an aunt during World War II. My brothers were away at school and at war; my mother was dying of tuberculosis; and the aunt, although she terrified my father, still seemed like the best solution. She lived in the foothills of the Blue Ridge Mountains, near Tryon, a winter resort.

I rode a train called the Carolina Special because it had one car, number sixty-one, that went all the way from Chicago to Spartanburg, South Carolina. On the last day, it made its way through the passes below Asheville, and I saw more physical beauty than I had ever seen before. Of course physical or psychological abuse, or the lack of them, is important in people's lives, but what if simply the quantity of natural beauty is the major thing? No, of course that isn't right. No one has treated their own citizenry or animals or prisoners of war more cruelly than Germany, yet Germany is an extravagantly beautiful country.

Still, beauty is something. On this particular autumn afternoon, the train creaked gingerly down the steepest grade in the United States. It dropped a thousand feet in the few miles between Saluda and Tryon, North Carolina. The track went round and round clinging to the mountainsides. It switch-backed upon itself in dozens of loops. The engine whistle wailed again and again, and the wheel flanges continually shrieked.

I was twelve. The porter let me lean on the platform dutch door with him. Whenever the forward section of train bent around rightward I could see both engines, the second joined on for extra braking power. Then the track flung us left and I saw only the spindling mountain woods, dynamited rock cuts, and clean, gashed clay nearly in my face. There had been a disease of Southern chestnuts; now the white chestnut trunks, frankly dead as bone, came right past us noble as pillars compared to the more spindling mountain growth. I smelled the rank ravines. Minnesota has nature pretty enough but it has no intensity—nothing you could call fastnesses. This North Carolina odor folded and folded in the air: I had never smelled anything like it: it felt like the odor of dead as well as live earth, seeping relaxedly from the brilliant clay. This smell had composure. I didn't feel alarmed, only surprised, as one is by some new but low-affect technology. Perhaps it was just a matter of geology. We were passing through stunning sections of anti-synclines, as my aunt told me later. A simple reality of long standing.

To a northern child the day seemed to blaze on forever. Finally, not an hour from Tryon, some January shadow said it was four o'clock. The train picked up speed. We were down on the bottomland now, well away from the mountain ravines. The train whipped along the valley of the Pacolet River.

I had the steadiness common to children from whom the parents haven't been able to hide their troubles—illness in my mother's case. I thought and daydreamed without panic, steadily. My ideas went this way and that way on some faint, colorless route of their own. I would guess one thing or another thing. I assumed such and such would happen. As the train took me to Tryon, I supposed, in a practical tone to myself, that I would draw pictures from nature that year. I supposed I would draw or paint these rocks and glossy laurel, or even the engines' wheels, strong-armed in a whirr by their pistons. I guessed I might draw them, since my sixth-grade teacher in Duluth had told my father that I was artistic. I could capture just about anything, she said. Art was to capture and make something pretty. It sounded like a permanent's work on hair, and in fact, the teacher smiled more easily as she got onto firmer ground, namely *character*. She pays attention, the teacher told my father. That was part of being an artist, paying attention was.

The aunt was a martinet with conscience. She took an interest in everything I did. When I came home from school one day, she said, "I think we had better get you some drawing lessons." She had found a sheaf of my drawings in my desk. On my construction paper, crayola-drawn Marines got bayonetted through the chest pockets. Gestapo officers wore peaked caps. They whipped people who wore pale grey and white striped clothing. I had had a number of dreams about concentration camps. That didn't surprise me. My best friend in Tryon was the daughter of an English Jewish couple, the wife an artist, the husband a banker. They had fled Paris when the Nazis invaded France. Tryon had several English families there for the Duration. We all knew their stories. And as for bad dreams, my mother had sometimes told me hers before she went into the sanitorium. Nightmares were one of life's verities, like everything else.

My aunt was holding, at arm's length, my drawing of an SS soldier torturing someone.

"This is terrible stuff," my aunt said. "If you're going to be an artist you had better take it seriously. This is ghastly. You must do decent work. I think I had better have Stella teach you charcoal and still lifes."

Stella Sassoon was my new best friend's mother. No sooner did my aunt telephone her than we were invited to drinks and dinner at the Sassoons'. Of all the contingent of English people stranded in Tryon, the Sassoons were the liveliest. They were always joyful, amused, hysterical, or infuriated. The whole family liked music and painting and despised cruelty. They were always asking one another, what sort of a clot would do something like that? The Sassoon family were heady stuff for me, a child raised on middle-ground opinions, middle-ground tastes. My feelings had no more weight to them than a lacing of first snow.

My aunt showed Mrs. Sassoon my work. "So you see what we are up against!" she said. "I thought you could give her a few lessons!"

But Mrs. Sassoon held up my drawings, one by one. "Oh, I say," she exclaimed about each one. "Look at these! These are quite wonderful! O my God, what's going on in this one?" she would ask. "Good God!" she shouted. "Look at *this* one! All that blood."

"Well, she needs to do some real work," my aunt said.

"But look at these wonderful pictures!" Mrs. Sassoon exclaimed, over and over. She moved fast around the studio in her expensive, perfectly pleated grey trousers, dropping cigarette ash everywhere, waving my drawings at everyone. "I think they're marvelous!" she shouted. "I say, Willie, look at these!" she howled.

Mr. Sassoon was a quiet, witty person whose eyes literally glowed. He stooped to pick up things his wife brushed off a table or an easel as she went past. He showed me how to praise. "I say," he said to me somberly, as if I were an adult, "Stella's awfully good, isn't she? Look at that expression! And the rich colors!"

"Have one of these," he would say to me, taking a silver plate of camembert and crackers from the maid. He lowered it before me. The cheese was not sanglant because of the war, but I admired its plunging flavor, a different thing from the yellow rat cheese I'd been raised on. When Willie Sassoon looked at me, I thought for the first time in my life, Why—that is a married man.

He is *married*. Marriage, then—but I could hardly think of it. Still, my heart took a different hold on things.

"But you *will* teach her still lifes—real art?" my aunt said.

We did work on still lifes. Each week, Stella Sassoon screwed up a tablecloth in the time-honored way. She placed on it an orange and a banana and a pewter pitcher with the first dogwood sprays. She taught me how to make shadow. "If you get the shadow of a thing you have it," she said in her British accent. Everything she said slid like a heavy continent under the tin of my old ideas.

After a few weeks' lessons she said, "I say, we don't like doing these still lifes, do we? I think you should work on what you want to work on!"

My aunt and I were at the Sassoons' for dinner. "You mean she hasn't enough gift to bother with?" my aunt asked.

"Oh! Gift enough!" Mrs. Sassoon shouted with one of her throaty laughs. She set down her martini and lunged across the studio to pick up an old crayon drawing of mine. "But she should follow her own direction I think. Look at this!"

The drawing showed a lance corporal being killed by a Feldwebel. I had the uniforms right because I was a morbid and patriotic kid. I knew that a soldier's shirt pocket tab is straight across, with clipped corners, but a Marine's shirt pocket tab curves down in a reverse arch to the center button. What I didn't have right was the locale. U.S. Marines didn't fight Germans in that war. Nor had I got the wounds exactly: drops of blood don't fly through the air with black waxy borders around them.

My aunt discontinued the lessons.

Fifty years went by. I had become a writer with an interest in social-work therapies, not a painter at all. One day I telephoned

Tryon, North Carolina, to see if I could find Mrs. Sassoon alive so I could thank her. I knew that her husband and the daughter who had been my friend had died some time ago. No sooner did she pick up the phone than I heard again that loud, friendly, curious voice.

"What?" she shouted into the receiver. "What? Carol? I say, is that you? My God!"

I began thanking her for her respect and kindness years before. I felt that my life had changed because of her—and Willie as well. I wondered aloud if she remembered that she had given me four or five art lessons.

"Remember!" she shouted. I had to hold the receiver a little away. "Remember! How could I not remember! I will never forget those drawings of yours, blood flying in all directions! Do you remember them? You had people being bayonetted and God knows what! You always drew blood flying in every direction! Well," she said, "you probably don't remember, but I do. I kept all those drawings, too. I come across them from time to time! Did you know that Willie died? I tell you, it's bloody hell."

CHARLES SIMIC
Three Fragments

I didn't tell you how I got lice wearing a German helmet. This used to be a famous story in our family. I remember those winter evenings just after the war with everybody huddled around the stove, talking and worrying late into the night. Sooner or later, somebody would bring up my German helmet full of lice. They thought it was the funniest thing they ever heard. Old people had tears of laughter in their eyes. A kid dumb enough to walk around with a German helmet full of lice. They were crawling all over it. Any fool could see them!

I sat there saying nothing, pretending to be equally amused, nodding my head while thinking to myself, what a bunch of idiots! All of them! They had no idea how I got the helmet, and I wasn't about to tell them.

It was in those first days just after the liberation of Belgrade, I was up in the old cemetery with a few friends, kind of snooping around. Then, all of a sudden, we saw them! A couple of German soldiers, obviously dead, stretched out on the ground. We drew closer to take a better look. They had no weapons. Their boots were gone, but there was a helmet that had fallen to the side of one of them. I don't remember what the others got, but I went for the helmet. I tiptoed so as not to wake the dead man. I also kept my eyes averted. I never saw his face, even if sometimes I think I did. Everything else about that moment is still intensely clear to me.

That's the story of the helmet full of lice.

Beneath the swarm of high-flying planes we were eating watermelon. While we ate the bombs fell on Belgrade. We watched the smoke rise in the distance. We were hot in the garden and asked to take our shirts off. The watermelon made a ripe, cracking noise as my mother cut it with a big knife. We also heard what we thought was thunder, but when we looked up, the sky was cloudless and blue.

My mother heard a man plead for his life once. She remembers the stars, the dark shapes of trees along the road on which they were fleeing the Austrian army in a slow-moving ox-cart. "That man sounded terribly frightened out there in the woods," she says. The cart went on. No one said anything. Soon they could hear the river they were supposed to cross.

DENISE LEVERTOV
Inheritance

In 1890, when my mother was five years old, staying with her grandmother in Caernarvon, North Wales, she was taken on a day's visit to an ancient great-uncle who lived alone by the sea, somewhere along the Caernarvonshire coast. His tiny whitewashed cottage had only one room, but that room was clean and neat and a kettle steamed on the hob. The floor was of earth, compacted, and decorated each day with patterns made by squeezing green juice from certain leaves. He had a long white beard, and wore knee-britches. His legs and feet were bare, for he had been mending his fishing nets on the strand. My mother's grandmother told her to remember what he said, and she did, although it was a number of years before she understood its interest: he recounted how he had been at the Battle of Waterloo, and had seen Napoleon—Boney himself—ride away on his towering horse. So I, living in the age of jets and nukes, am separated only by the life span of one person, my mother, from looking into the eyes of a relative who had seen the Emperor at the moment of his defeat; and whose mode of life differed in few respects from that of some ancestor of his (and mine) long before the Norman conquest.

LAWRENCE WESCHLER
Modern Times

The morning after the launching of Desert Storm, a group of us at my office were talking about this awesome new thing that has entered the world, these awesome new things: this unprecedented kind of warfare with its truly precision, pinpoint aerial bombing; this unprecedented kind of war where, thanks to the various satellite technologies, you get to hear the results of that bombing instantaneously, as it's happening. Modern, we said, high-tech, uncanny, eerie, futuristic. And yet, of course, at another level, there's nothing new here. On the ground, the carnage of war, the gore, the frantically desperate attempts at rescue, the bitterly expiring hopes—they're all the same as they've ever been.

One of my friends there at the office that day commented on the way he'd been haunted all morning by the memory of an article he'd read last year—he couldn't remember where—about the San Francisco earthquake. About this young couple who'd been buried alive together in a small room in their collapsed apartment, their bones crushed in debris up to their waists, the

two of them huddled together in this narrow air pocket. And of
how the rescuers finally got to them—but at that very moment
the wreckage caught fire; they were able to free up the husband,
but he was forced to leave his wife behind and she perished in the
flames.

We were all silent for a moment—CNN in the background
was crosscutting between the latest Pentagon briefing and live
coverage of a speech by the Turkish prime minister in Ankara.

"Wait a second," my friend said. "I remember: it was in the
Whole Earth Review. In fact, I bet we can even access it over
Nexus." Our office is tied into one of those computerized data
bases which offers continuously updated access to the complete
back-contents of hundreds of newspapers and periodicals. My
friend set himself down before the system's console, revved up the
machine, punched in a few key words—*earthquake* and *fire* and
rescue and *couple*—and instantaneously that very article appeared
on the screen. He punched a few more buttons and the console's
neighboring printer revved up and began spewing out a copy. The
whole process didn't take more than a few moments.

The account, by Stewart Brand, was every bit as compelling
as our colleague had remembered it. It turned out that Brand himself had happened to be visiting the neighborhood at the moment
the earthquake struck and that he'd played an impromptu part
in the volunteer rescue attempts: he'd been one of those on the
outside, scrambling through the wreckage. "Of course, it wasn't
as direct and purposeful as this brief account makes it seem," he
records. "A real rescue is dreamy and hesitant, full of false starts
and conflicting ideas, at times frantic and focused, at times dif-
fuse. It is a self-organizing process, neither quick nor tidy. . . ."
Much later, weeks after the disaster, he'd gone back and interviewed several of the principals from that evening's incident,
including Bill Ray, the husband, who was still recovering at a

hospital. In his article, Brand interwove their stories, and his account climaxed as the firemen were being driven back by the flames:

> "I told Janet," [this is Ray talking] "I told her 'I'm going to get free, and we're both going to get free.' I assumed that I was binding her and that if I could get loose, then she could get loose. You just start pulling with everything you've got. You reach up and you pull on the lathe and the plaster, and it's breaking off in your hand. . . . Janet was screaming because it was a lot of pain and her arms were trapped, and a picture frame of glass was cutting her.
>
> "Then I got free, but she still wasn't. I tried to pull her out. Smoke was coming in. You could hear the flames cracking and popping. She couldn't pull herself loose, and I couldn't get to her."
>
> What they said to each other then, Bill Ray prefers to keep private. "Then I left," [Ray recalls] "I crawled out that hole. . . ."

And so forth. That terrible lacuna—the private moment, what they possibly could have said to each other—has haunted me, too, ever since I read it. And, of course, I've been imagining the hundreds of variations of that scene being played out half a globe away; the fact that accidental strikes on civilian targets are purportedly being kept to a minimum doesn't comfort me in the least. I envision seventeen-year-old boys scrambling desperately to rescue their buddies, having to abandon the attempt in the face of further bombardments, and the image is in no way softened by the allegedly mitigating circumstance that the boys in question may be wearing uniforms.

But, strangely, the image that really haunts me, and the one I just can't shake, is that of my colleague in the eerie glow of his Nexus console, calmly punching that set of keys, activating the machine—the machine silently humming away, surveying the veritable continents of information before it, instantaneously targeting its quarry, yanking it out of the endless field and delivering it up to us whole. The surgical precision of the whole process. For a moment that morning, my colleague seemed to me like one of those amazing young officers strapped to his battle station aboard the AWACs control planes circling high above Saudi Arabia—coolly surveying his console, punching in the coordinates, splaying out the information, directing the entire battle.

CNN, Nexus, AWACs—they're all of a piece. And the carnage on the ground is something entirely else, almost infinitely removed.

ANDREI CODRESCU
Nostalgia for Everything

This time of year for some reason I get filled with nostalgia like a Jules Verne balloon. I'm like Marcel Proust, who smelled a cookie and couldn't stop remembering. Wood fires are my cookie. I remember walking through an old square in my hometown in Romania, late fall 1958, kicking leaves with my feet and feeling as nostalgic as I do now for something I remembered then. I remember sitting on the steps of the Santa Maria Maggiore cathedral in Rome in 1965, eating an apple while everything turned to nostalgic gold around me. I sat in a steamy café by the Spanish Steps later with a bitter, hot espresso, looking wistfully on the fashions of the year 1965, mini-skirts and polka dots, and feeling so terribly young and alone. I remember the wind whistling with snowflakes in it down Woodward Avenue in Detroit as I looked for a warm place to sit and contemplate the future year 1967, for which I already felt nostalgic though it hadn't even happened. I remember the Blimpie's on the corner of Sixth Avenue and Ninth Street in New York across from the long-gone Women's House of Detention where I sat writing nostalgically in my diary about the incredible year 1969 that was just around the corner. I remember the back porch of Gabriel's hilltop apartment in San Francisco in 1970, looking on a pastel blue and gold city and wondering where winter was. I went looking for it in Golden Gate Park, wrapped in its cocoon of eucalyptus and ocean salt, and rocked like a baby listening for hints of 1971. I remember the mists swirling above the Knotty Room in Monte Rio in 1974 while Pat and Jeff and I drank Rhoda's bad coffee and looked out to the huge redwood trees bending in an awesome wind announcing the torrential winter rains of 1975. I remember late fall, early winter, at the Mt. Royal Tavern in Baltimore in 1978, when all the lights went out and we continued drinking and talking by candlelight as the world fell apart. And the autumnal little café near Pont Neuf in Paris in 1981, where nostalgia was invented. I'm writing now at the Déjà-Vu in New Orleans at the end of 1992, and I miss this place already.

CAROL BURELBACH
On the Way Home

I glance at the paper thinking of Geraldine and Miguel in Costa Rica, and their Chichi, with her big eyes like chocolate drops in whipped cream and skin the color of the café con leche I have begun to think I cannot live without: Chichi, who begins every sentence with "¡no quero!", who this morning walked holding my hand on the way to the beach, this brown baby, so fully aware, who predictably, once at the beach, puts her thumbs inside the shoulder straps of her pink tank suit, pops the straps from her shoulders, and steps proudly out onto the white sand in her glowing altogether.

GERRY SHARP
Falling Stars

When Norton and I slept out we were always on the lookout for falling stars. In science class we learned that falling stars, or more correctly meteors, upon entering the protective layer of the earth's atmosphere burned up so rapidly that by the time you called another person's attention to them, they would be gone.

We spent many summer nights behind Norton's sagging barn, stretched out side by side in our sleeping bags, in the long grass of his overgrown back yard disproving this and other pieces of adult wisdom handed down from a world blind to the infinite possibilities of boyhood. Refuting something learned in school was a triumph easily expressed and relished, but loosing ourselves upon the vast summer skies and connecting at a small temporary flame arching upon the night was a quieter triumph, never expressed aloud. This feeling as delicate as night air between us was even more tenuous because half the time I didn't believe him. I hardly ever saw the stars he pointed out, but it seemed like he saw almost all of mine.

Occasionally I'd send out a false cry.

Hey Norton! Did you see that one?

More often than not he'd give out a quiet but enthusiastic, *Yeah Sharp. I saw it!*

I never said anything as we lay in our musty canvas bags, later sleeping while hard celestial bodies burned themselves out against the soft nothingness of air.

MICHAEL DORRIS
Three Yards

When I was five years old we moved to an old house in the Crescent Hill section of Louisville. The property was oddly shaped for an urban lot, and the backyard measured almost one-third of an acre. It seemed to me then—and still does, in memory—a vast, lumpy expanse, a veldt big enough to plant trees or till a garden or run in a straight line long enough to be winded. The story went that a century earlier, this property had been the city dump, and indeed a bit of digging was always rewarded. Over time I collected worn sherds of blue glass, broken tools, bits and pieces of detritus that, in its bounty if not its perfection, struck me as treasure worth preserving.

The backyard was a place of record, from the spreading oak against whose trunk I stood each birthday for a measuring snapshot, to the clovery dell where I retreated to write in my diary. The geography was generous and precise: a fire pit for burning trash and autumn leaves, a plain on which neighbor children and I staged theatrical performances (our parents assembled on the bleachers of the porch steps), a tangle of my grandmother's roses, a different variety planted every Mother's Day.

Our house wasn't rich, our neighborhood was unremarkable, but I was wealthy with privacy, affluent with quietude. By merely walking out the door I could reach a green island where the sounds of traffic were muted and, when I lay flat upon the earth, clouds were all there was to see.

●

Much later, in my twenties, I lived alone in a small cabin perched on a bluff overlooking Cook Inlet. I was in Alaska to conduct my first stint of anthropological field-work, observing the changes wrought in an Athapaskan native community by the discovery of offshore oil deposits. Doubly isolated by remote location and by my inability to speak the language, I spent many hours each day sitting at my table, staring through my one glass window at the grey-blue waters. As the seasons altered, the light changed from day to night and the surface from rough-waved to an opaque frozen marsh that reached all the way east to Kenai.

The ocean is a taciturn companion, giving up less than it takes. At first its sweep drained rather than replenished my enthusiasm: it seemed simply too big, too alien, too much beyond calculation. In contrast to the benign, mowed lawn of my childhood lot, this crooked finger of the Pacific was a wall that seemed to separate me from everywhere I wanted to be—until one sunrise when the tide was turning. From that bright, sparkling-smooth mirror shone a single piercing idea: to do something about my loneliness, to initiate a process that eventually resulted in the adoption of my eldest son. Contemplation of the depths had, without my realizing it, reached bottom and become buoyant. Ever after in that spot, whether on cloudy days or sunny, the sea looked familiar as tomorrow, and now, when I cast my thoughts back a quarter-century, its face is the one I most clearly recall.

For seventeen years I've lived as an adult with my family in a rambling New England farmhouse fronted by a dirt road that carries little traffic. Our six children have played among the stone fences that transect the property, dodging the thorns of raspberry bushes and hiding from each other behind the weave of grape vines that drape the giant elm. The land, in its known history, has been put to many uses—fed sheep and cows, nourished crops, gone to seed. My wife and I are the latest to be married within its boundaries, in a grove of slender willows.

Our farm's former tenants would be surprised and pleased at our improvements: a new pond fed by underwater streams, concrete laid upon the dirt of their basement floor, a second well. But these are superficial changes, scratches on the surface. The smell of alfalfa in August is the same as it was. The wind through the pines sounds just as clean. The rocks still rise through the soil and must be harvested every spring before the furrows are dug.

Wherever we go from here, a part of us will stay rooted in this patch of earth, buried like a cache, ready to be redeemed by memory or by return. Domestication is a product of habit, a series of adjacent yards whose only fences are the limits of imagination, the length and circumference described by a line of sight in any direction.

REG SANER
The Tree Beyond Imagining

Seeing is not believing. Any tree "acting out" in such hog-wild and crazy ways—or so I used to feel—can't be truly arboreal. This one thinks it's a mad dog. Here's another trying to prove chaos might be a conifer. Yet another so riven, so warped, it looks like self-knowledge. Or is it just pretending to summarize World History? During our first acquaintance I ran across examples so willful and creaturely that my glance often boggled at believing what it saw. How could a juniper, I would ask myself, be throwing a fit?

Botanically speaking, of course, a juniper can't be perverse. As a dirt-common member of the cypress family it can at worst be only an oddball conifer. Other arboreal species may echo states we recognize in ourselves, but none I've run across seems so moody and emotional. Lifelong, we humans conceal our intimate histories, even while a version of them gets slowly written into our faces. This tree's neurotic past, however, appears at a glance, visible through no matter how many feigned identities. And though cone-bearing species may be tricky to tell, one from another, the one I have in mind is easy.

Beneath erstwhile needles that evolution has smoothed like snakeskin, and under cones shrunk to beads, a greyish-brown welter of wood appears. If it looks like tensed muscle and sinew, that illusion and the preceding traits do add up to generic juniper. But if the bark is shaggy as hanks of unbraided sisal; if the absolutely motionless trunk seems to be groveling in frenzy or twisting like smoke; and if in even the best-behaved specimen you see branches that mime devastation having a temper tantrum, you know you're not only dealing with *Juniperus osteosperma,* Utah juniper. You know the example before your eyes is a special case: a high-desert strain of that species, one growing where it ought not to try.

If animal, such trees would be camels, and almost are. But what camel drinks sand? Hence the near-incredulity. On a sun-spattered, all-but-windless morning in Utah, for example, you stand smack in front of one, gasping at its self-tormented trunk fed by red sand; or fed by far less, a crevice in rock which that sand once was. Yet on naked stone those knotted roots have knuckled down to sipping a trunk and limbs into life. From a low writhing branch you might strip off a fibrous dangle of bark the creature seems clad in, all threads and shreds and tatters, like a beggar's rags. Obviously the bark's stringy hairs are real. Just as clearly, its tree *as tree* lacks full credibility. The riven trunk, the gesturing limbs in every style of passion, cannot be anything Nature approves, much less intended. So you're bound to wonder about botanical vandalism. Novice-like, you stand there in south-eastern Utah just staring and shaking your head: "Surely someone has *done* this?"

Fact is, among Utah juniper of the high desert, flabbergasting abnormality is the norm only among individual trees defying limitation. Lots of rock, lots of sand, lots of wind, and very little rain can make juniper stands growing there, at the far end of possibility, an outpost of marginalized eccentrics. Not the whole species. No, the stressed-out examples I'm talking about, the trees you can see without quite believing, grow where they almost can't—at their ecological edge. We think timberline a question of mountain altitudes beyond which no conifer can rise. For desert junipers timberline may be a limit drawn in the sand, not by rarefied air but by rain, lower than which there is none, or as good as.

Thus, it's by taking root at the threshold of impossibility that this most irrational tree grows against all reason. A Utah juniper at the edge of its range is either so distraught or far gone in perplexity it can't make sense of itself. "Do you suppose I'd have grown this way," it seems to snort, "if I'd had any idea what I was getting into?"

Although the specimens I admire would indeed make more interesting museum pieces than many a prize now under glass, I realize that bringing just the tree inside wouldn't do. You'd need to bring along with it the thin air of its Southwestern plateau. You'd need too that powdery fine sand red as rust, rippled dunes sparsely tufted with greasewood or Indian rice grass. And skies blue as chicory petals. Floating puffs of cumulus too, their undersides tinted by the red miles beneath them. Birdsong as well; rock wrens, horned larks, mockingbirds, vireos, piñon jays. And scrub jays, cowbirds, towhees. And vultures. Above all, you'd need desert sun with its glare, its incomparable clarities, deep shadows; its refusal to lie.

On the Grand Canyon's south rim, I have spent hours of clear weather, more intrigued by its pygmy forest of piñons and junipers than by the view. Happily roving among outcrops of chert and Kaibab limestone, well-content at being scolded by piñon jays, I have come upon deep depression and recovery—both alive in the same tree. How had it grown so depressed, I wondered. Through wrestling for its own affections? Or by being too much a shape-shifter ever to tire of dilemma? And how had recovery and relapse grown from the same trunk? Because its moods, like ours, don't believe in each other? There I found trees giving instructions in bravery. Found them more typical than not. To look at such lives and say "struggle" doesn't touch it.

During that same afternoon I stumbled upon a juniper who had once been a witch and couldn't quit practicing; then found countless others its bad example converted. As if they had used witchery to request eternal life and youth, they seemed the picture of what happens when only the first half is granted. The picture of how losers look when they win.

There amid the deranged and violent I also discovered "good" trees battening on the same rimrock; witnessed all the living optimism, all the hurt joy that can scuffle upward out of rock and suffer open. In wresting a living from limestone's long famines of rain they must sometimes have felt that enduring there was next to impossible, yet endure they had.

We admire most, I suppose, those virtues our souls utterly lack, or need more of. Even after twenty years, therefore, I'm apt to be spellbound by the drama of a particular trunk and limbs. Feeling sympathy and awe before such pure indomitability costs nothing, I know, because I've often stood that way a longish while, unaware that I was; as if hoping a touch of juniper courage might agree to come with me.

KIM R. STAFFORD
December Meditation at Camp Polk Cemetery

You have to listen real hard to hear anything at all: a little snow ticking down through juniper trees; the click of the
chain around a family plot flexing in the cold. Wind. You hear
it quite a while before it arrives. Then the eastern half of your face
might just as well be stone.

Ten years ago I was here to do a formal study of the cemetery
layout. As part of my folkloristic fieldwork, I made a systematic
ramble of thirteen central Oregon cemeteries, stepping respect-
fully in the August dust of memorial plots at Grizzly, Antelope,
Ashwood, Grandview, Madras, Hay Creek, Bakeoven, Warm
Springs, Simnashio, Camp Polk, and three without names. I
wanted to know how the adjacent communities of the living
marked, surveyed, and maintained these trim little cities of stone
and sage. I wanted to know how many gravemarkers listed family relations, military rank, professions, hobbies, wise proverbs,
and the verse of grief or hope. I wanted to know how these
stretches of sacred ground were isolated from the cattle range sur-
rounding them: wood fence, iron gate, barbed wire, poplar square.
On the main street of how many towns would there be a sign for

the "Cemetery: 2 miles"? How many plots would be simple local secrets tucked away up a side canyon?

I wanted to seek and listen, to map and ponder the visible artifacts of religious belief my people hold. I did all that. The study is in the archive. The memory works on me.

But now it's dusk at Camp Polk, and I'm visiting old friends. Here's Ray, by the champion juniper gnarl he loved to paint. His name in my mouth brings up a riff of banjo jangle I heard him play. There's a snow-swirl dancer over his place now.

I remember my discovery ten years ago, that graves everywhere planted heads to the west. This marks the Christian readiness to rise up facing Christ as He will bloom from the east on Judgment Day. And I remember how many of the thirteen cemeteries marked the end of a dead-end road: the Ashwood plot up a dirt track with no sign. The Grizzly cemetery at the ripe heart of a wheatfield with no road at all, forgotten like the town of Grizzly itself, which some prosperous corporation bought. I drove around and around that field, knowing I was close, my map fluttering from my hand in the heat, until finally I squinted my eyes past the shimmering wheat and saw the cemetery fence out there in the middle of everything.

Somewhere near the cemetery here at Camp Polk, a hundred odd years ago, the U.S. Army buried a cannon before fleeing from the Indians. Treasure hunters have sought it, as if it were a memory they owned by rights, as if that brass body might be raised up and carried away. You have to brave a series of "No Trespassing" signs to get to Camp Polk. Ten years ago there was a sign to invite visitors on toward the cemetery on its little hill beyond the most handsome of falling barns. This evening, there is no sign. You have to know.

Driving into Shaniko, I remember slowing the car to ask directions of an old-timer crumpled easily beside a shed, whittling steadily at a stub of wood. I didn't realize until too late the impertinence of my opening question, "Excuse me, sir, could you direct me to the cemetery?"

There was a tremendous pause, as he turned slowly up from his work to unroll a vacant smile. No answer was on the way. I thanked him, and drove on to the Eat Cafe. This time, I tried to be a bit more discreet, making my request in hushed tones to the waitress as she came rollicking across the room with half a dozen steaming plates along her arms.

"Excuse me, I'm trying to find the cemetery—for research."

She lurched expertly to a stop without jostling a plate, and shouted to the long table of white-haired ladies at the far end of the room, "Hey girls, we got a cemetery?" They vaguely shook their heads.

"Mister," she said, "we ain't got one. Try Antelope." I explained that I had already been there, and learned what I could.

"Well," she said, "then I don't think we can help you. We don't figure to do much dying in *this* town."

If you lie on your back to watch the snow come down, you will hear little rustlings in the grass, and you seem to see a long way up into the sky. You can try to be as still as everyone else, as hopeful and content.

I remember the gravestone at Agency Plains, the one with the sheriff's badge carved deep into the marble beside one name. Neighbors told me later he had never been Sheriff, but that was his life-long wish. Deputy, yes. Sheriff, never. Until then.

Religion in the desert has a lot to do with patience, and patience has a lot to do with silence. Beyond my feet where I lie at Camp Polk, there is a stone with an infant's oval ceramic photograph fixed to the pedestal. Someone sometime has used it for target practice, and the gray print of the bullet shies away low and to the left. There are so many children, and they are all so silent they are a chorus. The desert is big enough to hold it.

At Ashwood in that ten years back I heard a wind coming. All was still where I crouched, but I heard that wind. Hot. There was a permanence to every stone crumb and weedstalk in the little enclosure of wire where I stood up. About a quarter mile away, a single tree was moving. The others were inert. I folded my map and put it away. Then the little whirlwind moved down the hill into another tree and left the first tree alone. There was a weight to the afternoon. Then all the trees were still and the wind was a slender spiral of dust coming down toward me.

Even under the snow I can see the varieties of hope at Camp Polk: the ring of stone, the chain perimeter, the lichen-shredded picket fence, concrete moat, rusted cast-iron rail around a rich man's land. In the sweep of open desert ground, the grave plot is a pouch, a box, a small fenced span of certainty. That's all. That's enough. It's nearly dark.

As I rise up, fervent and happy for every movement I make, snow shakes off my coat into my body's print on the ground. There is one thing still I must do. One of Camp Polk's oldest stones has fallen from its pedestal. Carved on the stone are the twin gates of heaven thrust wide. An orange swathe of lichen has covered the spirit's name. I can see only a submerged swirl of graceful lettering where the stonecutter engraved a name, a year, a lamb, and a verse.

I bend to lift the stone back into place, but it is frozen to the earth. I try to kick it loose, but my toes go numb. Then I see the initials. Chipped ruggedly at the base of the stone, never intended to be seen once it had been fit forever to the pedestal, are the stonecutter's secret letters "J.A.W.O.S." What for immortality? Public proclamations are prey to time. Only the secrets survive.

Was it at Grizzly? Was it at Hay Creek: the nameless stone sunk almost gone into the earth, with its moss-word "Mother"? Or was that Warm Springs, among the gifts of favorite things, the scattered trinkets love makes us give back to a place where we believe?

Good night, Ray. Bit windy, wouldn't you say? One thing about snow, though. It don't ever last.

JOHN D'AGATA
Notes Toward Identifying a Body

Every day he poured himself into it, as water might pour from a flask. And every day, nothing poured back. So don't tell me it was an accident, don't tell me about the desert heat, about dehydration, or the way hikers get lost and burn inside-out. There was a moment when the water was not in him, nor in the flask, nor on the ground, but still pouring. He knew, in this moment, nothing; felt nothing, even as his own skin weakened to parchment, forfeiting itself to story. Later, he would remember thirst, and remember dreaming, but he would not remember death.

●

He is ten times bigger than he ever was in real life. The photograph is swollen, enlarged to the point of diffusion, so that all the brown, tan, beige, white dots that make up the image—like cells in his body, or atoms in the air—look bloated, the size of marbles. They are large enough to stick my hand through, and as I stare they skid further apart. *Soon I will be able to walk right into him,* I think. It's not the reason we're here, of course. But as we wait in line for the "Welcome to Death Valley" slide-show, who doesn't want to stare at this man rotting on the wall, and think, "Isn't death intriguing? Larger than life and still a mystery?" or, "When is a body no longer a body, and when does it become an artifact? Does it happen as soon as the soul exits the body, or as soon as the body is hollowed-out by bugs?" Or like the woman beside me, pointing out the second "E" in *unidentifiEd:* "That's a sign of instability!" she says, because it rises above the rest of the word. Hell on fire. She invokes an entire life from this conjecture, as if the man in the photo had anything to do with the words on the photo; as if the words had anything to do with anything.

●

It is not the kind of penmanship that anticipated scrutiny, so when the nervous quill misspells *Vally,* I don't care, I look away. There is more to the man than how the rangers catalogued him. More than this black and white version of post mortem— blasphemy, when you think about it and stare long enough at the shadows to catch a murmur of their unique dialects, the insinuation of late-afternoon colors, almost-gorgeous, almost-perfect if it weren't for this blemish in the landscape; or perhaps, because of it. The ranger sent to entertain us while we're waiting says the man probably died in 1898, and was found a year later by tourists. The ranger's voice is dry and empty; it doesn't say *please rest please.* It says *a 49er seeking gold in this dangerous environment;* it says *a macabre case of dehydration.* It does not say *wadder wadder wadder wadder wadder.* Or sound anything like death.

●

I wonder if he died before his body cracked open, or if he watched vultures tear into him and smaller animals nest inside. If the photo weren't so old, I could see his eyes and tell you, but his irises are blue and too pale to have been caught by the early camera's lens. So his eyes glare now in the purest white, and his eye sockets gape open where he might once have had the strength to scarcely stare at his body surrendering to his body, and his mind, like Prometheus wracked with guilt, burning-up and literally baking under the kind of torture that inflicts the damned with an eternity of their sinful passing whims.

•

They started coming in 1860: on foot, on mule, on a dare, sometimes they came on litters shouldered by black "amigos," and at least one person came on stilts to avoid inhaling the valley's deadly "sea of gas." Everyone was searching for gold and nobody ever found it. Not a speck, not even fool's gold, until finally someone found borax—not as sexy as gold, but just as lucrative—and the valley soon streamed with pack animals and mining carts and tracks from a new machine that propelled itself across the desert, which Henry Ford had called his industry's "clincher." Later, *The Death Valley Chuck-Walla* (a gentlemen's quarterly) advertised "An automobile trip through Hell. . . . It has all the advantages of hell without the inconveniences. The perfect Novelty!" Ten years later, the travel agency reported record earnings, and that same year *The Death Valley Chuck-Walla* reported the discovery of the man's body. He was found by motoring tourists on an adventurous jaunt off the trail. By that time he looked so unlike a man that not even the squeamish screamed, but had to ask themselves why there were men still dying in Death Valley. Why, with all the conveniences, the new resort, the golf course, talk of a highway?

•

Beside the body is a bottle of whiskey, now empty like the water flask but stained brown in the photograph where the brew must

have sat as he lay dying—slowly evaporating, afterward. Funny
that he drank his water, but saved his whiskey. . . .

    ●

Right now I'm paler than the least exposed patches in the
photograph—a walking negative you can almost see through.
But when I leave in a week I'll be red, my burn an emblem of a
nap I took half-naked at noon, swaddled in a piece of canyon that
cooked my skin to the same shade as sandstone. In a month I will
wake in an apartment in New York and roll onto a parody of myself, my shed-skin the rarest lace, an exfoliated lover—shoulder,
foot, bits of chest. And I'll want to name it, try to keep it, and
then remember the dead man who is still crumbling, still molt-
ing, still hurrying his life into heaven, unable to shake off the last
of his mortal ties, his fated rank in a purgatory of gawking tourists
hypnotized by this photograph, by the man, his body, its label—
"unidentifiEd man, 1899"—when all he really wants is to disappear into the next century, and then, into no time at all, and
finally, to catch up with his last breath that pours into everything,
and on a whim, pours back out.

    ●

Deadman's Pass, Coffin Peak, Funeral Mountains, Cemetery
Mine, Dry Bone Canyon, Skull Gulch, Dante's View, Hell's
Gate. Sometimes I think Death Valley was named by men who
hated life rather than by men who lived heroically. One night after
hiking I watched a man pour a personality into himself at the lone
end of a bar. He was a man I'd seen hiking without water, and
who—he admitted at the end of the night—wanted me, and
who—I'm willing to admit—I wanted too, although not in the
same way that he did, but in the way you thirst for an experience,
and the experience, like water, pours you out.

GRETEL EHRLICH
A Match to the Heart

Deep in an ocean. I am suspended motionless. The water is gray. That's all there is, and before that? My arms are held out straight, cruciate, my head and legs hang limp. Nothing moves. Brown kelp lies flat in mud and fish are buried in liquid clouds of dust. There are no shadows or sounds. Should there be? I don't know if I am alive, but if not, how do I know I am dead? My body is leaden, heavier than gravity. Gravity is done with me. No more sinking and rising or bobbing in currents. There is a terrible feeling of oppression with no oppressor. I try to lodge my mind against some boundary, some reference point, but the continent of the body dissolves.

•

A single heartbeat stirs gray water. Blue trickles in, just a tiny stream. Then a long silence.

•

Another heartbeat. This one is louder, as if amplified. Sound takes a shape: it is a snowplow moving grayness aside like a heavy snowdrift. I can't tell if I'm moving, but more blue water flows in. Seaweed begins to undulate, then a whole kelp forest rises from the ocean floor. A fish swims past and looks at me. Another heartbeat drives through dead water, and another, until I am surrounded by blue.

●

Sun shines above all this. There is no pattern to the way its glint comes free and falls in long knives of light. My two beloved dogs appear. They flank me like tiny rockets, their fur pressed against my ribs. A leather harness holds us all together. The dogs climb toward light, pulling me upward at a slant from the sea.

●

I have been struck by lightning and I am alive.

KATHLEEN NORRIS
Rain

Above all, it is a land in serious need of rain.
—WILLIAM C. SHARMAN, *Plains Folk*

Until I moved to western South Dakota, I did not know about rain, that it could come too hard, too soft, too hot, too cold, too early, too late. That there could be too little at the right time, too much at the wrong time, and vice versa.

I did not know that a light rain coming at the end of a hot afternoon, with the temperature at 100 degrees or more, can literally burn wheat, steaming it on the stalk so it's not worth harvesting.

I had not seen a long, slow rain come at harvest, making grain lying in the swath begin to sprout again, ruining it as a cash crop.

Until I had seen a few violent hailstorms and replaced the shingles on our roof twice in five years, I had forgotten why my grandmother had screens made of chicken wire for all the windows on the west side of her house.

I had not seen the whimsy of wind, rain, and hail; a path in a wheatfield as if a drunken giant had stumbled through, leaving footprints here and there. I had not seen hail fall from a clear blue sky. I had not tasted horizontal rain, flung by powerful winds.

I had not realized that a long soaking rain in spring or fall, a straight-down-falling rain, a gentle, splashing rain is more than a blessing. It's a miracle.

An old farmer once asked my husband and me how long we'd been in the country. "Five years," we answered. "Well, then," he said, "you've seen rain."

VICKI LINDNER
Proud Flesh

When I moved from New York to Laramie, Wyoming, I thought that for symbolic, if not practical reasons, I ought to learn how to ride a horse. So every Thursday afternoon, when I am supposed to be engaged in a "program of relevant academic research," I drive away from the University town's U-Bake-Em Pizzas and Cowboy Bars to the uncramped sky of The Sodergreen Ranch, where I study "Beginning Horsemanship" with Mrs. Ellie Prince.

A professor of equitation, who breeds and trains Arabian steeds, Mrs. Prince wears unironed lavender levis, grass green shirts, and unlike most Wyoming women, bright red lipstick. Her firm, gum-soled step and definitive voice allow her staff of eighteen horses the comfort of knowing they have no choice but to obey. Their obedience to Mrs. Prince, in fact, can frustrate the neophyte horsewoman's progress. When she stands in the center of the ring and calls, "Prepaaare to halt!" her horses shuffle to an obliging standstill, whether or not we crunch our seatbones into the saddle, pull back our shoulder blades, and stare straight ahead. When Mrs. Prince orders, "Walk!" her horses start up again—

223

automatically. "I tried spelling the commands for a while," she said. "But pretty soon, they learned how to spell!"

Our Thursday afternoon lessons begin in the panelled living room of Mrs. Prince's old stone house. From her dining room table turned into a desk (she's too busy with horses to give dinner parties), our teacher lectures on equine intricacies. We have memorized the parts of the horse—withers, pastern, croup and hock—identified the coffin and navicular bones that support its feet, and recorded a Prince family recipe for bacon grease horse dressing. Horses, I now know, are delicate creatures, prone to Monday morning sickness (too much grain and not enough exercise), agoraphobia, and poetic ailments like Proud Flesh, Mud Fever, Poll Evil, Moon Blindness, Parrot Mouth and Warbles. We have also been made privy to the secrets of horse training: "Basically you take the place of another horse," advises Mrs. Prince. "You lead him around walking and whoaing, until he gets the idea that you are a friend. Then you touch his ears and his mouth and try picking up his feet. It's not a normal thing for a horse to like— to be touched like that—but after awhile he learns to like it. When the time is right—and you just kind of feel it—you get on astride. Don't introduce him to a rubber bit, because horses hate the taste of rubber."

During the lecture, a Methuselah-aged dog limps agreeably from student to student, wagging her tail, and Mrs. Prince's husband, Bill, as silent as the oil beneath the prairie, caresses a kitten beside the antique wood stove with a bullet hole in it. On the vanity in the old-fashioned rose-colored bathroom, next to the claw-footed tub, a single green alfalfa horse cookie awaits a beneficent opportunity.

Mrs. Prince loves her horses. She calls them "Darling" and "Sweetheart," and fusses a good deal about their kidneys and the state of their feet, their safety, and caters to their idiosyncratic personal preferences. Gail, she warns us, does not like to be cinched, and Jinx and Blue cannot be tied, whereas Apple and Phoebe, close girlfriends from the East Pasture, have to be tied side by side. As we maneuver our mounts around the ring, reversing, circling in voltes, sitting, standing, then posting a trot, Mrs. Prince will call, "You on Eddie—sorry, I forgot your name—keep away from Pegasus for Heaven's sake! Those two don't like each other." We spent the first class learning to curry and brush our horses, and pick irritating stones out of their feet, because this grooming process makes a horse feel like we do after we've washed our faces in the morning—comfortable. "And when he's comfortable," states Mrs. Prince, "he gives you a good ride!" Although she encourages us to practice safety rules, lest we are cowkicked, bitten, stepped on, shied from, reared on, or scraped off on the side of the barn, my teacher's optimistic blue eyes registered wary, almost offended surprise when I confessed that I was slightly afraid of horses.

In *Basic Horsemanship,* a primer illustrated with amusing cartoons of fearful dudes hammering spurs into a grimacing gelding's contorted sides, Mrs. Prince warns, "Do not think you will control this animal with your strength." What this clearly implies is that horse control falls under the jurisdiction of mysterious, non-muscular powers—an emanation of psychic mastery over the world of beasts. Unfortunately, this power is not one even the most brash New Yorker can pretend to possess. Herb, a cowboy artist who lives all alone on a ranch up north, has told me that the exceptionally sensitive horse knows more about you than you know about yourself—what kind of day you've had, whether or not you are a decent human being, and certainly, your innermost feelings about horsemanship. With this in mind, after a morning of unseasonable flulike symptoms, I approach Chico, Sodergreen's oldest, slowest, smallest and most trusted mount.

Mrs. Prince advises us to talk as we groom, so that our horses get to know us, but she doesn't tell us exactly what to say. It seems an insult to Chico's ton of stolid bulk, his moist, unblinking Scheherazade eyes, his coarseness of hair, and rancid grass odor to beguile him with the affectionate nonsense that lured the weightless, scurrying Baby Blue to suck up strands of fettuccine, or to admonish him with the thoughtless curse uttered before squashing a tenement cockroach. On the other hand, to regale him with my trivial human fears—my mother's illness—or home-sick dreams of floating up the perfumed escalators of Saks Fifth Avenue disrespects his intuitive equinity. Whatever I say, he stands with the permanence of a stoic rock, stronger than his inherited frailties, and greater than the sum of his memorized parts. Like a child accepting the onus of a snowsuit, he waits with complacent, if not cooperative patience, as I cinch his back into the saddle, and only steps to the side and throws up his head when I press my fingers into the back of his mouth (where, Mrs. Prince swears, he has "bars" instead of teeth), and timidly attempt to insert his bit.

Once saddled and bridled, Chico is lazy—or, at least, has tran-scended this world's exigency for speed. "Get Chico moving!" cries Mrs. Prince. "Use your legs on him. Hit him with the reins! No, not there! Behind the girth—that's where a horse's motor is." The Wyoming students, thundering by on proud-crested Turol, and temperamental, prancing Twano, cluck "C'mon Chico!" to help us out. Mrs. Prince swats him on his chestnut rump and dropping the "Darling" hollers, *"Move!"* For a brief moment, Chico's hooves obediently gallivant into a rhythmic clip-clop. After class, Mrs. Prince defends her old horse's slowness. "It's not his age. He's a good little jumper. And he gets a second life on the trail. Going around and around an arena is just not his thing."

What I don't tell her, but I'm sure Chico knows, is that my illusion of power over him only emanates when he moves slowly.

April 15

Found a starved calf on the Big Hill today. She was with her mother but too weak to suck. We carried her in, trailed the cow. Her mother doesn't have much milk so we bottle-fed her. She's so weak she may not make it.

Gusts measured 63 mph at the Air Force Base, and it seemed even windier here. Cory took the tractor and pulled the drag over the Bar Circle meadow; the broken-up manure came along in waves. The sandhill cranes are here now, and the wind catches them when they try to rise up from the creek banks. They look like gawky gliders, about to crash. At one point, I watched Charlie open a gate and his unbuttoned jacket flared out in the wind. He is so tall and thin and long-limbed, I almost expected to see him rise up like one of the cranes. Later, we spooked a couple of mallards when we rode along the creek; they beat their wings just as hard as they could trying to get back to the water, but the wind carried them in the opposite direction. The wind has been picking up small rocks, hurtling them with such force that they break the skin. I have scratches on my cheeks and around my left eye. The big plank corral gates are impossible to handle. I needed three tries to close the gate on the north side of the horse corral yesterday, and the wind was coming from the west.

At lunch, Chris said he wanted to come with us in the pickup to check the Big Meadow and Charlie told him to meet us in the Quonset hut in half an hour. But when we were ready to go, we couldn't find Chris. We knew he had come out from the house, but we couldn't find him anywhere. We called for him, but the wind took our words away. We finally found him: he had thought Charlie said *behind* the Quonset and had been there all the time, out of sight and out of earshot. Charlie told Chris we'd been afraid that the wind had carried him away and that we'd find him splayed out on the barbed wire around the alfalfa, snagged like a tumbleweed.

It's too windy to feed hay, so the bulls come running for cake. One big Charolais likes to eat out of my hand and I try to keep a couple pieces in my pocket for him. Today I forgot and he was much offended. He's a broad-headed bull, jowly and freckle-faced, affectionate. If I rub the soft spot on his forehead, he leans into my hand and rolls up his eyes. I've named him John Bell after my great-uncle, whom he resembles. When he bellers, he even sounds like Uncle John calling to Aunt Marie: "Mahh-rhee!" Charlie is appalled that I would name a Charolais after a good Hereford man, but he has to admit the likeness.

I've come to think that the most frequently used phrase this time of year is "out of the wind." She's got a good place for him, out of the wind. I don't see how that little fellah can be so cold, he's out of the wind. Let's leave the pickup here, out of the wind. I'll just lay that hay here, out of the wind. The shed is noisy, but at least it's out of the wind.

Walking

It began in dark and underground weather, a slow hunger moving toward light. It grew in a dry gulley beside the road where I live, a place where entire hillsides are sometimes yellow, windblown tides of sunflower plants. But this plant was different. It was alone, and larger than the countless others that had established their lives farther up the hill. This one was a traveler, a settler, and like a dream beginning in conflict, it grew where the land had been disturbed.

I saw it first in early summer. It was a green and sleeping bud, raising itself toward the sun. Ants worked around the unopened bloom, gathering aphids and sap. A few days later, it was a tender young flower, soft and new, with a pale green center and a troop of silver-gray insects climbing up and down the stalk. Over the summer this sunflower grew into a plant of incredible beauty, turning its face daily toward the sun in the most subtle of ways, the black center of it dark and alive with a deep blue light, as if flint had sparked an elemental fire there, in community with rain, mineral, mountain air, and sand.

As summer changed from green to yellow there were new visitors daily, the lace-winged insects, the bees whose legs were fat with pollen, and grasshoppers with their clattering wings and desperate hunger. There were other lives I missed, those too small or hidden to see. It was as if this plant with its host of lives was a society, one in which moment by moment, depending on light and moisture, there was great and diverse change.

There were changes in the next larger world around the plant as well. One day I rounded a bend in the road to find the disturbing sight of a dead horse, black and still against a hillside, eyes rolled back. Another day I was nearly lifted by a wind and sandstorm so fierce and hot that I had to wait for it to pass before I could return home. On this day the faded dry petals of the sunflower were swept across the land. That was when the birds arrived to carry the new seeds to another future.

In this one plant, in one summer season, a drama of need and survival took place. Hungers were filled. Insects coupled. There was escape, exhaustion, and death. Lives touched down a moment and were gone.

I was an outsider. I only watched. I never learned the sunflower's golden language or the tongues of its citizens. I had a small understanding, nothing more than a shallow observation of the flower, insects, and birds. But they knew what to do, how to live. An old voice from somewhere, gene or cell, told the plant how to evade the pull of gravity and find its way upward, how to open. It was instinct, intuition, necessity. A certain knowing directed the seed-bearing birds on paths to ancestral homelands they had never seen. They believed it. They followed.

There are other summons and calls, some even more mysterious than those commandments to birds or those survival journeys of insects. In bamboo plants, for instance, with their thin green canopy of light and golden stalks that creak in the wind.

Once a century, all of a certain kind of bamboo flower on the same day. Neither the plants' location, in Malaysia or in a greenhouse in Minnesota, nor their age or size make a difference. They flower. Some current of an inner language passes among them, through space and separation, in ways we cannot explain in our language. They are all, somehow, one plant, each with a share of communal knowledge.

John Hay, in *The Immortal Wilderness,* has written: "There are occasions when you can hear the mysterious language of the Earth, in water, or coming through the trees, emanating from the mosses, seeping through the undercurrents of the soil, but you have to be willing to wait and receive."

Sometimes I hear it talking. The light of the sunflower was one language, but there are others, more audible. Once, in the redwood forest, I heard a beat, something like a drum or heart coming from the ground and trees and wind. That underground current stirred a kind of knowing inside me, a kinship and longing, a dream barely remembered that disappeared back to the body. Another time, there was the booming voice of an ocean storm thundering from far out at sea, telling about what lived in the distance, about the rough water that would arrive, wave after wave revealing the disturbance at center.

Tonight I walk. I am watching the sky. I think of the people who came before me and how they knew the placement of stars in the sky, watched the moving sun long and hard enough to witness how a certain angle of light touched a stone only once a year. Without written records, they knew the gods of every night, the small, fine details of the world around them and of immensity above them.

Walking, I can almost hear the redwoods beating. And the oceans are above me here, rolling clouds, heavy and dark, considering snow. On the dry, red road, I pass the place of the sunflower, that dark and secret location where creation took place. I wonder if it will return this summer, if it will multiply and move up to the other stand of flowers in a territorial struggle.

It's winter and there is smoke from the fires. The square, lighted windows of houses are fogging over. It is a world of elemental attention, of all things working together, listening to what speaks in the blood. Whichever road I follow, I walk in the land of many gods, and they love and eat one another. Walking, I am listening to a deeper way. Suddenly all my ancestors are behind me. Be still, they say. Watch and listen. You are the result of the love of thousands.

JERRY ELLIS
Into the Storm

I'm soaked to the bone as I walk through a storm down a country road in western Arkansas. I don't mind the wind and rain so much, but I'm scared to death of lightning. If a bridge or barn were in sight, I'd run for shelter. But forget it. There's just me and trees, swaying in the wind. For the first time in my life, I imagine how a mouse might feel the moment he looks up to see a hawk shoot from the sky to drive claws into his tiny heart.

I wear a hat; a black crow feather sticks from it, while a rattlesnake rattler with eight buttons rides snug under the band at the back of my head. Jeans cover my aching legs.

Lightning flashes yellow once again, as if to see if I'll try to run under a rock. I'm tempted.

The road is flooded and small waterfalls shoot from the rock banks. My feet are blistered and on my back is a red and blue backpack weighing fifty pounds. I've walked one hundred miles in six days and I have eight hundred more miles and seven states to go. I promised myself I'd walk the whole way. But have I lied?

I'm forty-one now, but when I was four years old my house was struck by lightning. I was home with my mother and two sisters and we smelled smoke coming from the attic. I was sure the house would disappear in flames and we'd have nowhere to live. My father, a carpenter, came home from work minutes later. He climbed into the attic with a bucket of water and threw it onto the fire. That put out the flames, but he slipped and fell through the ceiling. He crashed atop a piano and onto the floor. I learned then and there that lightning, as beautiful as it is, doesn't give a damn about man.

●

I walk facing traffic and a truck, hauling horses, roars toward me. The driver leans forward and squints in disbelief. A cigarette dangles from his mouth and he becomes a blur behind windshield wipers.

As the truck shoots past me I'm hit with a blast of wind and water; for a split second I can't see. My hand flies to my hat to grab it just as it jumps from my head. The snake rattler shakes and the smell of horses pierces my wet nose.

The lightning is much closer now, and I recall hiding behind a big chair in the corner of my house during a thunderstorm when I was in the fourth grade. A bolt of fire might get me, I reasoned, but it would have to find me first.

Boom! The thunder follows and a car stops. It's a station wagon with the front fender falling apart with rust. The back is loaded with lumber, plastic pipes, and a garden hose coiled like the snake from whom I got the rattler.

The driver motions for me to hop inside, but I hesitate. A little girl with a candy bar—there's chocolate on her chin—is propped against his shoulder. A Band-Aid is stretched across her temple. The driver rolls down his window.

Get in, he shouts.

The little girl smiles and it's so cozy and dry inside. Water runs down my nose.

I can't, I say. I'm walking the Trail of Tears.

●

In 1838, the Cherokee Nation thrived in Alabama, Tennessee, Georgia, and North Carolina. The eighteen thousand Indians had their own newspaper, *The Cherokee Phoenix,* published in both English and Cherokee. They raised corn, cotton, hogs, and cattle. They lived in log houses and had long ago put away their scalping knives. They hoped to live in peace where their ancestors had lived for over five hundred years.

But in 1838, President Martin Van Buren, pressured by Georgia, ordered seven thousand soldiers to round up the Indians at gunpoint. Their homes burned before their eyes, while soldiers dug into the family graves in search of gold and silver.

The Indians were thrown into thirteen forts newly built to act as concentration camps. I was born and raised in Fort Payne (Willstown), Alabama, between Lookout and Sand mountains, which was the site of one of those thirteen camps. All that remains of the fort today is its chimney, crumbling among oaks behind a burger joint and a tire company.

The eighteen thousand Indians were forced to march from their homes in Alabama, Tennessee, Georgia, and North Carolina to Oklahoma, then Indian Territory, in the heart of winter. Many had to walk, and their shoeless feet left tracks of blood on the earth and in the snow. Four thousand Cherokee, mostly children and old people, died along that route which has become known as the Trail of Tears.

●

You can't walk in this rain, says the driver. Swim, maybe.

I'll be okay, I say.

I hope you make it, he says.

He rolls up his window and the little girl waves good-bye with the hand holding the candy. They disappear into the storm and I walk on. I feel alone, naked with lightning. Where is my faith? Indeed, where is the strength and courage of my ancestors?

IAN FRAZIER
Crazy Horse

Personally, I love Crazy Horse because even the most basic outline of his life shows how great he was; because he remained himself from the moment of his birth to the moment he died; because he knew exactly where he wanted to live, and never left; because he may have surrendered, but he was never defeated in battle; because, although he was killed, even the Army admitted he was never captured; because he was so free that he didn't know what a jail looked like; because at the most desperate moment of his life he only cut Little Big Man on the hand; because, unlike many people all over the world, when he met white men he was not diminished by the encounter; because his dislike of the oncoming civilization was prophetic; because the idea of becoming a farmer apparently never crossed his mind; because he didn't end up in the Dry Tortugas; because he never met the President; because he never rode on a train, slept in a boardinghouse, ate at a table; because he never wore a medal or a top hat or any other thing that white men gave him; because he made sure that his wife was safe before going to where he expected to die; because although Indian agents, among themselves, sometimes referred to Red Cloud as "Red" and Spotted Tail as "Spot," they never used a diminutive for him; because, deprived of freedom, power, occupation, culture, trapped in a situation where bravery was invisible, he was still brave; because he fought in self-defense, and took no one with him when he died; because, like the rings of Saturn, the carbon atom, and the underwater reef, he belonged to a category of phenomena which our technology had not then advanced far enough to photograph; because no photograph or painting or even sketch of him exists; because he is not the Indian on the nickel, the tobacco pouch, or the apple crate. Crazy Horse was a slim man of medium height with brown hair hanging below his waist and a scar above his lip. Now, in the mind of each person who imagines him, he looks different.

STEVEN HARVEY
Nacoochee Indian Mound: Helen, Georgia

The power of the mound is at least sexual, the arched back of earth rising in desire here to as much of the sky as the mountains ever have to offer, announcing itself when we are in its presence as the center of all, the long grassy meadow strewn about it in the droopy shapes of detumescence. It conjures up images of gestation and nurture, a grassy place reminiscent of the breast and surrounded by cattle. Standing at its flattened top we take in, at a glance, acres of land that have fed people and live-stock for more than a thousand years. Built to ease death fear, the mound surveys prosperity and wealth—all that the living have to lose.

Spring happens easily here—the creek off to the south lined with budded laurel and rhododendron that hide the shaggy shanks of cottonwoods. The meadow itself is dotted with daisies and hung here and there with white patches of Queen Anne's Lace. The mound—eroded, smoothed by ages and mown— hunches, a light green shoulder of April grasses dotted with daisies. It is a place set aside, holy, the site once of a temple, and even though it sits exposed to traffic, cows, and a stream of curious tourists, it remains apart from all that it surveys.

The mound suggests all of this—desire, nurture, holiness—but it is in fact a grave, and like all grave markers it measures our loss and fits us for reality. Loss is the first impulse we feel in its presence, the sense that this is a remnant, a clue, to mysteries that escape us still—to losses that our wealth cannot protect us from. The gingerbread gazebo, built on top of the mound by a former governor and a hint of the present-day tourist-trap of Helen at its ancient source, is no doubt a gesture to compensate for that sense of loss, the intricate wood railings and ornamental red tin roof an attempt by a later time to fill a void.

Barn swallows nest in the gazebo now and fly into the evening meadow in a wild, tumbling search for insects. They look from here like Shaman hands fluttering from invisible sleeves. The mound, our source and culmination, casts an oblong shadow into the open field. Here the dead are buried with shells over their eyes and the past is forsaken for a continuous and increasingly gaudy present. A truck in low gear roars by. Loaded with goods, it is all that remains of the ancient, torch-lit Eagle dancers, its headlights casting eerie beams into the trees. It is headed into America, toward Atlanta and beyond, away from the dead that it never really leaves behind.

DEBORAH TALL
The Stories Tell the Land

*Tell these stories when you shouldn't and the bees will come
and sting your lips, your tongue will swell and fill your mouth, snakes
will crawl into your bed while you sleep and choke you . . .*

Certain stories weren't told by the Seneca Indians during the
summer months because they could offend the "little people," the
magical helpers of fruits and vegetables. Tale-telling was so powerful it could unbalance the seasons—creatures might become
entranced, wander dazed through forests and forget to go to their
winter homes. "To listen to stories made the birds forget to fly
to the south lands when winter came," Seneca scholar Arthur
Parker explained, "it made the animals neglect to store up winter provisions. . . ." Even plants would cross a threshold to hear
a story. "All the world stops when a good story is told."

The story of deer: black silhouettes on warning signs, shot up
for practice, for kicks, preseason; drunks in pickups (stay out of
the woods now); viewing stands in the crotches of trees; a stiff-
ened carcass mauled by dogs. Deer won't go near human hair—
if you want to protect young plants, drape them with your hair.

A woman who lost hers to chemotherapy told me this. How do you meet a deer?

The story of deer: when deer come near the house, they are like ambassadors from another realm, willing, for a moment, to flirt at the border. A listening pause. She holds. I stare, rigid lest I spook her. She is just outside my study window. But the span between us is an abyss neither of us can cross. It allows only our gaze, our alert meeting, a summit between two sovereigns with everything to negotiate, conducted in silence. I stress the need for compromise. But she is the first to turn, give up, leave, while I strain for the final white whip of her tail and am left empty-handed.

The story of poetry: thinking the conversation with the deer matters. Not simply, romantically, reading her as a sign, an outward sign of inward grace. Not superstitiously in the old magical way requiring divination, action. But a world to be attended to, silenced by, and recorded—even if I risk misreading her and myself. For this is the all, the only, the unavoidable *is.* It will assert itself despite us, inevitable as weather.

The story of weather: one spring, so cold and interminably wet that the dogwood never bloomed and the peonies disappeared before they could flower. Fierce storms—wind that would be gale force at sea, Seneca Lake slamming and moaning. The trees crying, a kind of keening, low and constant, unintelligible. The trees look to me like banished women, heads forlornly hung, arms sweeping toward earth in the whoosh of each wind blast. What are they grieving?

Story of the earth: my daughter wants to know if the earth is alive. I tell her yes. She wants to know why. I start talking about Gaia, the Iroquois notion of *orenda,* about the old myths in which women were turned into birds and trees, but she interrupts, says, "I know. It's alive because it moves without electricity."

Story of the earth according to a Dakota: "Everything as it moves, now and then, here and there, makes stops. The bird as it flies stops in one place to make its nest, and in another to rest in its flight. A man when he goes forth stops when he wills. So the god has stopped. The sun, which is so bright and beautiful, is one place where he has stopped. The moon, the stars, the winds, he has been with. The trees, the animals, are all where he has stopped, and the Indian thinks of these places and sends his prayers there . . ."

Stop and tell a story. The stories tell the land.

Sanctuary

"Oh God of mercy, oh wild God."
—GERALD STERN

It was in the Victor hills just south of Rochester, New York, where our cabin crouches near the pond in the last open space before the hills and woods begin, that we saw the doe. She had come out of the woods to feed late one August afternoon, as August was folding into September, as afternoon was giving way to evening, as the sun was clinging to the horizon and the hills were lifting, shining gold, from their green.

Near Ganondagan, sacred land, site of an ancient Seneca town, the place where a prophet known as the Peacemaker and the woman known as the Mother of Nations created the confederacy of the Iroquois and where she is buried. Iroquois: our word. Their word for themselves: Haudenosaunee.

We are Jewish. My husband, Bernard, is a survivor of what some call the Holocaust, others call World War II, others say never happened. It happened. It was fifty years ago, but it happened.

The Nazis wanted to kill him as they did his parents, three sisters, and one brother. But Bernie was young and strong and hid out from them in "friendly" barns for a time until they, too, turned unfriendly.

Then he lived underground, literally, in a hole he and several companions dug in the Polish forest, near what had been their village. They used a small tree for an entryway, lifting it up and replacing it whenever they went down into hiding.

For two years, from January 1943 until December 1944, they starved in that hole in the ground, breathing air let in by hollow pipes, sharing the space with cold and vermin and fear. Two years in that hole, days dark as night, winter and summer, somehow surviving, foraging, begging or stealing food, doing what they had to do, circling around and around in the snow to cover their tracks, in the moonless dark, hiding from the Poles who hunted them, who stalked above them, who did not find their hiding place. Not only snow, but mud, leaves, tall grass—any of these, oh God of mercy, could, but did not, betray them. When, at last, the war ended, they came out to a world that no longer held the world they had known.

That was fifty years ago, fifty anniversaries of days that come again, hidden from memory, living in dreams, in stories, in bits and pieces of recall, in the names of our children who were named after those from whom memory and all else was taken. Mother: Sarah. Father: Jacob. Sisters: Tzipporah, Mariashe, Devorah. Brother: Maishe. It happened.

We had spent a quiet day near the pond we both love, the pond that loves light, drawing it to itself to play with glint and slant; drawing, too, swallows and dragonflies who swoop in and out of the light and hover above the black depths.

The woods are posted: No Hunting, Fishing, Trapping, Trespassing. Forbidden. *Verboten.* Deer live in these woods. We see their hoofprints in the soft soil of the fields and in the displaced gravel of the driveway. When we have gone deeply enough into the woods, we have seen their spoor and the flat places where they sleep.

Bernie said that day along towards dusk, "Let's go and look for deer. Maybe we can see some."

"Aah," I answered, "what's the use? We won't see any." We'd gone looking before, without luck, even though our neighbors and Bernie, too, have seen deer grazing in the fields. I think it's me—too eager, perhaps, or unworthy. "Well, let's go anyhow."

We walked along the path between the woods and the wheat field, a field partially cut earlier that day. Clusters of wheat berries lay along the path. Bernie bent down, scooped up a handful of wheat, and blew, scattering golden dust.

"Wheat saved my life once," he said. "Did I tell you? Reuvack and I went out from our hole in the forest to beg for food, and some Poles caught sight of us and shot. We dropped. It was in a field of wheat just like this. That's why I'm sentimental about wheat."

•

You have to be lucky to see deer, and we were lucky this time. She must have seen us first, though, as she grazed behind some low bushes at the edge of the far field on the other side of the thicket, for it was her alarm, her sudden leap into the safety of the dark woods, that let us see her white rump and then the rest of her leaping into shadow. Oh, Holy to Haudenosaunee, you are young, not fully grown, and alone.

Grateful, we turned then and walked back. That's all that happened. But sometimes the doe still leaps past the edges of my mind, and the wheat glows in the fading light, and Bernie stoops low to scoop up handsful of grain and rises to scatter them, as if in offering to the god of deer and wheat and luck. And sometimes deer approach and accept the offering.

SCOTT RUSSELL SANDERS
Buckeye

Years after my father's heart quit, I keep in a wooden box on my desk the two buckeyes that were in his pocket when he died. Once the size of plums, the brown seeds are shriveled now, hollow, hard as pebbles, yet they still gleam from the polish of his hands. He used to reach for them in his overalls or suit pants and click them together, or he would draw them out, cupped in his palm, and twirl them with his blunt carpenter's fingers, all the while humming snatches of old tunes.

"Do you really believe buckeyes keep off arthritis?" I asked him more than once.

He would flex his hands and say, "I do so far."

My father never paid much heed to pain. Near the end, when his worn knee often slipped out of joint, he would pound it back in place with a rubber mallet. If a splinter worked into his flesh beyond the reach of tweezers, he would heat the blade of his knife over a cigarette lighter and slice through the skin. He sought to ward off arthritis not because he feared pain but because he lived through his hands, and he dreaded the swelling of knuckles, the stiffening of fingers. What use would he be if he could no longer hold a hammer or guide a plow? When he was a boy he had known farmers not yet forty years old whose hands had curled into claws, men so crippled up they could not tie their own shoes, could not sign their names. "I mean to tickle my grandchildren when they come along," he told me, "and I mean to build doll houses and turn spindles for tiny chairs on my lathe."

So he fondled those buckeyes as if they were charms, carrying them with him when our family moved from Ohio at the end of my childhood, bearing them to new homes in Louisiana, then Oklahoma, Ontario, and Mississippi, carrying them still on his final day when pain a thousand times fiercer than arthritis gripped his heart.

The box where I keep the buckeyes also comes from Ohio, made by my father from a walnut plank he bought at a farm auction. I remember the auction, remember the sagging face of the widow whose home was being sold, remember my father telling her he would prize that walnut as if he had watched the tree grow from a sapling on his own land. He did not care for pewter or silver or gold, but he cherished wood. On the rare occasions when my mother coaxed him into a museum, he ignored the paintings or porcelain and studied the exhibit cases, the banisters, the moldings, the parquet floors.

I remember him planing that walnut board, sawing it, sanding it, joining piece to piece to make foot stools, picture frames, jewelry boxes. My own box, a bit larger than a soap dish, lined with red corduroy, was meant to hold earrings and pins, not buckeyes. The top is inlaid with pieces fitted so as to bring out the grain, four diagonal joints converging from the corners toward the center. If I stare long enough at those converging lines, they float free of the box and point to a center deeper than wood.

I learned to recognize buckeyes and beeches, sugar maples and
shagbark hickories, wild cherries, walnuts, and dozens of other
trees while tramping through the Ohio woods with my father. To
his eyes, their shapes, their leaves, their bark, their winter buds
were as distinctive as the set of a friend's shoulders. As with
friends, he was partial to some, craving their company, so he
would go out of his way to visit particular trees, walking in a circle around the splayed roots of a sycamore, laying his hand against
the trunk of a white oak, ruffling the feathery green boughs of a
cedar. "Trees breathe," he told me. "Listen."

I listened, and heard the stir of breath.

He was no botanist; the names and uses he taught me were
those he had learned from country folks, not from books. Latin
never crossed his lips. Only much later would I discover that the
tree he called ironwood, its branches like muscular arms, good
for ax handles, is known in books as hop hornbeam; what he
called tuliptree or canoewood, ideal for log cabins, is officially the
yellow poplar; what he called hoop ash, good for barrels and
fence posts, appears in books as hackberry.

When he introduced me to the buckeye, he broke off a chunk
of the gray bark and held it to my nose. I gagged.

"That's why the old-timers called it stinking buckeye," he told
me. "They used it for cradles and feed troughs and peg legs."

"Why for peg legs?" I asked.

"Because it's light and hard to split, so it won't shatter when
you're clumping around."

He showed me this tree in late summer, when the fruits had
fallen and the ground was littered with prickly brown pods. He
picked up one, as fat as a lemon, and peeled away the husk to
reveal the shiny seed. He laid it in my palm and closed my fist
around it so the seed peeped out from the circle formed by my
index finger and thumb. "You see where it got the name?" he
asked.

I saw: what gleamed in my hand was the bright eye of a deer. "It's beautiful," I said.

"It's beautiful," my father agreed, "but also poisonous. Nobody eats buckeyes, except maybe a fool squirrel."

I knew the gaze of deer from living in the Ravenna Arsenal, in Portage County, up in the northeastern corner of Ohio. After supper we often drove the Arsenal's gravel roads, past the munitions bunkers, past acres of rusting tanks and wrecked bombers, into the far fields where we counted deer. One June evening, while mist rose from the ponds, we counted 311, our family record. We found deer in herds, in bunches, in amorous pairs. We came upon lone bucks, their antlers lifted against the sky like the bare branches of dogwood. If you were quiet, if your hands were empty, if you moved slowly, you could leave the car and steal to within a few paces of a grazing deer, close enough to see the delicate lips, the twitching nostrils, the glossy, fathomless eyes.

MARGARET B. BLACKMAN
August

Amigiksivik on the North Slope Borough calendar that hangs in the village store and post office. "Caribou skins are good for making parka." "The month for skinning caribou." Fall arrives, overnight it seems. By early August, green tundra grasses shimmer golden at their tips; patches of brilliant red dwarf birch and bearberry flash on the flanks of the Brooks Range. Scrubby willows in autumn yellow drop their leaves, smell like October back home.

The beginning of sheep season and the ripening of arctic blueberries. Men take leave of work to go into the mountains in search of dall sheep; women bend low on the tundra filling plastic bags and buckets with salmon-colored *akpiks*—cloudberries.

More and more the big U.S. flag flying above the tiny post office unfurls towards the south in the cold north wind that blows off the Arctic Ocean. On any August morning, the mountains might be dressed in snow down to their base; wet snow hangs on the willow branches and leaves, then melts under the midday sun. The light of August is softer, less intense than that of a few weeks ago. The sun is leaving. Night returns to the Pass, seven minutes more of it each day, the sun sliding below the mountains in its ever-dipping circle.

Fog rolls in, not on "little cat feet," but on a strong north wind, eating up the mountains in its path. The village becomes small then, isolated. We retreat indoors against the cold, closing the two doors of our little house to the outside, bumping against each other in its close confines as we negotiate our personal spaces. Kids don't come by "walking around"; we bury ourselves in our books. A weekend day goes by without any contact with villagers. The skies are silent—no planes land.

We leave the Pass the third week in August, watching autumn turn back to summer as we fly south over the Brooks Range to Fairbanks. Up north the caribou cows are starting to get fat. Soon it will be September, *Amigaiqsivik*—"when the velvet is shed from antlers"—and the caribou will gather in preparation for their southward journey through Anaktuvuk Pass, the "place of many caribou droppings."

CAROL LUCCI WISNER
Stonehenge and the Louvre Were Cool

Sometimes it happens this way: I am standing in chest-high muddy water in a vast, dim room, and all my things—my chairs and tables, my lamps and bookshelves and my china cabinet—are floating and bobbing all around me as they're carried away on a swift current. There is the roar of rushing water ringing in my ears, and with it, the feeling that something I could have prevented is about to happen or has already happened. Then I wake to the sound of my daughter's key in the door and her footsteps on the stairs. I hear water running in the bathroom sink.

She's eighteen now, and when I look at her, I feel I don't know her. Some days I don't even like her. I love her but I don't like her, and I think if I could just tell this to someone it wouldn't seem so scary. No matter what I say, it's not what she wants to hear. No matter what she does, I'm alarmed, and it's all I can do to stop myself from imposing some "curfew" or "rule" or "punishment" I haven't the energy to enforce.

She's afraid of nothing—including me, including the thought that she could do something to make me stop loving her, which is true. We argue and when it's over, I can't remember what either of us wanted or how it started or what it was about. I feel heavy and at the same time emptied out, as if a storm came through and didn't clear the air, but left it harder to move and breathe in.

Last summer she brought me a teacup from London—where, she said, my camera was stolen the first day, on one of those double-decker buses. In Paris, everyone tried on her sunglasses. With a throwaway camera she took pictures of a pair of pale pink ballet slippers and some wilted long-stemmed roses on Jim Morrison's grave, which, she told me, is not far from Chopin's.

It was in Paris, in a karaoke club, where a cute guy named Michael came up to her and said "I love you." An artist did her portrait on the street—eighty francs—and it's her, right down to that expression of inwardness that infuriates me. She and her friends ate fresh baguettes they broke open with their hands, ate them with the peanut butter I'd slipped into her bag. Stonehenge and the Louvre were cool, she said, but Versailles sucked: miles and miles of dirty wallpaper and old bedspreads.

The pattern on the cup she bought is "Lavender Rose"—sprays of cabbage roses, ferns, silver-green leaves on creamy white, a rim of gold. She brought it out of her backpack, wrapped carefully in tissue paper. She didn't have enough to buy the saucer, hoped that was okay. The next morning I drank my coffee from it, and believe it or not, a few weeks after that I found a matching saucer. It was in a stack of old china under a table, in a shop so close and musty I could taste it in the back of my throat.

Her dreams have a certain plainness and logic; they're as neat and precise and as legible as a cornfield in winter, its parallel lines of stubble poking out of the snow. At least that's how they seem on those mornings she feels like talking, when her face is soft and open, when we haven't argued yet and her hair is in her eyes. When we haven't argued and the day can still be perfect. She'll tell me she dreamed of a blue heron, and for the rest of the day I'll see it circling over a lake that is dark and still and smooth as a mirror, with cattails all around.

In her dreams she is always running; she dreams about flight, escape. Everything is wide-open and in a light so hard and bright, things stand apart from each other as if their edges are cut out with scissors. Everything is sharp and sudden like the ringing of a telephone, like the young, vaguely sullen male voices on the line, saying her name as if they know something I don't. Something I don't know when they speak her name, asking for her. Something I don't want to know.

I'd like to be the one who gets to slam the door, the one who'll eventually leave. I'd like to tell her I too had that fearlessness, and that it went away when I had her. When I looked into her face that first time, I understood that the universe couldn't care less, and that its blessings were bestowed at random. What was given could just as easily be taken away. And what was taken away could never be given back.

These days, and by that I mean years, the years since I stopped being in my thirties, I find myself thinking, *how did you get here?* I mean, where was I while all this time was going by? I can rifle through a drawerful of pictures and see so many versions of myself: bride, young wife, mother, and in all of them I look happy. I even look like I knew what I was doing. I ask myself what it was that I wanted then, and I don't know, I don't remember. I don't remember wanting anything, except maybe someone to talk to.

We lived in a little white house, and I used to put her in the baby seat on my bike and we'd ride to the Savoia Bakery for Italian pastries. Or we'd take the bus downtown. We visited the Sully branch of the public library, and there was an older black woman there who was nice to us.

In the pictures I look happy, though there were times I felt trapped, as if every choice I made was the slamming of another door. Doors I slammed behind me recklessly, as if a future of possibilities was dangerous, or more than I deserved, or more than I could live up to. I kept hearing about all these options I had and I didn't know what to do with all that freedom. I think I'd know what to do with it now.

•

A Saturday, in January: she sleeps till eleven, takes a leisurely bath, tries on my earrings, uses my powder, my kohl pencils. Walks around in nothing but a man's shirt, blue plaid flannel, her friend Quinn's. Draws smudgy lines on her lids and studies the effect with her eyes half shut, her mouth loose, pouting. Does her laundry and lies on the couch, watching re-runs of "The Real World"—a documentary about seven incompatible people living in a beach house. Waits for her clothes to dry and for the phone to ring.

This is the child, I tell myself, who'd play happily in her playpen so I could go downstairs to throw another load into the washer, who wouldn't keep her shoes on in school, who was always losing her lunch money, who sucked her thumb when she thought no one was looking. Who is she now—this touchy stranger with whom I seem to have no history? She has kept a journal since she was six years old, and she writes poems that make the hairs on the back of my neck stand on end. At her feet, lying open on the floor is a book, one I remember reading when she was just learning to run. I read it in five- and ten-minute installments.

Her aimlessness, her evident lack of a plan drives me crazy, and we're like two travelers stranded in a storm, stuck with each other.

Her father's out of town and with him gone, I wonder—will there be no one to referee, or will the level of intensity ease up just a little? I don't know. I mean, it could go either way.

We get into a discussion about words people don't use much anymore. Crestfallen, abyss, bereft. *Bereft.* I say I think it's still a good word, but one I've never used, never spoken out loud. She says, "What are you waiting for?"

When I look in the mirror, this is what I see: a woman who needs to try a little harder, to choose her clothes more carefully— simpler lines, more subdued, more flattering colors. No ruffles, and nothing belted or sleeveless or clinging to her body. I see a woman whose features seem less like her own, and more like her mother's aunts. A woman who appears to have put certain aspects of life and marriage in their proper places, which is on the back burner. A woman who doesn't seem, well, arranged quite properly.

I see a woman who's been waiting, ever so patiently, to take over my body and assume my identity. A woman everyone will believe is me, but I'll know she's not.

Snow falls, and goes on falling. There is something I need to tell my daughter, something I should have already told her. What I want to say is that I never could bear to see her unhappy, and that I didn't trust in her instinct to survive. I couldn't let go of her. I didn't know how to say "no" to her. What I want to say is that the test of a woman's endurance may be her ability to withstand disappointment.

Each morning there are fresh tracks around the crabapple tree in the front yard: deer. With this much snow, with food so much harder to find, they've had to come out of the woods. They've had to overcome that instinct to run, when their movements trip the sensor on the light over the garage. Someone told me, though, that deer will not flee unless two of their senses are alerted; they have to hear *and* see, see *and* smell.

I let the dog out and stand at the door, waiting for him. His grey back vanishes in blowing snow, and reappears. It could be any time of day. The light has no warmth, as if it is coming out of the ground, from the trunks of the bare trees.

By the calendar, we have passed the year's longest night. The Earth, in its elliptical orbit, has begun its tilt back toward the sun and will go on doing so, spinning out and back in space, whether I am around to think about it or not. Picking the newspaper up off the porch I turn my face to the sun and—nothing. The landscape changes hourly—hills where there were no hills before, all the boundaries softened, gradually erased.

Winter

For two months I have hardly seen one bird. In past years we would have flocks at the feeders in the back yard. Finches, nuthatches, at least five varieties of woodpeckers, mourning doves, sparrows, bluejays, cardinals, the occasional hawk hunting the birds at the feeders, and once a great horned owl. I will admit their numbers took quite a drop when Walmart bulldozed a couple of hundred acres of woods behind my house for one of their fine stores, but this year they have almost vanished. Once in a while a sparrow will chirp from the top of the crabapple tree next to the garage when I leave for work. I usually throw some seed in the driveway next to the bush though it seems never to be touched.

It has been a cold winter. Sixty days now without the thermometer going above freezing once. One day with the high temperature below zero. I find myself looking at the bare trees and wondering if the birds have somehow found shelter in crevices and overhangs, or are mostly frozen or starved to death.

This winter a ninety-year-old woman froze to death filling her birdfeeder. The police think she must have accidentally locked the door behind her when she went out. They found her on the steps outside her back door. Last week, when it was twelve below zero, I stood at the glass door in the back of my house, looking out through the back yard. On my side, I was fairly comfortable in shorts. On the other side, I would probably not have survived an hour. The snow washed towards me in waves driven by the wind over smooth drifts. Swirling in eddies around the tree trunks, it hollowed out circles at each tree then blew in little whirl-winds and long arching lines scurrying over the snow. When I touched my fingers to the glass, I could feel it push in from the pressure of the wind. When I pushed back, it seemed almost like something alive on the other side.

I am constantly amazed at how casually we take the thin veneer of our civilization which protects us from the forces of nature. How confident we are in the transparent technology—an eighth of an inch of melted sand—that separates us from the winter outside. How smugly we drive through the blizzard in our cars.

That is, until the earth moves. Or the lights go out. Or the water rises. Or the wind blows the walls of our house out from under the roof. Then we stand looking dumbly into the TV cameras asking "Why did this have to happen to us?" as if we were somehow a factor in the movement of tectonic plates or the direction a low pressure system takes out of the south Atlantic.

I think perhaps I will stop feeling sorry for the birds. They are, after all, probably snug in some place I know nothing of, quietly waiting out the storm.

JOHN LANE
Natural Edges

Once I lived on Cumberland Island, on the eastern margin of the continent, at a place of merging forms. It was a water land. The sea and marsh drew in around me with each tide, fell away as the tide receded. Live there long enough, Nate, one of the island people, would say, and I'd feel my own being—mostly water anyway—slosh from ear to ear at the pull of a full moon.

I felt the moon pull me often, late at night, away from a book or a letter I was writing and up the trail to leave me sitting for hours watching the water slip up and back. I learned much on these nights, mostly the math of connection: the common denominators among us all. To live on an island is to walk daily on that common ground, to walk the edges of many things.

A dead deer was my first denominator. Curled under live oaks, feet crossed under its body, it was 10 feet from the barn where I wrote and slept. It was a big buck, but each day a little more disappeared as the island recovered its own. I watched it decay for a month in the island heat. The body collapsed inward. The carcass supported a congress of insects. Red ants, beetles, flies, wasps and mosquitoes came and went, working day and night to carry off what they could, bickering and buzzing over the rest. One day the skull was empty. Ants moved out and over the eye ridges.

At night, when the wind shifted east off the marsh, I could catch a strong smell, thick and sweet, a reminder of how close to the edges I lived. It was a mixed smell, but if I worked my nose I could parcel out the matted green stench of the rotted marsh grass, the hanging salt mist, the dead deer mixed with the marsh and salt and the dryer breezes of the mainland.

I was beginning to see that the edge of life is death, or birth, depending on which end of the cycle I wanted to focus on. Both were all around me. The world was building the house of birth and death; I lived within it the way I live within my body. All around me the work was going on.

One day I focused on the falling apart, the slowing down, death in all its island colors and states. I walked for hours in the oak forest, stepping around clusters of palmettos and over logs and branches. There was no shortage of company; I followed a pileated woodpecker half the distance to the sea, about a half a mile, and never lost the hive of mosquitoes circling my head.

There was no loneliness in the woods. I sensed a certain kinship, even with the mosquitoes and ticks; to travel so far and persistently at only the hope of a warm attachment is an act not uncommon to my tribe.

The air hummed with the hope of sweet conjunction as I fanned away the mosquitoes. To learn to love these creatures was a long mile on the road to heaven.

As I walked, I began to pick up bones in the woods. Deer, turkey, horse. Even a box turtle's shell. As life scaled my boots and buzzed in my ear, the signs of death were everywhere. I walked and counted out to myself the long list of the dead and dying: dead deer, limb, caves, log, dead wasp suspended by one small strand in a slanting light, a fern broken by strong wind (the wind itself gone now to nothing), a horse hair rubbed against a pine, a standing oak gone to beetles, bones at the base of an osprey's perch, fish skulls, fish ribs.

But soon I had walked out of the woods to the first dunes where the forest smells ceased and the air took on the salt smell of the sea.

Another margin. The dune slipped grain by grain into the oak woods, pushing the dunes inward, inland, taking the island three feet eastward every ten years. Suddenly, in the darkness of the oaks, the dunes were a white shock, a running range of sand, a white, head-high wall. I squatted and tried to find the spot where the woods ended and the dunes began, where sand lodged and tumbled among rotting leaves, and leaves rested, half-buried, among sand.

When I thought I'd found the place where the dunes became forest, the forest became dunes. I realized my discovery wouldn't last long. The wind stirred, and the edges shifted as new sand settled in the woods. One day I put my finger on the edge of woods. "Here," I said and planted a twig.

The next day I walked back to find the edge. The twig was gone from the spot. I dug a little and found the twig, not gone, but collapsed under a wash of sand, a small dune. The twig had created a new margin. I felt a strange assurance. I followed twin crescents of a deer trail over the rising dunes into the light outside the oaks.

DONALD HALL
Good Use for Bad Weather

My grandparents nailed two thermometers side by side on the porch of their New Hampshire farmhouse. One registered ten degrees cold, the other ten degrees hot, so that there was always something to brag about. Every morning when my grandmother sat in the rocker under Christopher the canary, writing three postcards to three daughters, she could say, "Thirty below this morning. Seems like it might get cold." Or, "Ninety already and the sun's not over the mountain."

In New England we take pride in our weather because it provides us with pain and suffering, necessities for the spirit, like food and clothing for the body. We never brag about good weather. Let Tucson display self-esteem over eighty-three days without rain. Let Sarasota newspapers go free for the asking when the sun doesn't shine. We smirk in the murk, superior. It's true that we have good weather; we just don't pay it any mind. When summer people flock north to the lakes and the mountains, they do not gather to enjoy our foggy rain. If they're from Boston, they don't come *for* bright sun and cool dry air; they migrate north *against* the soup-kettle mugginess of home. It seems more decent.

In good weather—apple days of October, brilliant noons and cool evenings of August—we remain comfortable despite our pleasure by talking about pleasure's brevity, forecasting what we're in for as soon as the good spell is done with. Winter is best for bragging. For a week or two in March, mud is almost as good. (Mud is weather as much as snow is; leaves are landscape.) "Tried to get the Buick up New Canada this morning. Have to wait for a dry spell to pull it out, I suppose. Of course, we'll have to dig to find it, first."

Black ice is first rate, but most of us who cherish difficulty will settle for a good ten feet of snow. We get up about five-fifteen, make the coffee, check the thermometer: ten degrees above. The warmth must account for the snow. Highway department plows blunder down Route 4 in the dark outside. We get dressed, dragging on flannel-lined chinos, flannel shirt, sweater, down jacket, and boots. Then we broom one car, headlights and taillights, gun it in reverse over the hump of snow Forrest's plow left, swing it up Forrest's alley, and swoop it down to the road, scattering ridges of snow.

Only two miles to the store. It's not adventurous driving, but it pays to be attentive, to start slowing for a turn a hundred yards early. The store opens at six. Because this is New Hampshire, somebody's bound to be there by five-forty-five. We park with the motor running and the heater on—it'll get warm while we pick up the *Globe*—to go inside. Bob's there with his cup of coffee, and Bill who owns garage and store, and Judy the manager who makes coffee and change. We grin at each other as I stamp my boots and slip my paper out of the pile. We say things like, "Nice weather!" "Bit of snow out there!" "Hear we're getting two feet more!" but what we're really saying is *It takes more than a couple of feet of snow to slow us down!*

Weather is conversation's eternal subject, lingua franca shared by every New Englander with sensory equipment. When Rolls-Royce meets junker, over to the dump, they can talk about the damned rain. Weather talk helps us over difficult subjects. On one Monday morning some years ago, Ned said to Will, "Too bad about Pearl Harbor. I hear there's ten feet over on Five-A." Will said to Ned, "I suppose we'll lick 'em. They say a bread truck got through."

In a boring patch when the weather's mild, we talk about disasters and catastrophes of the past. As a child I heard endless stories about the Blizzard of '88. My Connecticut grandfather belonged to a club that met once a year on the anniversary to swap reminiscences—by which, of course, we understand that they met to tell lies. As I stagger into codgerhood, I discover that my own Blizzard of '88 is the great wind of 1938. I was in Connecticut for that one, which first visited our house in my father's disgust over his new barometer. He won it in a putting contest, and he was proud of it, pretty in its rich brown wood and bright brass. Then when he hung it on the wall it busted; at least it sank way, way down until the foolish thing predicted hurricane.

Most of the time, weather is relative. Every year when an August morning is forty degrees, we shiver and chill: It's *cold* out there! But when a February morning rises to forty, we walk around with our coats unbuttoned, enjoying the heat wave. Next day an icestorm, and we take relief in the return of suffering. It's true—if you don't have to drive in it—that there are few things in Creation as beautiful as an icestorm. Much bad weather is beautiful: dark days when it never quite rains and never quite doesn't, English weather cozy around the fire; wild rains of summer after high heat, compensation and relief; drizzle in autumn that drains color from the trees, quiet and private; the first snow, which steps my heartbeat up; the first *big* snow, which steps it higher; winter thaw, with its hesitant promise; gothic thunderstorms with bolts of melodrama—we quicken, we thrill, we comfort the dog.

Every now and then we have an open winter, as we call it when we have no snow; it's psychic disaster. It's disaster also for shrubs and bulbs, but it's the soul's woe because we haven't suffered enough. The earth can't emerge because it never submerged. We don't deserve the milder air and the daffodils rising because we haven't lost our annual battles with the snow—fender benders, bad backs from shoveling the mailbox, rasp of frozen air in the lungs, falls on ice, chunks of snow down our boots. The only bad weather in New England is when we don't have any.

Greenhouse

Last November a night wind tore the plastic sheathing from the ribs of our greenhouse, and the exposed frame became one more stark contour in a land of bare trees and empty fields. The inside froze and filled with snow. Now, after a month of melt and spring mud, I can walk through what remains. The ribs still arch strong above me. Below, watering cans and plastic trays are strewn across the benches and floor. A stack of four-inch pots lists next to a heap of potting mix. There's a stray nozzle, baskets and hoes that belong in the shed, an uncoiled hose. It looks as if a night wind had also torn through the inside, or that we'd fled—from what?—overturning everything on the way out. But it proves only that, way back in June, we had never taken the time to clean up.

I have registered so many winter months since, so much orderly time, that it's hard for me to comprehend the summer rush now. The mess seems only senseless, and I want to set it right, to check the hose for leaks, to rinse the pots, and wash down the benches.

It's more work than I think, taking me a long day to sort through the pots, discarding much and rinsing every salvaged thing with a weak solution of bleach. It takes even longer for my father and brother to raise a new roof over the old ribs. The poly is light but cumbersome to draw up and over the frame, and it's subject to the smallest breeze until secured to the wood and metal. Once that roof is on, though, the greenhouse feels almost new. If I stand in its center, the shapes and colors of the world outside—seen through translucent plastic—seem to be muted versions of themselves. It's warmer inside than out, and I can no longer smell the spring thaw—soft air, sap, the pliant earth—for the peat.

The day begins with a flat of tomato seedlings that need to be transplanted into pots of their own. I break open a bale of potting mix—closer to chaff than to soil it's so light—and fill each pot nearly to its rim. It takes a long time to saturate the pots with water since the mix contains peat, so I pass over the pots again and again with a running hose until they finally take on water, becoming dark and nearly faithful to earth. I make a hole in the center of each pot, then pull a seedling from the flat. Each one has already sprouted a set of true leaves beneath the growing tip, yet the entire seedling is hardly longer than half my little finger. I never feel my bulk so much as now, bent over these small starts with a wisp of a seedling grasped between my forefinger and my thumb. It would take no effort at all to bruise the cells in those stems, and I have to transplant five hundred of them.

By the end of the morning the greenhouse once again seems as it should: filled pots spread across the benches, the air warm and humid. It is a day without wind in the spring of the year. The roof above me is so thin it's hardly measurable—a frame for the ephemeral—half work, half dream, sited, squared-off, saying *Here.* Here is your house built nearly of air.

Nature's See-Saw

I live at the top of Vermont, next to Canada, and moose leave their tracks in my garden occasionally, investigating the vegetables out of curiosity without eating them, in the same way that they may emerge from the trees onto the lawn to stare at my crowing rooster to see what he is. With no wolves around, they are increasing by 15 percent a year, though the pioneers had wiped them out, along with the wolves. But caribou, which originally shared that old-growth forest, have not come back because the caribou's mossy, lichenous diet was destroyed along with those virginal woods.

Instead, deer (called "Virginia" deer at first) moved north, thriving on the cutover vegetation. So I have deer, too, around my place, which are periodically thinned back by a severe winter, when the snow gets taller than their legs. Moose, being bigger, don't mind the snow, but will die from a brainworm that deer carry (and seem immune to) if the deer get too thick. The two animals are in balance here, in other words. The moose can't move too far south because of the deer and the deer can't go much further north on account of the snow.

Opossums also migrated up, finding the new habitat to their liking—in old books they too boast the sobriquet "Virginia"—but they stopped short of my latitude simply because their naked tails froze in Vermont north of approximately the White River. Raccoons and skunks are similarly opportunistic creatures but have no such problem with frost, so I do see them. My rabbits are snowshoe rabbits, however. The cottontails' northward swarm stopped at about the White River because of the depth of our snow and our mean winters.

Canada lynx, like the caribou, had disappeared when our primeval forests were felled for charcoal. But bobcats, more versatile, moved up from cottontail country to fill the lynxes' ecological slot, toughing out the cold weather by ambushing a deer in a snowdrift, perhaps, and strangling it, then camping for a month by the carcass. In the summer they eat rodents, birds, everything, and I hear them scream from the mountain ledges above my house. Or my dog may tree one, growling from a spruce limb above my head in the dark of the night.

The balance between predators and prey—bobcats and rabbits, fisher and porcupine—is different from the relationship between parallel species, such as moose and deer, fisher (a large form of weasel) and fox, fox and coyote, or coyote and bobcat.

Red foxes thickened to fill the void in predators as 19th-century sheep farming and 20th-century dairying replaced the charcoal industry, and hedgerows, underbrush and woodlots grew back. Foxes eat what cats eat, plus impromptu berries, nightcrawlers, slugs, grasshoppers, woodchucks and cows' afterbirths, while combing the meadows for voles. I've had them so bold that, chasing that rooster of mine, they've slammed right into my knees. Even southern gray foxes, a slinkier, nocturnal, tree-climbing species, have recently materialized in the north country.

And turkey vultures have begun to follow the interstate north every summer to compete for carrion with our wilderness ravens and farm-field crows, which are resident all year. Ravens nest on my cliffs, driving off the crows, though they are very much shyer toward people than crows. Nor do they mob hawks and owls as boisterously as crows do.

Red-tailed hawks and barred owls patrol the notch where my house is, but if I walk downhill for an hour or so to the swamps along Willoughby Lake, I will see red-shouldered hawks instead, or hear the five-hoot tattoo of a great horned owl at dusk.

Though the trout-fishing will probably never equal the prodigality of pioneer times, the crash in fur prices has brought beaver and even otter back, while bears—an estimated 2,000 inhabit Vermont's 9,000 square miles—are making out fine, fattening in derelict orchards on defunct farms and upon old-field budding aspens in early spring. One bear tried to hibernate in my hayloft, after climbing an apple tree next to the garage and biting apart a birdhouse that a mother deermouse was nesting in, after the swallows had gone south. After I repaired the box, a flying squirrel settled in.

When mice colonize my house, I can't bring in a bear to stop their scuttling, but what I'll do is catch a 3-foot garter snake and insert him through a hole in the ceiling to eat the babies. During the summer, this stratagem works. In winter an ermine moves in and does the trick.

Less tractable was the problem of the porcupines that for years kept chewing on the floor of my garage in their hunger for salt. Fishers had preyed on porcupines on the frontier, as martens had preyed on red squirrels, but the fishers and martens had been trapped out. The marten's demise was a boon to goshawks, Cooper's hawks, horned owls, bobcats and other enterprising hunters that can grab a quick squirrel. But the porcupines, equipped with quills, had no such effective secondary enemies, at least after country people stopped eating them (and squirrels), around the 1950s. In 1957, the state of Vermont, responding to complaints, started to release the nucleus of a new population of fishers, 124, acquired from Maine. One site happened to be close to my house, and quite soon I began finding porcupine skins inside-up on the ground and picked clean, until their numbers were in reasonable balance again.

Fishers, like bears and beavers, in taking to civilization, have spread through New England, prompting the recent reintroduction of 60 marten, too, in central Vermont. Vermont alone has perhaps 100,000 deer, and wild turkeys, reintroduced to the state in 1969, are nearly all over—so that, altogether, the New England region is richer in wildlife than when Henry David Thoreau was writing *Walden* 150 years ago.

There are exceptions, of course. Loons (which require an undisturbed lake to nest on), wood turtles (which frequently try to cross roads), warblers and other songbirds that winter in Latin American rainforests, are stymied and gradually vanishing, even as more protean actors elbow in. The busy coyote, which has migrated east through Ontario from the prairie Midwest in the past 40 years, eating housecats, road kills, wild grapes, leopard frogs, coon pups, and whatnot, may be the most notable of these. Though the settlers killed off the wolves and "catamounts" (mountain lions), they didn't shut off the future need for a middle-sized predator, and the "brush wolf" or "trickster" of 19th-century lore turns out to fill the bill.

Flux itself is balance of a kind; and along my stream, which feeds eventually into Lake Memphramagog and the St. Lawrence River, the local pack of coyotes has thrown the foxes and bobcats into a tizzy. Coyotes will kill and eat grown foxes (as they did the cocker spaniel next door), so the foxes simply withdraw from our mountain notch in years when I hear the coyotes' flamboyant howls. The coyotes also answer my harmonica, and may sneak into the garage and drag a 25-pound sack of dog food into the woods. They search the stream bank for fishermen's discards, flush and leap high for a woodcock, then eat its eggs, or discover a fawn. They can't kill a bobcat, but will sweep through in January and devour the bobcat's hoarded winter larder, creating a very grim situation for the bobcat. Being as versatile as African jackals, coyotes prosper in the tracks of humans in the way that jackals follow lions—and we're doing better than lions.

In the years when coyotes den on the mountains above, my fields aren't scoured for meadowmice as thoroughly as they would be if the foxes were at work. Coyotes range further out, so there is a surplus of rabbits and mice close in. Marsh hawks and red-tails then take over some of the foxes' micromanagement role, as well as owls, fluttering like gigantic butterflies in the moonlight, as I sit outside watching them and the bats. Coons, too, help take up the slack, afraid of the coyotes but at least able to scramble up a tree if they have to.

One banner noontime in August a flock of real butterflies descended upon my goldenrod—hundreds of Monarchs fattening for their autumn flight toward Mexico. Half a dozen snakes, safe from any hawk because they were next to the house, and my special garden toad who has swelled so big that no snake can swallow him, were basking in the sun.

A few years before I had paid $110 to have a pond bulldozed; and already a great blue heron was frogging in it; bear, moose, and deer tracks marked the margins; and the sky's mysteries were reflected on the surface.

I could see all these things because I had just paid $15,000 to have my vision restored—a cheap price for new eyes that, with plastic implants, saw as I did 50 years ago.

Plastic eyes—and more wildlife running around in New England than when Thoreau was alive? Nature is complicated.

MARVIN BELL
Outside's Not What We Think

Most people believe that poetry has a special relationship to nature. Aristotle said that art imitates nature, thereby giving rise not only to the great neo-Aristotelian literature teachers at the University of Chicago, but also to an infinitude of acrobatic theories intended to turn that analysis of art into a prescription for virtue. In the classroom, the term "art" has been reserved to effects of humankind, and human beings have been redefined as natural parts of the entirety of nature. Hence, to say now that art imitates nature is to say that art is art, nature is nature, art is nature, nature is art, anything is everything, and everything is anything. And that's just the beginning. The mind is a wonder, not least when language can be used to erase distinctions that language was created to define. Fuzzy is fuzzy. In literary studies, the natural (!) subjectivity and relativity of language has been used against itself so that now it bites its own tail and flies up its own ass. It has been left to the writers of poetry, fiction, and plays—at many schools, the lowly composition teachers—to teach literature. The literature departments of large universities are now chockablock with wannabe mandarins.

In an era of fuzzy logic and vague language, when random information overwhelms understanding and the statistics on computer ownership belie the truth that computers are used largely for sedentary games, chitchat, and busywork, it can be no surprise that people maintain a fuzzy, romantic sense of some ideal nature with which they associate poetry. In other words, Pals of Mine, out there in what is sometimes referred to by professorial types as "The Real World," we poets are still seen as soft-headed sissies.

But Thomas was hardy just as Robert was frosty, and Stevens could be an iceman. The poets Thomas Hardy, Robert Frost, and Wallace Stevens (whose poem "The Snowman" begins, "One must have a mind of winter . . .") represent what it means to be a grownup. Grownups know that things end. Children live in fantasy. I want to stay a child. So do you. I have been granted the wish, in a way, by becoming a poet: the one who is permitted to play with language for greater or lesser ends, however the chips fall. I learned to write by word-play, just as most poets do, whether they admit it or not. When I was a child, I thought as a child and spoke as a child, and it was natural. That is, it was in my nature to do so.

I want to save the planet. So do you. It's not just one of many, it's our home, and we have the blind faith or *chutzpah* to believe that our very substance is entitled to continue living here. We act as if we prefer the very form of our own lives to those of other creatures. Thus, we feel a special affection for those creatures that exhibit human qualities: the dolphin, for example, because we think it talks; the dog, because it listens. We say that we live, as we must, as parts of a whole: as John Donne reminded us, no man or woman an island. Yet Rilke speaks of an impenetrable solitude even in the midst of company, and then there is Georges Bataille's mortal pronouncement in *Death and Sensuality:* "We are attempting to communicate, but no communication between us can abolish our fundamental difference. If you die, it is not my death."

Nature is nature. Did the volcano at Haleakala care if I completed the Honolulu Marathon later that week? Does the water listen when I try to buy wishes from the bridge above? (Do others, like me, hedge their bets, or at least alter the stakes, by making wishes only for others, never for themselves? I have never asked anyone lest the silence be destroyed that attends one's inner thoughts.) Did the blue glacier care that I took a piece to eat?

For ten consecutive years, early in May, Dorothy and I have driven Interstate 90 from Iowa to Seattle on our way to a summer house in Port Townsend, Washington. We have not yet grown tired of it and don't expect to. We begin in eastern Iowa, where the land is various, subtle, contoured like the human body. We move past the Black Hills of South Dakota, along the high plains of northern Wyoming. We cross spectacular passes for the width of Montana, we slice the panhandle of Idaho (a pass called "4th of July"!), we descend into eastern Washington with its open vistas and distant buttes, we parallel the powerful Columbia in its stone corridor (and of course we sing, "Roll on, Columbia, Roll On" like David Carradine playing Woody Guthrie in *Bound for Glory*).

We drive up and over the pass at Snoqualmie into western Washington, and then we hang a right before Seattle to take the car ferry to Bainbridge Island and drive north to the long floating bridge spanning the Hood Canal ($2.00 a crossing until the locals found out that the bridge was paid for and refused to pay any more). After the bridge, we travel the Olympic Peninsula westward until finally we turn onto the smaller Quimper Peninsula where we drive to the end. Sometimes we come home through Canada: Lake Louise!, Banff!, Medicine Hat!, Moose Jaw! (where our muffler and tailpipe fell off on *Canada Day*).

Dorothy wants her ashes scattered where Wyoming meets

Montana. A friend of ours, a potter, wants her ashes used in a glaze to be applied to a ceramic vase to be dropped into the Mediterranean so a baby octopus can live in it. I myself have considered burial in Iowa City, where I teach, but only if the University will agree to keep me in the Faculty Directory and my gravestone can read, "Office Hours 2–4." I suppose the University would never consent, not because of an institutional lack of humor but because those who think man the measure of all things resent death.

Two friends were discussing where to be buried. One said she wanted to be buried in a beautiful spot in the countryside, among swaying grasses with a view of the sea. But the other said no, he preferred to be buried in the city. "There's so much more to do in the city," he said.

So every year we cross the country in which so many lie buried, making the return trip to Iowa in August. We have sometimes continued on from Iowa to New England before turning home for good. And there's more: each December, we drive from Iowa to eastern Long Island, to a place near where I grew up, and in January back to Iowa. We drive to Mexico and New Mexico, to California, to Tennessee, to Utah. We have seen a good bit of this country, and some parts of a few others.

Is it us—this nature, this out-of-doors, this scenery, this geography, this landscape? No, it is entirely outside us. That's the point. We can't take credit for it, nor have we any stake in judging it. It is neither a garden to be organized, nor a personal claim to be cultivated. It neither smiles nor weeps, nor does it look to see what we think or feel. Rather, it is perfectly—perfectly!—indifferent to us.

People like to think nature had humankind in mind. After all, we have survived—for now—where others suffered extinction. Humankind would like to believe that nature "knew what she was doing" when she gave us opposable thumbs, let us stand up, and complicated our brains. In truth, our vision of cause-and-effect is after-the-fact. Our charming mythologizing of the workings of nature into a Mother or the gods is wishful thinking. As far as we can tell, we are more likely, as James Wright wrote in a poem, "an accidental hump of chemistry."

But what chemistry! We like our own smell, we trust our senses, we sanctify our ideas. Nature, meanwhile, so fills our view that we cannot see our lives for the intervals that they are.

I still find clarity thrilling. When it comes to definition, nature is out-the-window. I myself would rather visit a canyon, a cliff, or a crater than a good restaurant. But a blade of grass will do and has often had to. I pocket stones, I pick up shells and envelopes of shark's eggs, I carry in my pocket a piece of hematite. The sound of the universe is music to my ears. It is a wonder to me, not a mystery, that things end. Is it such a big deal? There is a broken mirror in every lake but the fish do not pause to take a look. Of all the animals, only Man has to remind himself that he possesses life. Only Man invests nature with emotion and intention. I myself have heard laughter in the spring and a clucking in the trees, but to have thought it more than electrochemical fortune would have been to wake bathed in sap.

Falling

The movement of snakes, of water, of leaf shadows striking three-dimensional patterns into the *tabula rasa* of the dusty path—hypnotic. The cat scaling a straight wall, the hawk stooping—these are essays in abandonment, lessons in falling. They could be carrying messages in the waves of their bodies. Loosed from gravity, their movements serve no purpose, unless it's that redundancy the information theorists tell us is necessary to separate message from the constant background "noise" of the universe. Tongues loosed from the mouths that once held them, they could be speaking the gossip of God.

This is why boys throw cats in the air. Perhaps why they shoot at birds and throw stones and sticks (and knives) until their arms are sore. The pure useless beauty of flight and falling. Once or twice I've seen flying squirrels drift out of a distant tree. Unlike a bat competing with nighthawks for evening insects or chasing my fishing fly past my head, the flying squirrel constantly adjusts for the drag of its unaerodynamic hair. Common gray or red squirrels in free fall are as impressive. They fall, and this is the beauty of flight.

SUEELLEN CAMPBELL
Grubby

Consider the progression of the ages. Continental plates drift and collide, oceans rise and fall, inland seas advance and recede. Volcanoes spew out new earth. Mountains grow tall, then erode flat. Layers of sand and dust fill lake beds and ancient rivers, harden, wash away, settle again.

Chaos scientists call it "self-similarity across scale"—the way structures stay the same whether they're large or tiny. A cascade the size of your hand and Victoria Falls. The lines in a piece of driftwood, the contours of dunes, and the shapes of the Colorado Plateau seen from high above the land. Sedimentation and grubbiness.

Perhaps you begin with a layer of sunblock. Then you sweat. It's so dusty that every step you take sends eruptions of fine debris into the air. The mosquitoes in the trees are thick, so you add bugjuice, the more toxic the better. It tastes awful. The wind kicks up more dust—into your hair, lungs, nose. It sticks to your chapped lips and your teeth. At lunch you dribble some jelly on your jeans, smear it in with your palm. Or peanut butter. Or melted chocolate. (Spilled food is always sticky.) You envision big bear tongues licking you clean. In the afternoon you add more layers of sunblock, sweat, dust. A few drops of rain make it to the ground and tiny rivulets of mud appear here and there on your arms, neck, cap, knees, then dry to arroyos. At dusk the mosquitoes swarm: more bugjuice. Aluminum dust from your tent poles and greasy black soot from your cooking pot and backpack stove settle first on your hands, then transfer to your jeans. If you're a fire builder, you add splinters and sap, the fine black dust of decaying wood and the penetrating smell of smoke.

If you're lucky, your hair will accumulate more dust than oil, in an effect not unlike that of dry shampoo. No shine, no flexibility, but not slimy, not glued to your head with a tube of nature's Brylcream. In either case you'll have hat hair—smashed flat on the crown, maybe a Woody Woodpecker flourish around the back.

Perhaps you try to clean up. The clothes, of course, are hopeless, and new ones get dirty so fast it's hardly worth changing. Face and hands, then. The stream water is icy, and you don't want to pollute it with your soap. So you fill a small pot, maybe heat it up a bit if you're really energetic, squat on your heels, and attack a few layers with bandana and Dr. Bronner's magical 18-in-1 Peppermint Soap—brush your teeth! your dentures! wash your hair! keep off bugs! 100% biodegradable! smells great! tingles! cleans and freshens from head to toe! OK! You'll feel cleaner for a little while. But nothing will get rid of the silt that's filled every tiny line in your hands.

Bedtime is the hour of erosion. Producing what geologists call unconformity, some layers disappear completely, erasing chunks of history. During the night, remaining sediments undergo metamorphosis, recombine and harden in place. With breakfast, deposition begins anew.

Different landscapes, of course, produce different earth-forms. On the beach, fine sharp sand and sticky salt water interlayer with sunblock and lemonade. In the desert, sand, sunblock, and sweat dominate. If you died here, you'd become sandstone. In a rainforest, your skin turns liquid and slick, decaying leaves cling to your clothes, leeches crawl through your socks and suck on your ankles. Here you'd become coal.

Sometimes cataclysmic events occur, volcanoes, floods, earthquakes, mudslides. You slip pushing your canoe into the swamp and sink hip deep in rank black muck, then drift through a spider web so enormous that the individual strands tug at you as they stick to your humid, sweaty, bugjuiced skin. You slide down an abandoned coal chute, dying your clothes permanently grey, filling boots and pockets and scalp with black gravel and dust. Mysterious bug bites swell up to the size and color of squashed plums, and you smear them with cakey pink calamine lotion that hardens into the cracks of dried mudflats. A patch of wet brush leaves thin black whip stripes across your legs and torso and face. It rains hard and you ferment under your poncho, your soggy socks coagulating with your prune feet. You slip in a fresh cow pie.

In time, if you lie still on the ground, you will disappear from view. Like petrified wood, like a fossil in slate, your living pores will be filled with the matter of the planet, your shape preserved for the ages. Exquisite camouflage. At one with the earth.

Children in the Woods

When I was a child growing up in the San Fernando Valley in California, a trip into Los Angeles was special. The sensation of movement from a rural area into an urban one was sharp. On one of these charged occasions, walking down a sidewalk with my mother, I stopped suddenly, caught by a pattern of sunlight trapped in a spiraling imperfection in a windowpane. A stranger, an elderly woman in a cloth coat and a dark hat, spoke out spontaneously, saying how remarkable it is that children notice these things.

I have never forgotten the texture of this incident. Whenever I recall it I am moved not so much by any sense of my young self but by a sense of responsibility toward children, knowing how acutely I was affected in that moment by that woman's words. The effect, for all I know, has lasted a lifetime.

Now, years later, I live in a rain forest in western Oregon, on the banks of a mountain river in relatively undisturbed country, surrounded by 150-foot-tall Douglas firs, delicate deerhead orchids, and clearings where wild berries grow. White-footed mice and mule deer, mink and coyote move through here. My wife and I do not have children, but children we know, or children whose parents we are close to, are often here. They always want to go into the woods. And I wonder what to tell them.

In the beginning, years ago, I think I said too much. I spoke with an encyclopedic knowledge of the names of plants or the names of birds passing through in season. Gradually I came to say less. After a while the only words I spoke, beyond answering a question or calling attention quickly to the slight difference between a sprig of red cedar and a sprig of incense cedar, were to elucidate single objects.

I remember once finding a fragment of a raccoon's jaw in an alder thicket. I sat down alongside the two children with me and encouraged them to find out who this was—with only the three teeth still intact in a piece of the animal's maxilla to guide them. The teeth told by their shape and placement what this animal ate. By a kind of visual extrapolation its size became clear. There were other clues, immediately present, which told, with what I could add of climate and terrain, how this animal lived, how its broken jaw came to be lying here. Raccoon, they surmised. And tiny tooth marks along the bone's broken edge told of a mouse's hunger for calcium.

We set the jaw back and went on.

If I had known more about raccoons, finer points of osteology, we might have guessed more: say, whether it was male or female. But what we deduced was all we needed. Hours later, the maxilla, lost behind us in the detritus of the forest floor, continued to effervesce. It was tied faintly to all else we spoke of that afternoon.

In speaking with children who might one day take a permanent interest in natural history—as writers, as scientists, as filmmakers, as anthropologists—I have sensed that an extrapolation from a single fragment of the whole is the most invigorating experience I can share with them. I think children know that nearly anyone can learn the names of things; the impression made on them at this level is fleeting. What takes a lifetime to learn, they comprehend, is the existence and substance of myriad relationships: it is these relationships, not the things themselves, that ultimately hold the human imagination.

The brightest children, it has often struck me, are fascinated by metaphor—with what is shown in the set of relationships bearing on the raccoon, for example, to lie quite beyond the raccoon. In the end, you are trying to make clear to them that everything found at the edge of one's senses—the high note of the winter wren, the thick perfume of propolis that drifts downwind from spring willows, the brightness of wood chips scattered by beaver—that all this fits together. The indestructibility of these associations conveys a sense of permanence that nurtures the heart, that cripples one of the most insidious of human anxieties, the one that says, you do not belong here, you are unnecessary.

Whenever I walk with a child, I think how much I have seen disappear in my own life. What will there be for this person when he is my age? If he senses something ineffable in the landscape, will I know enough to encourage it?—to somehow show him that, yes, when people talk about violent death, spiritual exhilaration, compassion, futility, final causes, they are drawing on forty thousand years of human meditation on *this*—as we embrace Douglas firs, or stand by a river across whose undulating back we skip stones, or dig out a camas bulb, biting down into a taste so much wilder than last night's potatoes.

The most moving look I ever saw from a child in the woods was on a mud bar by the footprints of a heron. We were on our knees, making handprints beside the footprints. You could feel the creek vibrating in the silt and sand. The sun beat down heavily on our hair. Our shoes were soaking wet. The look said: I did not know until now that I needed someone much older to confirm this, the feeling I have of life here. I can now grow older, knowing it need never be lost.

The quickest door to open in the woods for a child is the one that leads to the smallest room, by knowing the name each thing is called. The door that leads to the cathedral is marked by a hesitancy to speak at all, rather to encourage by example a sharpness of the senses. If one speaks it should only be to say, as well as one can, how wonderfully all this fits together, to indicate what a long, fierce peace can derive from this knowledge.

MICHAEL SHAY
We Are Distracted

I. WE ARE DISTRACTED

We are distracted by the agility of my eight-year-old son
Kevin as he clambers up the slick granite rock formation near
Rocky Mountain National Park. He is fifty feet above us; we are
a bit frightened by the risks he takes, the way he clings like a
human fly to the sides of the rock. We all look up and watch one
of Kevin's handholds become a fingerhold and just when it's
about to become a no-hold, he pushes off the rock with his feet,
leaps a three-foot gap between spires and wraps his arms tightly
around the precious purchase he has made with this part of the
Rockies.

We are like three slugs on a slab—Kevin's classmate Freeman,
his father, Randy, and I. We lean against the cool rock surface of
this six-million-year-old mountain and watch Kevin. We look up
and Kevin never looks down. It would break his concentration,
interrupt his communion with the rock, I think. To concentrate
is everything for Kevin. He can't do it for extended periods of time
unless he is under the influence of Ritalin, a drug that helps him

control his hyperactivity-inspired impulsiveness. Right now, as he climbs toward the sharp blue Colorado sky, the Ritalin, a central nervous system stimulant, is working on my son's brain stem arousal system causing it to *not* be aroused. Medical researchers are not sure why a stimulant has the opposite effect on hyperactive kids. Says the 1994 *Physicians' Desk Reference:* There is no "specific evidence which clearly establishes the mechanism whereby Ritalin produces its mental and behavioral effects on children, nor conclusive evidence regarding how these effects relate to the condition of the central nervous system."

II. HYPER/ACTIVE

When Kevin is in a classroom and a bird flies to a branch on a tree across the street, he will stop everything and look at the bird. A whispered comment at the opposite end of the classroom might as well be a sonic boom. If he is surrounded by too much energy in his orbit, he absorbs that energy. It sometimes causes him to twist and whirl and slam into his playmates; not so much now as when he was a toddler and his way of play was FULL BODY CONTACT. Slam, bam—and there was a kid crying, one nonplussed Kevin and usually a very pissed-off parent, who soon would be in my face, asking me why I didn't control my son on the playground because he was really going to hurt somebody somehow someday.

III. NAMES, ALPHABETS, NAMES

Physicians have been prescribing Ritalin (a.k.a. methylphenidate) for more than 30 years for a condition that has been known as Minimal Brain Damage (MBD), Minimal Brain Dysfunction in

Children (MBDC), Attention Deficit Disorder (ADD) and ADD with Hyperactivity (ADHD). If some progressive therapists and groups such as ChADD (Children with Attention Deficit Disorder) have their way, the official designation will be changed to Attention Deficit *Syndrome* with Hyperactivity (ADHS). This alphabet soup can be confusing. Once, on his first day at a new school, my son announced in front of the class that he had ADHD. The next day, several very nervous parents called the school, concerned about the new student that had AIDS. Being a "hyper" kid turns you into one type of pariah; AIDS carriers get special mistreatment. It was weeks before the confusion was straightened out. But the impression had been made. Kevin was different; different is bad.

IV. SOME THEORIES

There are those, notably psychiatrist Peter R. Breggin, who regard ADD as a chimera, a non-condition, a conspiracy by the entrenched psychiatric establishment to dose our children with drugs. "Just Say No to Ritalin!" could be their battle cry.

Thom Hartmann runs the Attention Deficit Disorder (ADD) bulletin board on Compuserve. In 1993 he published *Attention Deficit Disorder: A Different Perspective.* Writing on the Prodigy BBS, he summed up his book: "If you lived 10,000 years ago, before the agricultural revolution, and were part of a hunting society, then the 'ability' to have an 'open, highly distractible' state of mind would be an *asset*. Walking through the woods/jungle, if you didn't notice that flash of light out of the corner of your eye, you may miss either the bunny which is lunch, or get eaten by a tiger."

Hartmann surmises that the ADD hunters were survivors and

their DNA went into the gene pool. "Modern people with ADD are those with leftover 'hunter' genes."

There are a few problems with this theory. Since impulsiveness is one of the hallmarks of ADD and ADHD, isn't it likely that the hunter with hyperactivity might charge headlong into a herd of charging mastodons without considering the consequences? Maybe he would neglect to tread carefully in sabertooth tiger country?

V. CONTRAINDICATIONS

The pharmacy clerk always gives me a yellow sheet with Kevin's Ritalin prescription. Under "Side Effects" it reads: "Decreased appetite; stomach ache; difficulty falling asleep; headache." Under "Cautions": "DO NOT DRIVE, OPERATE MACHINERY, OR DO ANYTHING ELSE that might be dangerous until you know how you react to this medicine." It says nothing about rock climbing, although you might infer that comes under "dangerous," or at least, risky.

VI. TO FALL . . .

Kevin never has fallen. When he was two, he climbed the highest trees in the park near our Denver home. Fifty-foot-tall pines and spruces. The first time he did this, he looked down at me and yelled, "You worried, Daddy?"

"Yes!" I said, which seemed to please him.

So what if he falls? Randy, Freeman and I watch him climb and it occurs to them because Randy says, "Does this worry you?"

"Yes," I say, "It worries me." And it thrills me too. I've seen him all alone in the playground because the mothers won't let their kids near him. I've seen him mark time in his room, usually because he's been restricted in some way because he's had trouble at home or on the school bus or in the playground.

VII. TO FLY . . .

Do rock climbers dream of falling or of flying? Do hyperactive kids dream of solitude on a granite mountain? Or do they dream of this: dancing and laughing, surrounded by friends, the mountains a distant mirage?

One Human Hand

I remember how on certain Sunday evenings my father would show us his best-loved possessions, unrolling across our dining-room table the hundred-year-old scrolls he'd carried over the sea from China. He showed them to us in the order he remembered having collected them, and the first one, unscrolled, revealed first the black claws, and then the long legs, and at last the whole height of a standing crane, long-beaked, with coarse head and neck feathers, and one fierce eye. The second scroll was mostly white except for the blight-struck pine, and one bird perched at the tip: a shrike, surviving, last carrier of seed and stones in his little gizzard. The scrolls in my father's house, stored in room after room, or hung in the halls, were so many any breeze could send their silk dancing and their bones all knocking against the walls. He spent every day in August, his vacation time, painting from morning to evening, filling sheet after sheet of rice paper with washes of ink. I watched him lean over the table and his hand flee, or seem to flee, the ink running past the brush and into the very bird. It was birds he painted, one after another. To make you see flying in a standing body, he said, his arm moving up and down to be flying, pushing backward to be drawing nigh, backing up into the future in order to be coming into what's passed. One human hand, a bird, resigned to let time resolve it in paper and ink. It takes one bird to write the central action of the air, lending its wings to gravity, in order to be aloft.

Mute Dancers: How to Watch a Hummingbird

A lot of hummingbirds die in their sleep. Like a small fury of iridescence, a hummingbird spends the day at high speed, darting and swiveling among thousands of nectar-rich blossoms. Hummingbirds have huge hearts and need colossal amounts of energy to fuel their flights, so they live in a perpetual mania to find food. They tend to prefer red, trumpet-shaped flowers, in which nectar thickly oozes, and eat every 15 minutes or so. A hummingbird drinks with a W-shaped tongue, licking nectar up as a cat might (but faster). Like a tiny drum roll, its heart beats at 500 times a minute. Frighten a hummingbird and its heart can race to over 1,200 times a minute. Feasting and flying, courting and dueling, hummingbirds consume life at a fever pitch. No warm-blooded animal on earth uses more energy, for its size. But that puts them at great peril. By day's end, wrung-out and exhausted, a hummingbird rests near collapse.

In the dark night of the hummingbird, it can sink into a zombielike state of torpor; its breathing grows shallow and its wild heart slows to only 36 beats a minute. When dawn breaks on the fuchsia and columbine, hummingbirds must jump-start their hearts and fire up their flight muscles to raise their body temperature for another all-or-nothing day. That demands a colossal effort, which some can't manage. So a lot of hummingbirds die in their sleep.

But most do bestir themselves. This is why, in American Indian myths and legends, hummingbirds are often depicted as resurrection birds, which seem to die and be reborn on another day or in another season. The Aztec god of war was named Huitzilopochtli, a compound word meaning "shining one with weapon like cactus thorn," and "sorcerer that spits fire." Aztec warriors fought, knowing that if they fell in battle they would be reincarnated as glittery, thuglike hummingbirds. The male birds were lionized for their ferocity in battle. And their feathers flashed in the sun like jewel-encrusted shields. Aztec rulers donned ceremonial robes of hummingbird feathers. As they walked, colors danced across their shoulders and bathed them in a supernatural light show.

While most birds are busy singing a small operetta of who and what and where, hummingbirds are virtually mute. Such small voices don't carry far, so they don't bother much with song. But if they can't serenade a mate, or yell war cries at a rival, how can they perform the essential dramas of their lives? They dance. Using body language, they spell out their intentions and moods, just as bees, fireflies or hula dancers do. That means elaborate aerial ballets in which males twirl, joust, sideswipe and somersault. Brazen and fierce, they will take on large adversaries—even cats, dogs or humans.

My neighbor Persis once told me how she'd been needled by hummingbirds. When Persis lived in San Francisco, hummingbirds often attacked her outside her apartment building. From their perspective she was on *their* property, not the other way round, and they flew circles around her to vex her away. My encounters with hummingbirds have been altogether more benign. Whenever I've walked through South American rain forests, with my hair braided and secured by a waterproof red ribbon, hummingbirds have assumed my ribbon to be a succulent flower and have probed my hair repeatedly, searching for nectar. Their touch was as delicate as a sweat bee's. But it was their purring by my ear that made me twitch. In time, they would leave unfed, but for a while I felt like a character in a Li'l Abner cartoon who could be named something like "Hummer." In Portuguese, the word for hummingbird *(Beija flor)* means "flower kisser." It was the American colonists who first imagined the birds humming as they went about their chores.

Last summer, the historical novelist Jeanne Mackin winced to see her cat, Beltane, drag in voles, birds and even baby rabbits. Few things can compete with the blood lust of a tabby cat. But one day Beltane dragged in something rare and shimmery—a struggling hummingbird. The feathers were ruffled and there was a bit of blood on the breast, but the bird still looked perky and alive. So Jeanne fashioned a nest for it out of a small wire basket lined in gauze, and fed it sugar water from an eye dropper. To her amazement, as she watched, "it miscarried a little pearl." Hummingbird eggs are the size of coffee beans, and females usually carry two. So Jeanne knew one might still be safe inside. After a quiet night, the hummingbird seemed stronger, and when she set the basket outside at dawn, the tiny assault victim flew away.

It was a ruby-throated hummingbird that she nursed, the only one native to the East Coast. In the winter they migrate thousands of miles over mountains and open water to Mexico and South America. She may well have been visited by a species known to the Aztecs. Altogether, there are 16 species of hummingbirds in North America, and many dozens in South America, especially near the equator, where they can feed on a buffet of blossoms. The tiniest—the Cuban bee hummingbird—is the smallest warm-blooded animal in the world. About two and one-eighth inches long from beak to tail, it is smaller than the toe of an eagle, and its eggs are like seeds.

Hummingbirds are a New World phenomenon. So, too, is vanilla, and their stories are linked. When the early explorers returned home with the riches of the West, they found it impossible, to their deep frustration, to grow vanilla beans. It took ages before they discovered why—that hummingbirds were a key pollinator of vanilla orchids—and devised beaklike splinters of bamboo to do the work of birds.

Now that summer has come at last, lucky days may be spent watching the antics of hummingbirds. The best way to behold them is to stand with the light behind you, so that the bird faces the sun. Most of the trembling colors aren't true pigments, but the result of light staggering through clear cells that act as prisms. Hummingbirds are iridescent for the same reason soap bubbles are. Each feather contains tiny air bubbles separated by dark spaces. Light bounces off the air bubbles at different angles, and that makes blazing colors seem to swarm and leap. All is vanity in the end. The male's shimmer draws a female to mate. But that doesn't matter much to gardeners, watching hummingbirds patrol the impatiens as if the northern lights had suddenly fallen to earth.

ALBERT GOLDBARTH
Farder to Reache

Kepler was born in 1571. He knew about as much of the night sky and its mysteries as anyone alive in his time. We might say his skull contained the sky of the 16th and early 17th centuries, held it in place like a planetarium dome. Today we still haven't improved on his famous three Laws of Planetary Motion.

And yet the notion that the universe might be infinite—that there wasn't an outermost sphere of stars that bound it all in—terrified him, filled him with what he termed "secret, hidden horror. . . . One finds oneself wandering in this immensity in which are denied limits and center."

This is, of course, the dread of free verse, that one might fall into Whitman and freefloat directionlessly forever. Whitman calls himself "a Kosmos," and in "Song of Myself" the vision is of a creation whose parts are "limitless" and "numberless"—these words and their kin are used with manic glee and with a great intentionality. This is poetry's announcement of the given of 20th century astronomy: the universe is, so far as we know, unbounded.

But it isn't easy to walk through a day of fists and kisses, paychecks, diaperstains, tirejacks, and our buildingblock aspirations, with the mind fixed on infinity. Every year in beginning poetry classes hands startle up in protest of free verse, "it isn't poetry," which is metered and rhymed, and so is a kind of map of Kepler's universe.

John Donne's poems, for instance—he was born one year after Kepler. And he praises his lover by placing her at the center of an onion-ring sky: "so many spheres, but one heaven make," and "they are all concentric unto thee."

And yet as early as 1577—Kepler was only six years old—the British astronomer Thomas Digges undid the outer sphere, and published a vision of stars in endlessness: "Of which lights celestiall, it is to bee thoughte that we onely behoulde sutch as are in the inferioure partes . . . even tyll our sighte being not able farder to reach or conceyve, the greatest part rest by reason of their wonderfull distance invisible unto us."

Perhaps infinity isn't discovered along a timeline of gathering progress, but by certain sensibility, no matter when it lives.

In that land of simultaneous sensibility, I think that I could knock on Kepler's door and invite him out for some beers with Whitman. Really, he's flinging his cloak on now.

It's a foggy night as we sit around the veranda overlooking the lake. The sky is cloudy, and so are my two friends' faces—they don't know each other, are guarded, and rely on me to ease the conversation.

I do, though; or maybe it's the beer. It turns out we can shoot the shit all night, stein after stein, anecdote on anecdote, until the first light swarms over the water like thistledown on fire. Then the fog disappears—which is, of course, the day clearing its throat for clear speech.

BERNARD COOPER
The Fine Art of Sighing

You feel a gradual welling up of pleasure, or boredom, or melancholy. Whatever the emotion, it's more abundant than you ever dreamed. You can no more contain it than your hands can cup a lake. And so you surrender and suck the air. Your esophagus opens, diaphragm expands. Poised at the crest of an exhalation, your body is about to be unburdened, second by second, cell by cell. A kettle hisses. A balloon deflates. Your shoulders fall like two ripe pears, muscles slack at last.

My mother stared out the kitchen window, ashes from her cigarette dribbling into the sink. She'd turned her back on the rest of the house, a sentry guarding her own solitude. I'd tiptoe across the linoleum and make my lunch without making a sound. Sometimes I saw her back expand, then heard her let loose one plummeting note, a sigh so long and weary it might have been her last. Beyond our backyard, above telephone poles and apartment buildings, rose the brown horizon of the city; across it glided an occasional bird, or the blimp that advertised Goodyear tires. She might have been drifting into the distance, or lamenting her separation from it. She might have been wishing she were somewhere else, or wishing she could be happy where she was, a middle-aged housewife dreaming at her sink.

My father's sighs were more melodic. What began as a somber sigh could abruptly change pitch, turn gusty and loose, and suggest by its very transformation that what begins in sorrow might end in relief. He could prolong the rounded vowel of OY, or let it ricochet like an echo, as if he were shouting in a tunnel or a cave. Where my mother sighed from ineffable sadness, my father sighed at simple things: the coldness of a drink, the softness of a pillow, or an itch that my mother, following the frantic map of his words, finally found on his back and scratched.

A friend of mine once mentioned that I was given to long and ponderous sighs. Once I became aware of this habit, I heard my father's sighs in my own and knew for a moment his small satisfactions. At other times, I felt my mother's restlessness and wished I could leave my body with my breath, or be happy in the body my breath left behind.

It's a reflex and a legacy, this soulful species of breathing. Listen closely: My ancestors' lungs are pumping like bellows, men towing boats along the banks of the Volga, women lugging baskets of rye bread and pike. At the end of each day, they lift their weary arms in a toast; as thanks for the heat and sting of vodka, their a-h-h's condense in the cold Russian air.

At any given moment, there must be thousands of people sighing. A man in Milwaukee heaves and shivers and blesses the head of the second wife who's not too shy to lick his toes. A judge in Munich groans with pleasure after tasting again the silky bratwurst she ate as a child. Every day, meaningful sighs are expelled from schoolchildren, driving instructors, forensic experts, certified public accountants, and dental hygienists, just to name a few. The sighs of widows and widowers alone must account for a significant portion of the carbon dioxide released into the atmosphere. Every time a girdle is removed, a foot is submerged in a tub of warm water, or a restroom is reached on a desolate road . . . you'd think the sheer velocity of it would create mistrals, siroccos, hurricanes; arrows should be swarming over satellite maps, weathermen talking a mile a minute, ties flapping from their necks like flags.

Before I learned that Venetian prisoners were led across it to their execution, I imagined that the Bridge of Sighs was a feat of invisible engineering, a structure vaulting above the earth, the girders and trusses, the stay ropes and cables, the counterweights and safety rails connecting one human breath to the next.

Biographical Notes

Diane Ackerman lives in upstate New York, travels widely, and writes both poetry and nonfiction. Her nonfiction books include *A Natural History of Love, The Moon by Whale Light,* and the best-selling *Natural History of the Senses,* all published by Random House. In her new collection of nature essays, *The Rarest of the Rare,* she explores the plight of and fascination with endangered animals.

Sherman Alexie is a Spokane/Coeur d'Alene Indian living in Seattle, Washington. His nonfiction has appeared in *Edge Walking on the Western Rim, Left Bank, Indian Market Magazine, The New York Times,* and *The Seattle Weekly.* He has published six books of poetry, one book of short stories, and, most recently, *Reservation Blues,* a novel from Atlantic Monthly Press.

Will Baker lives in northern California on a fruit and hay farm. His nine books include *Mountain Blood* (University of Georgia Press), winner of the Associated Writing Programs Award in nonfiction; *Hell, West, and Crooked* (stories); *Shadow Hunter* and *What a Piece of Work* (both fiction).

Marvin Bell teaches at the University of Iowa and lives part time in Port Townsend, Washington. The latest of his thirteen books are *The Book of the Dead Man* (poems) and *A Marvin Bell Reader* (selected prose and poetry). His writing has earned him awards from the Guggenheim Foundation and the Academy of American Poets, among others. Though primarily a poet, he writes essays "whenever asked to."

Bruce Berger is the author of two collections of desert essays, *The Telling Distance,* which won the 1990 Western States Book Award, and *There Was a River* (University of Arizona Press, 1994). His essays have appeared in *Sierra, Orion, The Yale Review,* among others. He has worked as a pianist, and is currently writing a book on Baja California.

Margaret B. Blackman is a cultural anthropologist who has done field research with the Haida in the Pacific Northwest and the Inupiat Eskimo on Alaska's north slope. She is currently writing a collection of essays on the village of Anaktuvuk Pass, Alaska. She is the author of two life histories of Native American women (University of Washington Press).

Carol Bly teaches in the University of Minnesota's Master of Liberal Studies program. Her nonfiction books include *Letters from the Country, The Passionate, Accurate Story,* and most recently *Changing the Bully Who Rules the World* (Milkweed, 1996). Among her many awards are a Minnesota State Arts Board Grant and a Bush Foundation Artists Fellowship.

Jane Brox is a recipient of literature grants from the National Endowment for the Arts and the Massachusetts Cultural Council. She lives on her family's farm in the Merrimack Valley and teaches at the Harvard Extension School in Cambridge, Massachusetts. Her first book, *Here and Nowhere Else: Late Seasons of a Farm and Its Family,* was published by Beacon in 1995.

Sharon Bryan's third collection of poems, *Flying Blind,* will be published by Sarabande Books in 1996. She is the editor of *Where We Stand: Women Poets on Literary Tradition* (W. W. Norton, 1993) and is currently a Visiting Professor at Dartmouth College and the University of Houston. "Around the Corner" is from a memoir in progress.

Carol Burelbach, from Irondequoit, New York, spent 1993–94 teaching in Nanjing, China. She is currently working on a collection of essays about that year.

Franklin Burroughs teaches English at Bowdoin College, Maine, and is the author of *Billy Watson's Croker Sack* and *Horry and the Waccamaw,* both published by Norton. His essays have been included in *Best American Essays* and *The Pushcart Prize,* and he has received a National Endowment for the Arts Fellowship for creative nonfiction.

John Calderazzo teaches creative nonfiction workshops at Colorado State University and is the author of the how-to textbook, *Writing from Scratch: Freelancing.* Essays from his new collection, *Portraits from the Open Road,* have appeared in *Audubon, The Georgia Review, Orion,* and elsewhere. He has also written a children's book on volcanoes.

SueEllen Campbell lives in Bellevue, Colorado, not far from Colorado State University, where she teaches literature about nature and the environment, literary theory, and various other topics. Her book *Bringing the Mountain Home* (University of Arizona Press, 1996) is a collection of short essays about what it's like to spend time in wild places.

Norma Elia Cantú, a native of the U.S.-Mexico borderlands, is professor of English at Texas A&M International University and lives in Laredo, Texas, a few blocks from the Rio Grande. Her books include *Canícula: Snapshots of a Girlhood en la Frontera* (University of New Mexico Press) and *Matachines de la Santa Cruz: An Ethnography of a Folk Religious Performance in Laredo, Texas.*

Bill Capossere teaches high school in Victor, New York. His latest work was a collaborative effort with his second-grade reading group.

Kelly Cherry's books of creative nonfiction are *Writing the World* and *The Exiled Heart.* She has also published five books of fiction, including *My Life and Dr. Joyce Brothers,* and four of poetry, including *God's Loud Hand* and *Natural Theology* (LSU Press). Her awards include the Hanes Prize, an O. Henry Award, and a Pushcart Prize. She teaches at the University of Wisconsin, Madison.

Andrei Codrescu lives and teaches in Louisiana. He is an editor and translator, as well as a writer of poetry, fiction, and nonfiction. His books include *Zombification: Stories from National Public Radio* and *Road Scholar: Coast to Coast Late in the Century,* which was made into a film.

Judith Ortiz Cofer is the author of *Silent Dancing,* a collection of essays and poetry; *The Latin Deli: Prose and Poetry;* and two books of poetry and one novel. A recipient of fellowships from the National Endowment for the Arts and the Witter Bynner Foundation, she teaches at the University of Georgia. Her most recent book is a collection of short stories, *An Island Like You: Stories of the Barrio.*

Bernard Cooper lives in Los Angeles and teaches the personal essay at the UCLA Writer's Program and Antioch University/Los Angeles. He has received a PEN/Hemingway Award and an O. Henry Prize. His work has appeared in numerous publications, most recently *The Paris Review, Harper's,* and *Best American Essays.* His books include a novel, *A Year of Rhymes,* and two collections of essays, *Maps to Anywhere* and *Truth Serum* (Houghton Mifflin, 1996).

Stephen Corey is Associate Editor of *The Georgia Review.* Author of six collections of poetry, he also writes essays which have appeared in *Poets & Writers, The Laurel Review, Tampa Review,* and in the anthology *Writing It Down for James: Writers on Life and Craft* (Beacon Press, 1995).

John D'Agata received a B.A. from Hobart and William Smith Colleges in 1995 and now attends the University of Iowa's graduate writing program in nonfiction. "Notes Toward Identifying a Body" is his first publication.

Jim DeCamp's essay, "MRI," is his first appearance in print. He is a combat veteran of Vietnam and twenty-eight years of teaching in public schools. He works exclusively in the "short" form and lives in Geneseo, New York.

Michael Dorris's 1989 book, *The Broken Cord,* won the National Book Critics Circle Award for nonfiction. He is the author of a novel, *A Yel-*

low Raft in Blue Water; a collection of short stories, *Working Men;* essays, *Paper Trail;* and two children's books. His next novel, *Cloud Chamber,* will be published by Scribner's in 1997.

Rita Dove was Poet Laureate of the United States and Consultant in Poetry at the Library of Congress (1993–95). She has published a number of poetry collections, most recently *Mother Love* (W. W. Norton, 1995). In 1987 she received the Pulitzer Prize in poetry. She is currently Commonwealth Professor of English at the University of Virginia and lives near Charlottesville with her husband and daughter.

David James Duncan is the author of *River Teeth: Stories and Writings* (Doubleday, 1995) and two novels, *The River Why* and *The Brothers K.* Both novels won the Pacific Northwest Bookseller's Award. Duncan's nonfiction appears in *Harper's, Big Sky Journal, The Los Angeles Times Magazine, Northern Lights,* and many other publications. He lives on a troutstream in western Montana.

Stephen Dunn has published a book of essays, *Walking Light: Essays & Memoirs* (W. W. Norton), and nine books of poems, most recently *New & Selected Poems: 1974–1994* (also Norton). He teaches at Richard Stockton College in New Jersey.

Stuart Dybek is the author of three books—*The Coast of Chicago* his most recent—and a chapbook of short short stories. He teaches at Western Michigan University. His awards include an Award in Fiction from the American Academy of Arts and Letters and a PEN/Malamud Award.

Gretel Ehrlich has received awards from the National Endowment for the Arts, the Guggenheim Foundation, the Whiting Foundation, and the American Academy of Arts and Letters. She is the author of *The Solace of Open Spaces; Islands, the Universe, Home;* and *A Match to the Heart.* She now divides her time between the central coast of California and Wyoming.

Jerry Ellis is the author of a series of nonfiction books that combine personal experience and a study of history, especially Native American history. They include: *Bareback! One Man's Journey Along the Pony*

Express Trail; Marching Through Georgia; and *Walking the Trail* (Delacorte, 1991), from which the first chapter is reprinted here as "Into the Storm."

Ian Frazier is a writer of humor, essays, and longer nonfiction. His books include *Nobody Better, Better than Nobody; The Great Plains;* and *Family.* He currently lives in Montana.

Henry Louis Gates, Jr., is the author of many books of literary theory and criticism, among them *Loose Canons, Figures in Black,* and *Signifying Monkey,* winner of the American Book Award. He is W.E.B. DuBois Professor of Humanities at Harvard University. *Colored People,* a memoir, won the *Chicago Tribune's* Heartland Award and the Lillian Smith Prize.

Reginald Gibbons has published four books of poems and two books of fiction. His novel, *Sweetbitter,* won the 1995 Anisfield-Wolf Book Award and the 1995 Jesse Jones Award of the Texas Institute of Letters. He has edited anthologies of fiction and essays, and since 1981 has been the editor of the literary journal *TriQuarterly* at Northwestern University, where he also teaches.

Albert Goldbarth currently lives in Wichita, Kansas. He has received a fellowship from the Guggenheim Foundation and three fellowships from the National Endowment for the Arts. His collections of poetry include *Heaven and Earth,* recipient of the National Book Critics Circle Award. He has also published two volumes of essays, *A Sympathy of Souls* (Coffee House Press) and *Great Topics of the World* (David R. Godine).

Vivian Gornick has been a staff writer for *The Village Voice* and contributes regularly to *The New York Times* and other journals. Her books include her memoir, *Fierce Attachments; Women in Science: Portraits From a World in Transition;* and *Essays in Feminism.* Her awards include a Guggenheim Fellowship and a grant from the Ford Foundation. She lives in New York City.

Lee Gutkind lives in Pittsburgh, Pennsylvania, and is editor of the new journal *Creative Nonfiction.* He is the author of eight books of nonfiction, most recently *Stuck in Time* (Henry Holt), a novel, and an award-winning documentary film. "On Two Wheels" is taken from *Bike Fever,* about his cross-country travels on a motorcycle.

John Haines's Collected Poems, *The Owl in the Mask of the Dreamer,* was published by Graywolf Press in 1993. His numerous books of nonfiction include *You and I and the World; The Stars, The Snow, the Fire: Twenty-five Years in the Alaska Wilderness*; and *Fables and Distances.* He lives in Fairbanks, Alaska.

Donald Hall lives in New Hampshire. He has published many volumes of poetry, most recently *The Old Life* (1995). His prose collections include *Principal Products of Portugal* (1995), *Death to the Death of Poetry* (1994), and *Life Work* (1993).

Joy Harjo, of Creek and Cherokee descent, lives in Albuquerque, New Mexico. Among her books of poetry and prose are *She Had Some Horses; Secrets from the Center of the World*; *In Mad Love and War*; and *Woman Who Fell from the Sky.* She has also written film scripts. "Suspended" will appear as part of "A Love Supreme" in *The Jazz Anthology,* to be published by W. W. Norton.

Steven Harvey is the author of a book of personal essays entitled *A Geometry of Lilies: Life and Death in an American Family.* He is also the editor of *In a Dark Wood: Personal Essays by Men About Middle Age,* to be published by the University of Georgia Press. He teaches English at Young Harris College and lives with his family in the mountains of North Georgia.

Emily Hiestand, essayist, poet, and visual artist, lives in Massachusetts. Her literary awards include the National Poetry Series Award and a Whiting Writers' Award. Her publications include *Green the Witch-Hazel Wood* (poems) and *The Very Rich Hours* (travel essays). A second book of nonfiction, *Travels at Home,* is forthcoming from Beacon Press. She is the literary and poetry editor for *Orion* magazine.

Edward Hoagland lives in Vermont and teaches at Bennington College. Best known as a master of the essay form, he contributes to numerous periodicals such as *Esquire* and *The New Yorker.* His fifteen books include seven collections of essays, among them *Balancing Acts, The Tugman's Passage, The Edward Hoagland Reader,* and *The Courage of Turtles.*

Linda Hogan is a Chickasaw poet, novelist, and essayist, living in Colorado. She has received an American Book Award, a grant from the National Endowment for the Arts, and the Five Civilized Tribes Museum playwriting award. Her most recent book of essays is *Dwellings* (W. W. Norton, 1995).

John Holman lives in Atlanta and teaches at Georgia State University. He has published one book of short fiction, *Squabble and Other Stories,* and is the recipient of a Whiting Writers' Award. He was recently selected to teach teachers in a special program designed by the Associated Writing Programs.

Art Homer lives in Omaha, where he teaches at the University of Nebraska in the Omaha Writer's Workshop. He has published three collections of poetry and a book of nonfiction, *The Drownt Boy: An Ozark Tale* (University of Missouri Press). He received a 1995 Pushcart Prize.

David Huddle has published nonfiction in *Southern Review, Details,* and *Playboy.* His collection of essays, *The Writing Habit,* was reprinted by University Press of New England in 1994. He is also the author of a novella, three collections of poetry, and four collections of short stories. He teaches at the University of Vermont and the Bread Loaf School of English.

Pico Iyer is a longtime essayist for *Time* magazine and a contributing editor to *Condé Nast Traveler.* His books include *Video Night in Kathmandu, The Lady & the Monk, Falling Off the Map,* and a recent novel, *Cuba and the Night.*

Mary Paumier Jones's essays have appeared in *The Georgia Review* and in *Creative Nonfiction.* She is currently completing a book of personal essays. A public librarian in Rochester, New York, she was the originator of the idea for this anthology.

Teresa Jordan is the author of two works of nonfiction, *Cowgirls: Women of the American West*, an oral history; and *Riding the White Horse Home*, a memoir. She has edited two collections of Western women's writing. She is the recipient of fellowships from the National Endowment for the Arts and from the Nevada State Council on the Arts. She lives in rural Nevada with her husband, Hal Cannon.

Bhanu Kapil lives mostly in Fort Collins, Colorado. Although her parents were born in India, she is a native of England and an immigrant to the United States. "Three Voices" is her first major publication.

Susanna Kaysen has published two novels—*Asa, As I Knew Him* and *Far Afield*. "Ice Cream" is taken from her memoir, *Girl, Interrupted* (Random House, 1993). She lives in Cambridge, Massachusetts.

Judith Kitchen has published books of poetry, criticism, and essays, and has received grants from the National Endowment for the Arts and the New York Foundation for the Arts. *Only the Dance: Essays on Time and Memory* (University of South Carolina Press) was published in 1994. She is currently poetry reviewer for *The Georgia Review* and lives in Brockport, New York.

William Kittredge teaches in the writing program at the University of Montana. His books include several works of fiction, as well as a collection of essays, *Owning It All*, and a memoir, *Hole in the Sky*. His most recent book is *Who Owns the West?* (Mercury House, 1996).

Ted Kooser is an insurance executive, a poet, a painter, and a sometime essayist. He lives on an acreage near Garland, Nebraska. His most recent book of poems is *Weather Central* (University of Pittsburgh Press).

Maxine Kumin won the Pulitzer Prize for poetry in 1973, served as Poetry Consultant to the Library of Congress in 1981–82, and has been named a Chancellor of the Academy of American Poets. She has published eleven books of poetry, most recently *Connecting the Dots* (W. W. Norton, 1996), two books of essays, and one book of essays and stories. She and her husband live on a farm in New Hampshire.

John Lane lives in Spartanburg, South Carolina. His full-length narrative, *A Stand of Cypress,* was the runner up in the 1994 Associated Writing Programs creative nonfiction award. He has two collections of poetry, most recently, *Against Information* (1995).

Li-Young Lee lives in Chicago. He has received a fellowship from the National Endowment for the Arts, the Lamont Award, the Delmore Schwartz Award, a Whiting Fellowship, and, most recently, a Lannan Award for his poetry. "One Human Hand" is taken from his memoir, *The Winged Seed* (Simon & Schuster, 1995).

Denise Levertov has won numerous awards for her poetry, including a Senior Artists Award from the National Endowment for the Arts. She has published over twenty books of poetry and a book of essays. "Inheritance" is taken from *Tesserae: Memories & Suppositions* (New Directions, 1995).

Vicki Lindner, a fiction writer, essayist, and journalist, lives in the Shoshone National Forest in Dubois, Wyoming, and teaches at the University in Laramie. Her short fiction and essays have recently appeared in *Northern Lights, Witness,* and *Chick Lit: New Writing by Women.*

Barry Lopez is the author of several books, among them, *Arctic Dreams: Imagination and Desire in a Northern Landscape* (for which he received the National Book Award), *Crossing Open Ground*, and *The Rediscovery of North America.* His many awards include a Guggenheim Fellowship and a Lannan Foundation Award. He lives on the McKenzie River in western Oregon with his wife, Sandra, an artist.

Bia Lowe lives in Los Angeles. Her work has appeared in *The Kenyon Review, Salmagundi,* and *Harper's.* A collection of her essays, *Wild Ride: Earthquakes, Sneezes and Other Thrills,* was published by HarperCollins in 1995.

William Matthews is the author of a book of essays, *Curiosities* (University of Michigan Press), and ten books of poems. He teaches at The City College of New York. His most recent book is the culmination of a translation project on Martial, the first-century Roman poet: *The Mortal City: 100 Epigrams of Martial.*

Judson Mitcham's first collection of poems, *Somewhere in Ecclesiastes,* won the Devins Award from the University of Missouri Press. His novel, *The Sweet Everlasting,* is forthcoming from the University of Georgia Press. Winner of fellowships from the National Endowment for the Arts and the Georgia Council for the Arts, he chairs the Psychology Department at Fort Valley State College, Macon, Georgia.

Gwendolyn Nelson lives near the south shore of Lake Ontario, teaches literature and composition in Henrietta, New York, and has had poems published in various journals.

Kathleen Norris's most recent books are *The Cloister Walk* (Riverhead, 1996) and *Little Girls in Church* (University of Pittsburgh Press, 1995). She is the author of *Dakota: A Spiritual Geography,* and lives in northwestern South Dakota. She has received fellowships from the Guggenheim and Bush Foundations.

Naomi Shihab Nye's collection of personal essays is entitled *Never in a Hurry: Essays on People and Places* (University of South Carolina). She has published five books of poetry (most recently *Red Suitcase,* BOA Editions) and five books for young readers, as well as *Mint,* a collection of paragraphs (State Street Press). She lives in San Antonio, Texas.

Tim O'Brien is the author of *Going After Cacciato,* which received the 1979 National Book Award in fiction. Other books include *The Things They Carried* and *In the Lake of the Woods,* named by *Time* magazine as the best work of fiction published in 1994. He is the recipient of literary awards from the Guggenheim Foundation, the National Endowment for the Arts, and the American Academy and Institute of Arts and Letters.

Michael Ondaatje was born in Ceylon (now Sri Lanka) and lives in Toronto, Canada. He is well known for his many novels and collections of poetry, as well as his memoir, *Running in the Family.* He has twice been given the Governor-General's Award for Literature.

Cynthia Ozick is the author of ten books, the most recent of which is *Fame & Folly,* a collection of literary essays. She has won numerous awards for her short stories, novels, and essays. Other books include *Art & Ardor: Essays*; *Metaphor & Memory: Essays*; and *The Shawl,* a novel. She lives in New Rochelle, New York.

Brenda Peterson is the author of three novels and three works of non-fiction. Her most recent novel, *Duck and Cover,* was selected as a Notable Book of the Year by *The New York Times,* and a book of nature writing, *Living by Water,* was chosen as an *Editors' Choice* Best Book of 1990 by the American Library Association. She lives in Seattle, Washington.

Aleida Rodríguez was born in Cuba, and at the age of nine traveled to the United States via Operation Peter Pan. She has lived in Los Angeles for more than ten years. Her work has appeared in *Prairie Schooner* and *Ploughshares,* and in such anthologies as *Hers* and *Grand Passion.*

Richard Rodriguez lives in San Francisco. A regular essayist on the former MacNeil/Lehrer NewsHour and the current NewsHour with Jim Lehrer, his books include an autobiography, *Hunger of Memory: The Education of Richard Rodriguez,* and a collection of essays, *Days of Obligation: An Argument with My Mexican Father.*

Scott Russell Sanders is the author of fifteen books. His selections of essays include *Writing from the Center* (University of Indiana, 1995); *Staying Put: Secrets of the Universe*; and *The Paradise of Bombs,* which was awarded the Associated Writing Programs Award in creative nonfiction. His work has been selected for *Best American Essays,* and he received a Lannan Literary Award for nonfiction in 1995. He teaches at Indiana University, in Bloomington.

Reg Saner lives and writes among the flora, fauna, and human presences of the Rockies and the high deserts of the Southwest. *The Four-Cornered Falcon: Essays on the Interior West and the Natural Scene* was published by Johns Hopkins in 1993. His books of poetry have won several major prizes, among them the Walt Whitman Award and the State of Colorado Governor's Award.

Jane Moress Schuster lives in Rochester, New York. She recently completed her master's degree in English at SUNY Brockport, where "Sanctuary" won an award in the W. C. Randels Essay Contest. This is her first appearance in other than local print.

Fred Setterberg lives in Oakland, California, and works as a staff writer with the *East Bay Express* in Berkeley. He won the Associated Writing Programs Award in creative nonfiction for *The Roads Taken: Travels Through America's Literary Landscapes,* and is the co-author of *Toxic Nation.* Other awards include a fellowship from the National Endowment for the Arts, and the California Newspaper Publishers' Association writing award.

Gerry Sharp lives in Penfield, New York, where he works as a carpenter. "Falling Stars" is his first major publication.

Michael Shay is director of the literature program for the Wyoming Arts Council, and in 1993–95 was assistant director of the literature program for the National Endowment for the Arts. His fiction and essays have been published in *High Plains Literary Review, Visions, Colorado Review,* and the *Denver Post's Empire Magazine.* He is working on a book about hyperactivity.

Richard Shelton is a Regents Professor of English at the University of Arizona in Tucson. He is the author of nine books of poetry and most recently the nonfiction book *Going Back to Bisbee,* which won the Western States Arts Federation Award for creative nonfiction. His other books include *Hohokam* and *Selected Poems: 1969–1981.*

Larry Sill is a machinist who lives in Greece, New York. He is working on a graduate degree in English.

Charles Simic is Professor of English at the University of New Hampshire. Among his awards for poetry are a MacArthur Fellowship, National Endowment for the Arts fellowships, a Guggenheim Foundation Fellowship, and the Pulitzer Prize. He has also written a book of essays, *The Unemployed Fortune Teller* (University of Michigan Press).

Kim R. Stafford has published fiction, poetry, and essays, including *We Got Here Together*; *Lochsa Road: A Pilgrim in the West*; and *Having Everything Right: Essays of Place,* which won a Western States Book Award Citation for Excellence in 1986. He lives and teaches in Portland, Oregon.

Deborah Tall, poet and nonfiction writer, lives in Ithaca, NY. Her books include *The Island of the White Cow: Memories of an Irish Island* and *From Where We Stand: Recovering a Sense of Place* (Knopf, 1993), forthcoming in Johns Hopkins University Press's "American Land Classics" series. Co-editor of *The Poet's Notebook: Excerpts from the Notebooks of Twenty-Six American Poets* (Norton), she teaches at Hobart and William Smith Colleges, where she edits *Seneca Review.*

Jerome Washington lives on the Mendocino Coast of California. While incarcerated in upstate New York, he received a grant from the New York Foundation for the Arts. His collection *Iron House: Stories from the Yard* was awarded the 1994 Western State Arts Federation Award for creative nonfiction. He is a member of the PEN America Center's Prison Writing Committee.

Lawrence Weschler has been a staff writer at *The New Yorker* since 1981 and is a two-time winner of the George Polk Award. His books include *Seeing Is Forgetting the Name of the Thing One Sees*; *A Miracle, A Universe: Settling Accounts with Torturers*; and *Mr. Wilson's Cabinet of Wonder.* He lives in Westchester County, New York.

Paul West's thirteenth novel, *Love's Mansion,* won the Lannan Prize for fiction in 1993. He has published over a dozen nonfiction books, ranging from the best-selling *Words for a Deaf Daughter* to *A Stroke of Genius* and the three-volume collection of essays, *Sheer Fiction.* His honors include an Award in Literature from the American Academy and Institute of Arts and Letters. He makes his home in upstate New York.

Alec Wilkinson has published five books, including *Big Sugar* and *A Violent Act*. He has been a Guggenheim Fellow and has won a Robert F. Kennedy Book Award and a Lyndhurst Prize. Since 1980, his work has appeared regularly in *The New Yorker*. He lives in New York City.

Terry Tempest Williams lives in Salt Lake City, where she is naturalist-in-residence at the Utah Museum of Natural History. Her first book received a Southwest Book Award. Her most recent publications are *Refuge: An Unnatural History of Family and Place* and *An Unspoken Hunger: Stories from the Field*.

August Wilson lives in Seattle, Washington, where he is at work on a series of plays about the black experience in America. His plays have won numerous awards, among them the New York Drama Critics Circle, the Tony, and two Pulitzer prizes. They include: *The Piano Lesson, Two Trains Running, Ma Rainey's Black Bottom,* and *Fences*.

Carol Lucci Wisner is a nurse employed at a 72-bed rural community hospital in upstate New York. She has published occasional short stories, poems, or essays in various local magazines and newspapers.

Tobias Wolff is the author of *This Boy's Life: A Memoir,* which won the *Los Angeles Times* Book Prize, and *In Pharaoh's Army: Memories of the Last War* (Knopf, 1994). He has also published two collections of short stories, *Back in the World* and *In the Garden of the North American Martyrs,* and a novel, *The Barracks Thief.* He teaches at Syracuse University, New York.

Permissions

Index

Index

Index

Index